JAZZ
THEORY & WORKBOOK

By Lilian Dericq & Étienne Guéreau
Translated by Eileen Rezwin

HAL•LEONARD®
7777 W. BLUEMOUND RD. P.O. BOX 13819 MILWAUKEE, WI 53213

ISBN: 978-1-4950-6200-1

In Australia Contact:
Hal Leonard Australia Pty. Ltd.
4 Lentara Court
Cheltenham, Victoria, 3192 Australia
Email: ausadmin@halleonard.com.au

Visit Hal Leonard Online at
www.halleonard.com

Contents

Foreword

Given the large number of harmony books on the market, it can be difficult for students of jazz, and music in general, to find the reference text that suits them best. Many of these methods propose a theoretical approach with an excessive amount of descriptive information, and abstract explanations of harmonic notions that are far removed from the real musical and aural challenges students have to deal with.

The approach of Lilian Dericq and Étienne Guéreau is particularly unique in that it provides an extraordinary balance between the rational explanations of the theoretical elements presented and the physical and empirical aspects of these harmonic notions. This makes for a highly structured and practical method designed to help students acquire an understanding of musical theory and put this knowledge directly into practice.

This method is based on the teachings and practical approach handed down by our dearly departed colleague, Bernard Maury, and indirectly draws on the musical concepts of the undisputed master of harmony, Bill Evans, the same concepts Maury so brilliantly systemized and made available to many musicians during his lifetime, and which Dericq and Guéreau skillfully retransmit in this book. Thanks to this method, the precious legacies of Evans and Maury are now accessible to everybody.

By drawing on their extensive knowledge, Dericq and Guéreau have tapped into this timeless legacy to create a method that is both rich and dynamic in its theoretical and practical approach.

Enrico Pieranunzi
May 2015

INTRODUCTION

While harmony is about logic and listening, it should not be reduced to an overly abstract science: it has to live.

—Bernard Maury[1]

Musical harmony involves the study of chords, their construction, and the rules governing their progressions. These "rules" are based on a set of concrete procedures that summarize the theoretical principles of certain aesthetic choices made by the composer and the performer.

The teaching of harmony as we perceive it and in the way it is presented here is the result of these rules: an approach that is a coherent and hierarchical system, one that defines its concepts and determines objectives are explained in precise musical terms.

While this book essentially deals with jazz harmony, many of the elementary principles developed here are rooted in classical harmony and apply to all musical genres. These principles provide a foundation common to all tonal and tempered music; that is to say, almost all Western music — with the notable exceptions of modal music and free jazz which, because of its nature, rejects any system that can be taught. This foundation covers notions such as intervals, cadences, tonality, three- and four-note chord constructions, and modulations, etc. It serves as the basis for many types of music that differ mainly because of their respective style and the application of a set of subjective criteria.

Frequently, the only factor that distinguishes classical music from jazz is how these rules are applied. For example, in jazz, we refer to the "chromatic dominant" (or sub V), which, in the classical world is known as the "augmented sixth." However, both these nomenclatures designate the same principle, the only difference being the selection of context, position, and harmonic rhythm.

Moreover, the boundaries between the different musical worlds are extremely permeable, as exemplified by Bill Evans, who was classically trained, and Maurice Ravel, who was influenced by jazz, and by the fact that these notions diverge within the same musical universe. Indeed, while the rules governing cadences, for example, are the same in all musical genres, it is difficult to compare the works of Bach with those of Messiaen, or the compositions of Jelly Roll Morton with those of Clare Fischer. Nevertheless, all these composers had one thing in common: their knowledge of these harmonic rules, and the fact that any decision to digress from these rules was based on a conscious choice. These composers followed the same harmonic tradition, a tradition presented in this book.

This may be summarized by drawing a parallel with the culinary arts: While the harmony of jazz and "classical" music (including tonal music, of course) use the same ingredients and share many recipes, the "dishes" they produce are different because they are prepared according to the individual taste of each musician.

Jazz Theory & Workbook is designed for all instrumentalists eager to understand how the jazz tunes, and, more specifically, the standards they play and improvise over, are constructed, as well as for arrangers and composers seeking new writing tools. Although some of the musical examples are pianistic, this book is not exclusively for keyboard players. Traditional musical notation, in treble and bass clef, is a writing convention that can be read by most musicians. Nonetheless, students who are seriously interested in harmony should learn the keyboard basics. The fact that the notes on the keyboard are arranged in a logical order offers unparalleled advantages in terms of tessitura and visual projection.

---

[1] French pianist, arranger and teacher, Bernard Maury (1943-2005) played with numerous French and American musicians, including, among others, Johnny Griffin, Hal Singer, Toots Thielemans, Michel Petrucciani, and Didier Lockwood. His friend Francis Paudras introduced him to Bill Evans, with whom he remained friends for many years and became a specialist in Evans's musical language, jazz harmony, and solo piano style in France. In 1996, he founded the Bill Evans Piano Academy, a jazz school in Paris where the two authors of this book still teach.

Contrary to the many available musical theory books that provide a more general approach, we have deliberately limited the scope of information contained in this book and presented concepts we consider the most important and the most original. This choice is the fruit of our pedagogical experience, which has enabled us to identify the key elements students and newcomers to jazz need to learn in order to advance without being burdened by unuseful or premature information. With this in mind, we have excluded any analysis related to musicology or acoustics, and everything else we considered superfluous.

Our aim is to create a structured method whereby every musical concept is clearly presented and explained, put in context with one or more musical examples, and then consolidated with a set of written exercises. In addition, the method is progressive; beginning with a lengthy and comprehensive presentation of intervals (which we explore in great detail, since it is vital students acquire a thorough understanding of this area of study) and culminating with an in-depth review of the synthetic modes.

While most of the concepts developed in *Jazz Theory & Workbook* already exist in classical music, and in certain general harmony books (where they are merely cited), the way they are presented in this book, and the pedagogical tools used are, to our knowledge, unprecedented. Our study of the modes, for example, is based on the analysis of the Natural and the Altered Characteristic Degrees of "five" diatonic systems, compared with only "two" (the major and the melodic minor) in most methods. In addition, our approach proposes a classification of these five systems by nomenclature and by new and specific relationships. Furthermore, we have endeavored, as far as possible, to provide a concrete example to illustrate the specific color of each mode. Most often, modes are taught in an isolated manner, with no contextual link to the standards, an approach that tends to leave students with the impression that modes are complicated and, even worse, useless. Although jazz harmony remains a theoretical field of study, in this book, we have sought to create a method that is both practical and immediately applicable.

We have organized and created a system for many concepts that will help the student understand and acquire the musical language of Bill Evans, Clare Fischer, and many others. This choice is based on the fact that these two musical giants incarnate the essence of the harmonic vocabulary of modern and tonal music (which de facto excludes free jazz and atonal, or "chromatic," jazz), and the fact that their place in the history of music makes them precursors (having influenced such notable musicians as Keith Jarrett, Herbie Hancock, and Chick Corea — to name but a few).

The aim of this book is to present both a vertical and a horizontal study of jazz harmony. Although jazz is based essentially on a progression of chords, where each chord is heard vertically in a given moment, students who are unaware of the linear mechanisms that also determine this style of music are denied the precious concepts often required for their musical expression. These mechanisms are characterized by different conjunct melodic movements, such as voice leading, which make it possible to transcend the isolated expression of each harmonic element. In other words, these two approaches are complementary, and even indispensable, to understand the specific requirements of techniques (such as appoggiaturas) based on a horizontal approach.

For the most part, *Jazz Theory & Workbook* is based on Bernard Maury's harmony classes, which we have endeavored to present in a way that respects the logic and subtlety of his teachings, plus additional explanations and simplifications, when necessary, derived from our own experience. Bernard Maury is at the origin of an unparalleled and ambitious harmonic paradigm, a doctrine whose apparent complexity is fully justified by the musical teachings and insight it offers. Maury's musical discoveries (which some would call his "genius") have until now been reserved for those who had the chance to benefit from his teachings. With *Jazz Theory & Workbook*, our goal is to make these treasures accessible to all.

Our encounter with Bernard Maury was a musical revelation. He was a great master and a true friend. It is an honor for us to be able to transmit his teachings in this book.

The authors

CHAPTER 1
INTERVALS

This chapter focuses on the identification and classification of intervals which, as we will later see, are essential for analyzing melodic phrases, scales and chords, etc.

❶ Intervals: definition

An **interval** is determined by the **distance** between any two given notes, the smallest distance being a half-step (or semitone). There are two types of intervals:

- **melodic intervals:** when two notes are played successively, and
- **harmonic intervals:** when two notes are played simultaneously.

1.1 Melodic intervals

A **melodic interval** comprises two notes played successively, in ascending or descending order:

Ascending intervals: the first note is lower than the second.

Descending intervals: the first note is higher than the second.

Melodic interval motion may be conjunct (moving by step) or disjunct (by skips).

Conjunct motion: the second note of the interval is a neighboring diatonic degree[1] above or below the first note.

The two examples below illustrate an ascending conjunct-motion of one whole step (F to G) and a descending conjunct-motion of one half step (C to B).

Conjunct motion   Ascending   Descending

---

1 A diatonic degree is a note in a given tonality. A diatonic movement specifies that the two notes belong to the same tonality.

There are two types of half-steps:

- diatonic half-steps: here the two notes of the interval have **different names**.

- chromatic half steps: both notes of the interval have the **same name**.

Disjunct motion, the second note of the interval is not a neighboring tone above or below the first.

A **chromatic movement** designates a diatonic or non-diatonic half-step interval.

1.2 Harmonic intervals

A **harmonic interval** refers to two notes played simultaneously.

In the chapters on chord construction, we will see that by superimposing (or "stacking") intervals, it is possible to form triads (three-note chords), tetrads (four-note chords), and more complex chords (comprising five or six notes, and polychords,[2] etc.).

Summary table of interval-motion possibilities

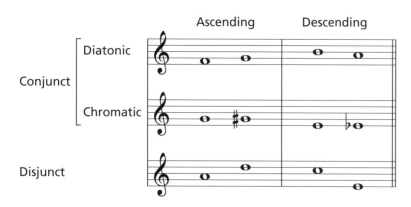

---

2 Stacking of two or more triads.

❷ Interval components

An interval is defined by a set of two criteria, namely:

- its name (2nd, 3rd, 4th, etc.), and
- its quality (major, minor, etc.).

2.1 Interval name

The **name** of an interval indicates the number of degrees it comprises. This is calculated by counting the degrees between, and including, the first and the second notes of the interval.

Intervals may be simple (spanning up to an octave) or compound (more than an octave).

There are:

Six simple intervals

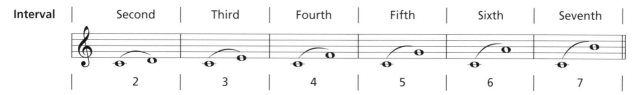

Four compound intervals

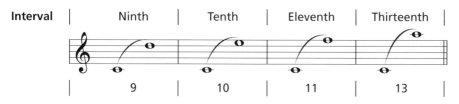

Note that all compound intervals have a simple-interval equivalent, and vice versa:

- the compound 9th interval is equivalent to the simple 2nd;
- the 10th is equivalent to the 3rd;
- the 11th is equivalent to the 4th;
- the 13th is equivalent to the 6th.

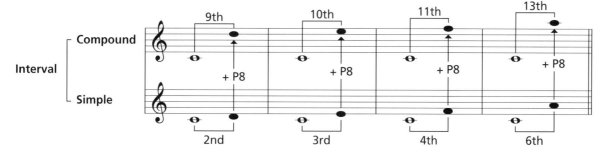

12th and 14th compound intervals also exist but are rarely used.

2.2 Interval quality

The type of interval is defined by its **quality**. By analyzing the number of whole steps (1) and half steps (1/2) separating the two notes, it is possible to determine whether the quality of the interval is **major**, **minor**, **perfect**, **diminished**, or **augmented**.

These five qualities are indicated by interval size in the table below:

	Major	Minor	Perfect	Diminished	Augmented
Second	X	X			X
Third	X	X			
Fourth			X		X
Fifth			X	X	X
Sixth	X	X			
Seventh	X	X		X	
Ninth	X	X			X
Tenth	X	X			
Eleventh			X		X
Thirteenth	X	X			X

In theory, other intervals exist (notably the diminished 2nd, diminished 3rd, augmented 3rd, diminished 4th, augmented 6th, and augmented 7th) but these are rarely used.

Interval quality table

The number of whole-steps (1) and half-steps (1/2) by interval type are indicated in the table below. The quality of compound intervals is the same as for their simple-interval equivalents (minor 9th = minor 2nd; augmented 11th = augmented 4th, etc.)

	Diminished	Minor	Perfect	Major	Augmented
Second		½		1	1 ½
Third		1 ½		2	
Fourth			2 ½		3
Fifth	3		3 ½		4
Sixth		4		4 ½	5
Seventh	4 ½	5		5 ½	

When several sets of intervals contain the same number of whole steps and half steps, the names of the notes determine the quality of the interval in question. In the following example, the intervals C-D♯ and C-E♭ both contain three half steps and sound identical. The only difference lies in their names, C-D♯ being an augmented 2nd and C-E♭ a minor 3rd:

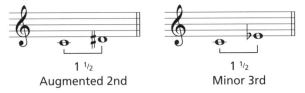

1 ½
Augmented 2nd

1 ½
Minor 3rd

This underscores how important it is to use the precise names of the notes to distinguish the difference between the two intervals. Because D♯ and E♭ share the same sound, but not the same pitch name, they are called "enharmonic equivalents."

2.3 Enharmonic intervals

As the preceeding example shows, the **enharmonic intervals** C-D♯ and C-E♭ sound the same and contain the same number of whole- and half-steps, but have different **pitch names**.

While using enharmonic intervals has certain advantages, it can also have some drawbacks. The strongest argument in its favor is that it offers the possibility of replacing altered notes (such as E♯, B♭♭, F×, etc.) with their respective enharmonic equivalents (F, A, and G), which makes music easier to read and write. The main disadvantage, however, is that its use can lead to confusion when analyzing music, and make it impossible to establish chord and scale relationships. We will examine this paradox in greater detail when we come to analyzing chords, scales, and modes.

2.4 Principles of writing music

The type of interval is always determined, first by its name (3rd, 5th, etc.), then by its quality (major, perfect, etc.).

> **Important**
>
> When writing intervals, follow this two-step approach:
>
> 1. Calculate the size of the interval (as defined by its name) without taking into account its quality (major, minor, etc.); then,
>
> 2. Add an accidental, if necessary, to reflect whether the interval quality is major, minor, perfect, etc.
>
> Respecting this order will help avoid making enharmonic mistakes.

EXAMPLES

To find the minor 3rd above F:

- first, calculate the size of the interval; the 3rd above F is A:

- then, add an accidental, if necessary; in this case, because the interval is a minor 3rd, lower the A to obtain three half steps (1-1/2 whole steps) between F and A♭:

To find the major 6th above E:

- first, calculate the size of the interval; the major 6th above E is C:

- then, add an accidental, if necessary; in this case, raise the C to obtain four and a half steps between E and C♯:

2.5 Interval inversions

In the case of **inverted intervals,** the order of the notes is inverted so that the lowest pitch is raised one octave to become the highest-sounding pitch, and vice-versa.

The sum of an interval and its inversion is always equal to 9; these are called **complementary intervals:**

- an inverted unison is always an octave (1 + 8 = 9);
- an inverted 2nd is always a 7th (2 + 7 =9);
- an inverted 3rd is always a 6th;
- an inverted 4th is always a 5th;
- an inverted 5th is always a 4th;
- an inverted 6th is always a 3rd;
- an inverted 7th is always a 2nd.

The quality of most intervals changes when they are inverted:

- major intervals become minor, and vice versa;
- augmented intervals become diminished, and vice versa.

Exceptions to the rule are perfect intervals (perfect 4ths, 5ths, unisons, and octaves), which remain unchanged when inverted.

2.6 Unisons and octaves

Unisons and **octaves** differ from other intervals in that they have only one quality and are always perfect.

The unison comprises two identically pitched notes that are played simultaneously:

The octave comprises two notes played eight degrees apart.

2.7 Primary intervals

Fourths and 5ths are primary intervals and correspond to **tonal degrees** IV and V relative to the root.

Their qualities may be:

- perfect;
- augmented (perfect + 1/2 step);
- diminished (perfect − 1/2 step).

The Ist degree is also a tonal degree. The root cannot be modified since it serves as the base upon which the different intervals are built.

2.8 Secondary intervals

The 2nd, 3rd, 6th, and 7th are secondary intervals and correspond to **modal degrees** II, III, VI, and VII relative to the root. Their qualities may be:

- major = the reference interval;
- minor = a major interval minus a 1/2 step;
- augmented = a major interval plus a 1/2 step;
- diminished = a major interval minus 1 whole step.

A thorough understanding of interval inversions, and knowing how to notate them correctly, is not only essential to tackle the chapters ahead, but also a prerequisite for identifying and voicing notes in chord symbols. Indeed, chords sound quite different depending on how they are voiced. For example, play the 1-3-5 (root, 3rd, 5th) and 1-5-3 voicings of the A major chord below. Can you hear the difference? The importance of this writing principle will become apparent when we look at four-, five-, and six-note chords.

❸ Different intervals

When it comes to recognizing and reproducing intervals, a useful tip is to memorize some well-known tunes that begin with the intervals in question. These tunes can be simple children's songs or more complex themes. When studying intervals, it is important to adopt a three-fold approach that includes aural **recognition**, **writing**, and **singing**.

3.1 Enharmonic intervals

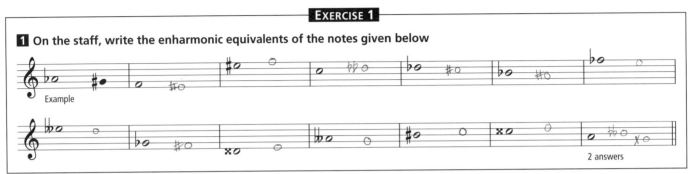

EXERCISE 1

1 On the staff, write the enharmonic equivalents of the notes given below

Example

2 answers

Answers, p. 23

3.2 Seconds

3.2.1 Minor seconds

Choose a melody you know that begins with each of the following intervals and write it on the staff:

Ascending minor seconds

Write your melody

Descending minor seconds

Write your melody

EXERCISE 2

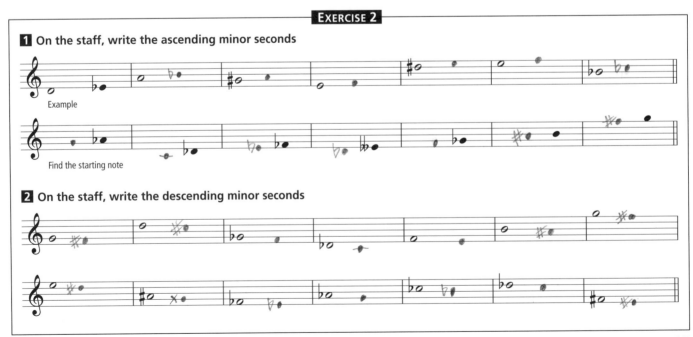

1 On the staff, write the ascending minor seconds

Example

Find the starting note

2 On the staff, write the descending minor seconds

Answers, p. 23

3.2.2 Major seconds

Choose a melody you know that begins with each of the following intervals and write it on the staff:

Ascending major seconds

Write your melody

Descending major seconds

Write your melody

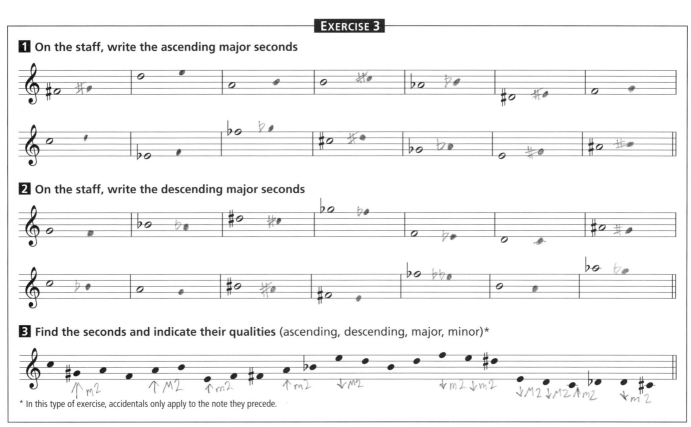

EXERCISE 3

1 On the staff, write the ascending major seconds

2 On the staff, write the descending major seconds

3 Find the seconds and indicate their qualities (ascending, descending, major, minor)*

* In this type of exercise, accidentals only apply to the note they precede.

Answers, p. 24

3.3 Thirds

3.3.1 Minor thirds

Choose a melody you know that begins with each of the following intervals and write it on the staff:

Ascending minor thirds

Write your melody

Descending minor thirds

Write your melody

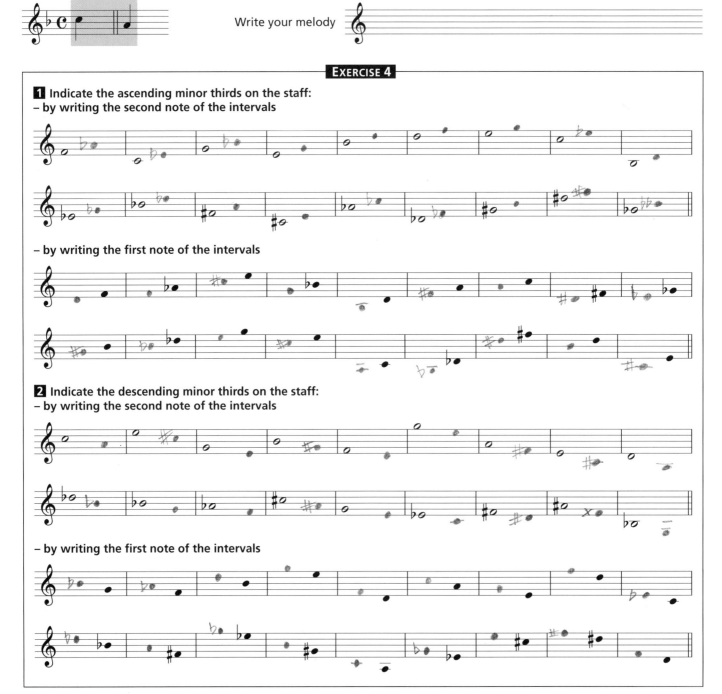

EXERCISE 4

1 Indicate the ascending minor thirds on the staff:
– by writing the second note of the intervals

– by writing the first note of the intervals

2 Indicate the descending minor thirds on the staff:
– by writing the second note of the intervals

– by writing the first note of the intervals

Answers, p. 24

3.3.2 Major thirds

Choose a melody you know that begins with each of the following intervals and write it on the staff:

Ascending major thirds

Write your melody

Descending major thirds

Write your melody

EXERCISE 5

1 Indicate the ascending major thirds on the staff:
– by writing the second note of the intervals

– by writing the first note of the intervals

2 Indicate the descending major thirds on the staff:
– by writing the second note of the intervals

– by writing the first note of the intervals

3 Find the intervals and indicate their qualities (ascending, descending, major, minor)

Answers, p. 25

3.4 Fourths

Choose a melody you know that begins with each of the following intervals and write it on the staff:

3.4.1 Perfect fourths

Ascending perfect fourths

Write your melody

Descending perfect fourths

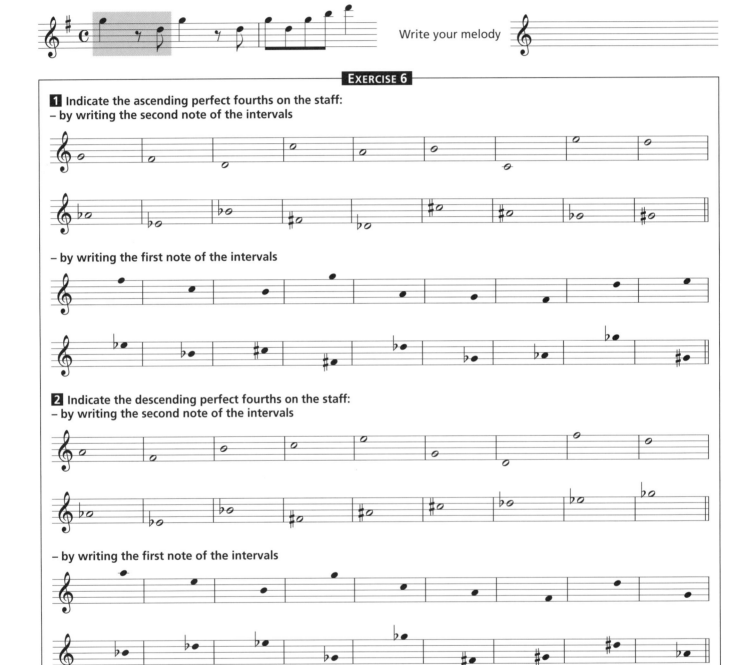

Write your melody

Answers, p. 25-26

3.4.2 Augmented fourths

Choose a melody you know that begins with each of the following intervals and write it on the staff:

Ascending augmented fourths

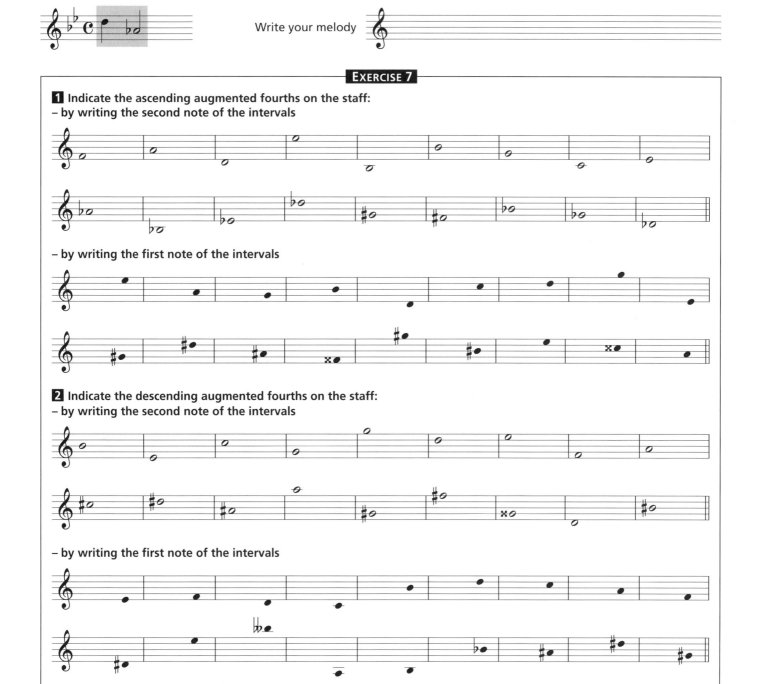

Write your melody

Descending augmented fourths

Write your melody

EXERCISE 7

1 Indicate the ascending augmented fourths on the staff:
– by writing the second note of the intervals

– by writing the first note of the intervals

2 Indicate the descending augmented fourths on the staff:
– by writing the second note of the intervals

– by writing the first note of the intervals

3 Find the intervals and indicate their qualities (ascending, descending, major, minor)

Answers, p. 26

3.5 Fifths

3.5.1 Diminished fifths (also known as the tritone)

While the diminished fifth is the enharmonic equivalent of the augmented fourth (three whole tones), it is rarely used in melodies. This interval is essentially used in chords and scales.

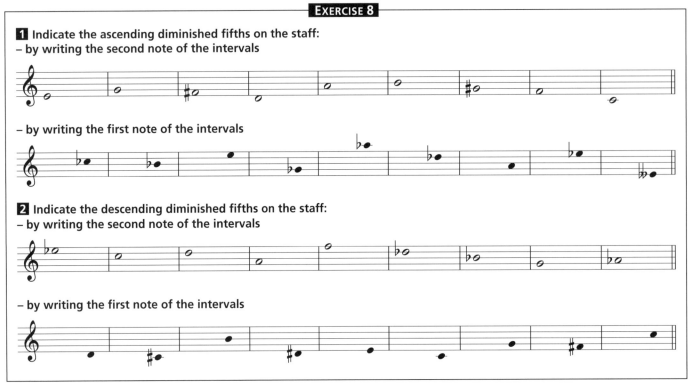

Answers, p. 27

3.5.2 Perfect 5ths

Choose a melody you know that begins with each of the following intervals and write it on the staff:

Ascending perfect 5ths

Descending perfect 5ths

Useful tip

In a perfect 5th, the accidental applied to the Vth degree is generally the same as that applied to the root (e.g., C# and G#). The two exceptions to this rule are B (in which case the Vth degree is F#) and B♭ (where the Vth degree is F).

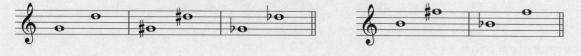

1 Indicate the ascending perfect fifths on the staff:
– by writing the second note of the intervals

– by writing the first note of the intervals

2 Indicate the descending perfect fifths on the staff:
– by writing the second note of the intervals

– by writing the first note of the intervals

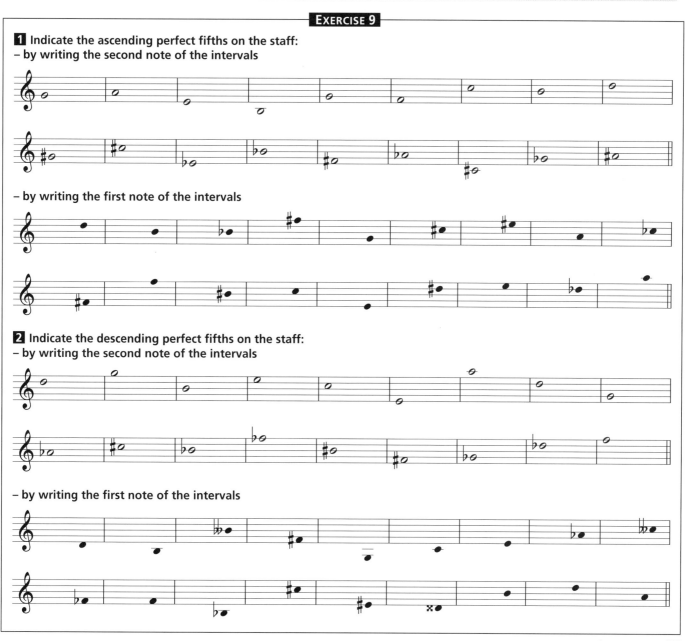

Answers, p. 27

3.5.3 Augmented 5ths

Choose a melody you know that begins with each of the following intervals and write it on the staff:

Ascending augmented 5ths

Write your melody

Descending augmented 5ths

Write your melody

EXERCISE 10

1 Indicate the ascending augmented fifths on the staff:
– by writing the second note of the intervals

– by writing the first note of the intervals

2 Indicate the descending augmented fifths on the staff:
– by writing the second note of the intervals

– by writing the first note of the intervals

3 Find the intervals and indicate their qualities (ascending, descending, major, minor)

Answers, p. 28

3.6 Sixths

Choose a melody you know that begins with each of the following intervals and write it on the staff:

3.6.1. Minor sixths

Ascending minor 6ths

Write your melody

Descending minor 6ths

Write your melody

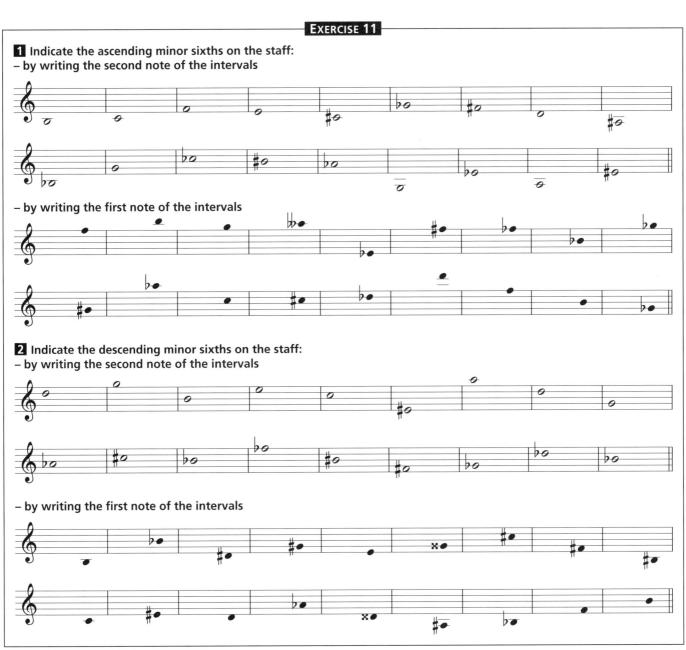

EXERCISE 11

1 Indicate the ascending minor sixths on the staff:
– by writing the second note of the intervals

– by writing the first note of the intervals

2 Indicate the descending minor sixths on the staff:
– by writing the second note of the intervals

– by writing the first note of the intervals

Answers, p. 28-29

3.6.2 Major 6ths

Choose a melody you know that begins with each of the following intervals and write it on the staff:

Ascending major 6ths

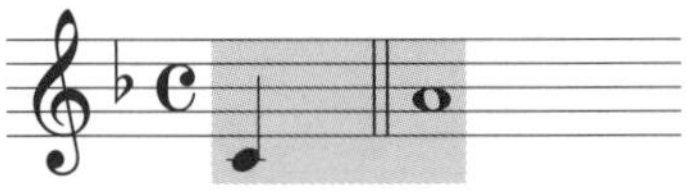

Write your melody

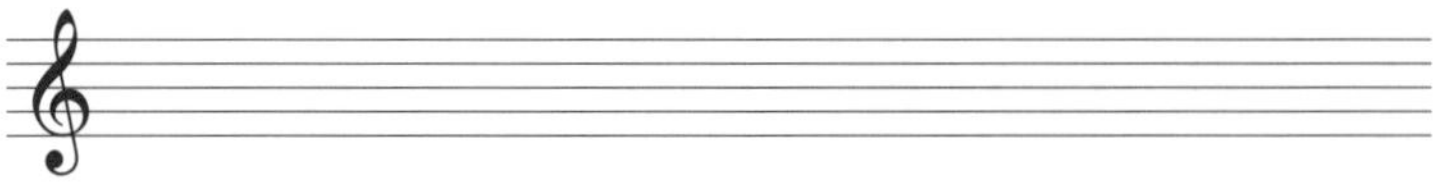

Descending major 6ths

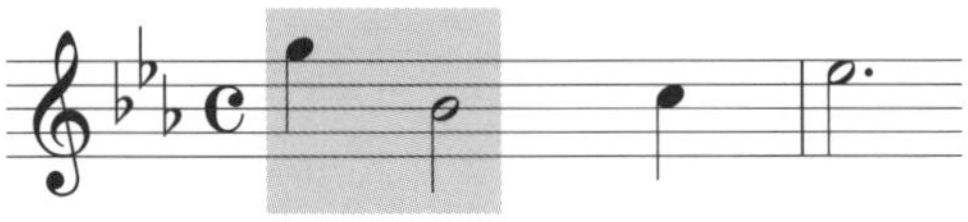

Write your melody

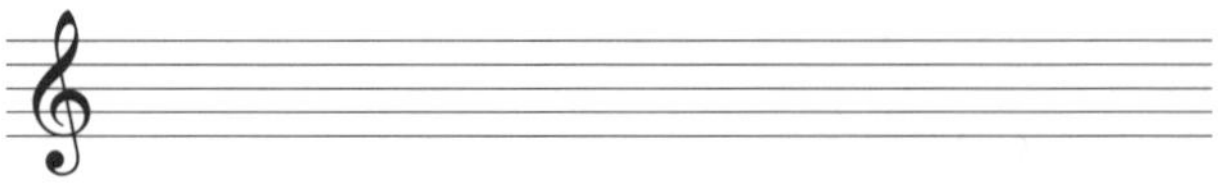

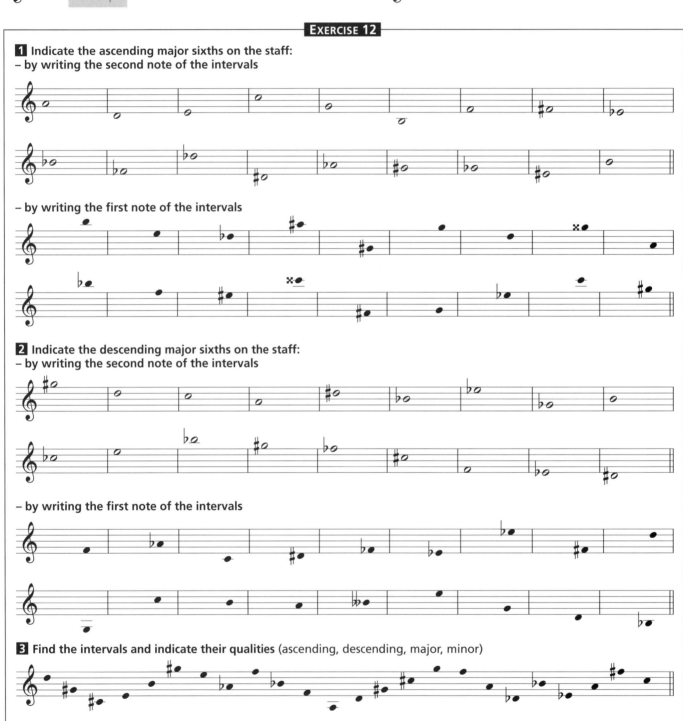

EXERCISE 12

1 Indicate the ascending major sixths on the staff:
– by writing the second note of the intervals

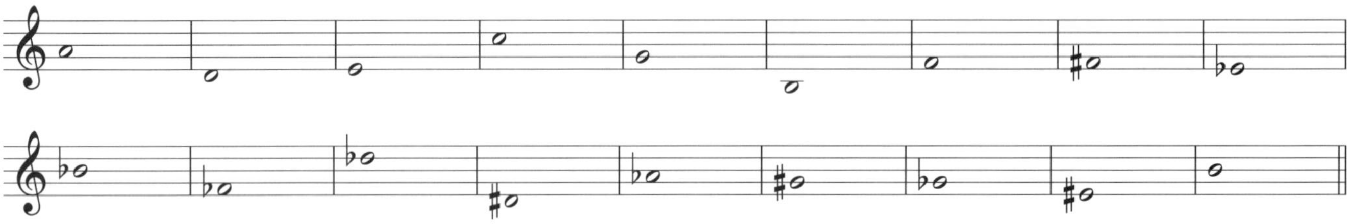

– by writing the first note of the intervals

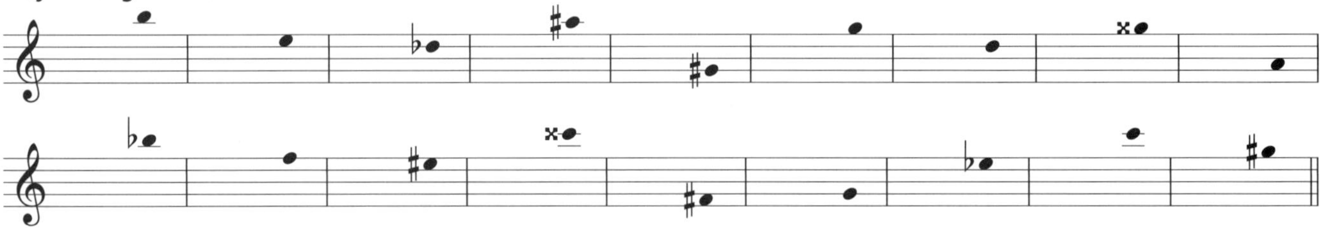

2 Indicate the descending major sixths on the staff:
– by writing the second note of the intervals

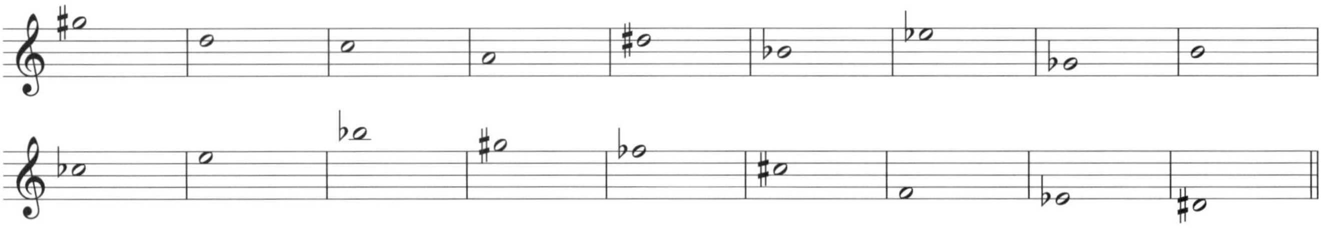

– by writing the first note of the intervals

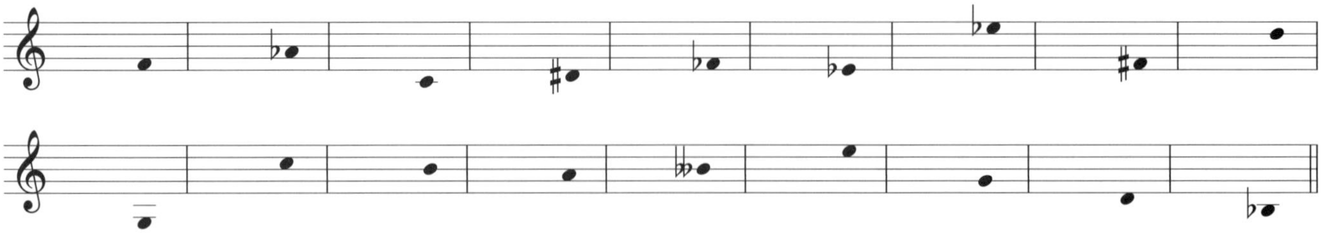

3 Find the intervals and indicate their qualities (ascending, descending, major, minor)

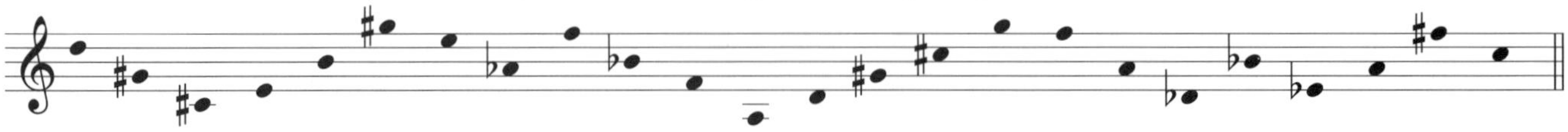

Answers, p. 29

3.7 Sevenths

3.7.1 Diminished 7ths

The diminished seventh is the enharmonic equivalent of the major sixth (4-1/2 steps). This interval is used mainly in diminished chords, but rarely in melodies.

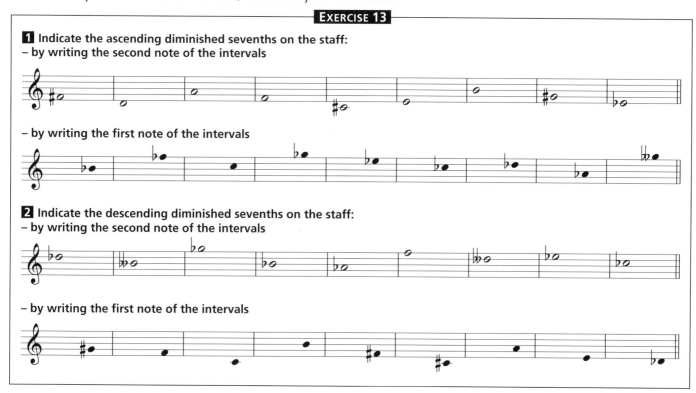

Answers, p. 30

3.7.2 Minor 7ths

Choose a melody you know that begins with each of the following intervals and write it on the staff:

Ascending minor 7ths

Write your melody

Descending minor 7ths

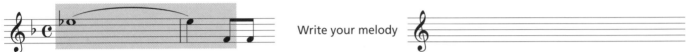

Write your melody

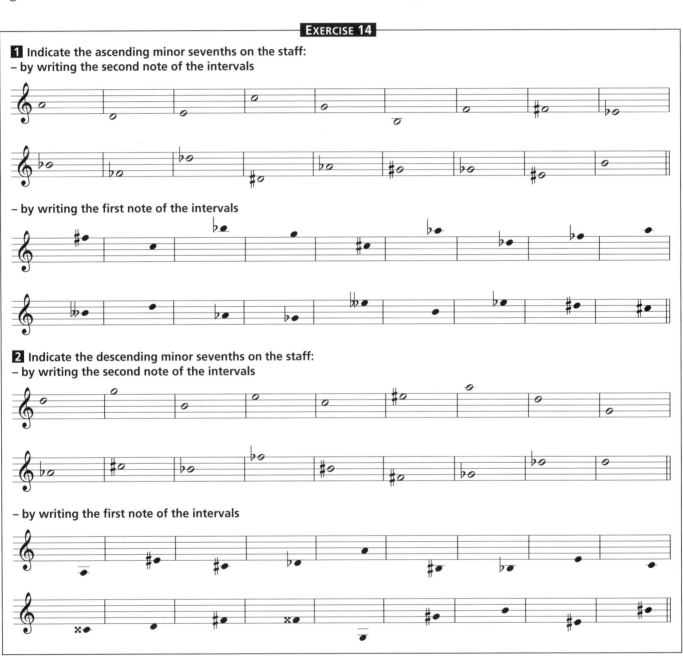

EXERCISE 14

1 Indicate the ascending minor sevenths on the staff:
– by writing the second note of the intervals

– by writing the first note of the intervals

2 Indicate the descending minor sevenths on the staff:
– by writing the second note of the intervals

– by writing the first note of the intervals

Answers, p. 30

3.7.3 Major 7ths

Choose a melody you know that begins with each of the following intervals and write it on the staff:

Ascending major 7ths

Write your melody

Descending major 7ths

Write your melody

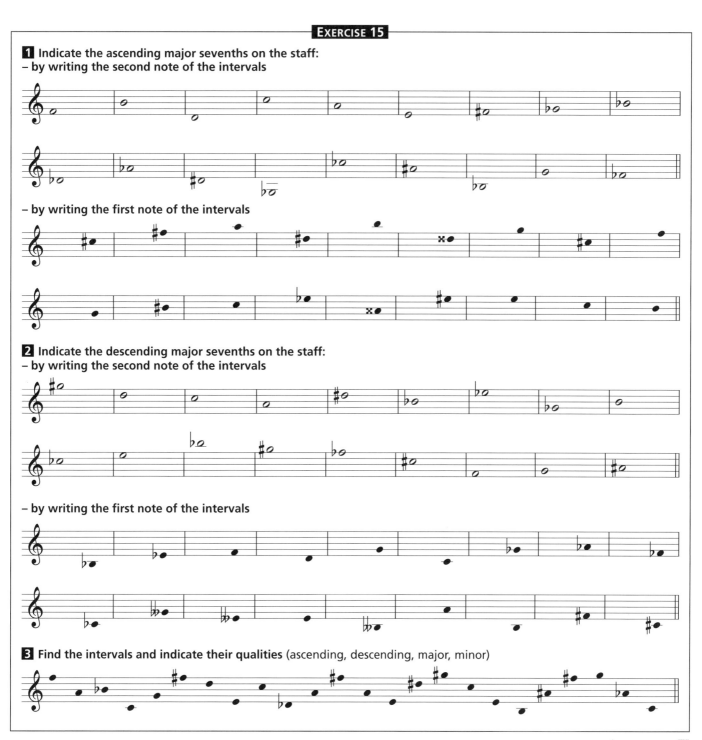

EXERCISE 15

1 Indicate the ascending major sevenths on the staff:
– by writing the second note of the intervals

– by writing the first note of the intervals

2 Indicate the descending major sevenths on the staff:
– by writing the second note of the intervals

– by writing the first note of the intervals

3 Find the intervals and indicate their qualities (ascending, descending, major, minor)

Answers, p. 31

3.8 Octaves

Choose a melody you know that begins with each of the following intervals and write it on the staff:

Ascending octaves

Write your melody

Descending octaves

Write your melody

❹ General review

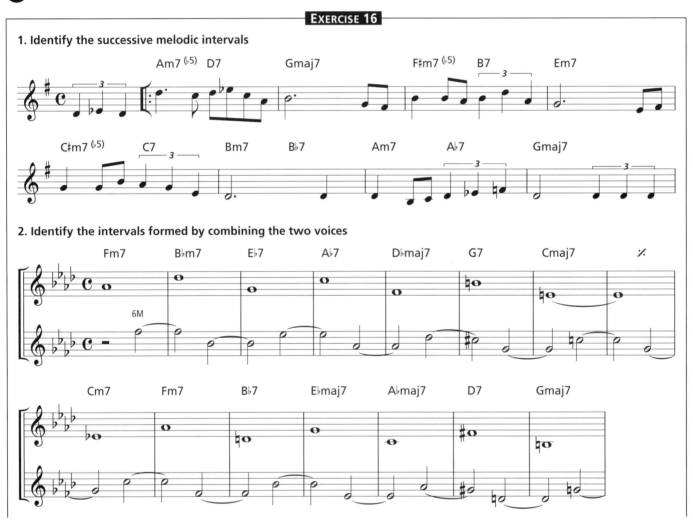

EXERCISE 16

1. Identify the successive melodic intervals

2. Identify the intervals formed by combining the two voices

Little Prelude in Cm, BWV 934 / Johann Sebastian Bach

3. Identify the intervals formed by combining the melody and the root of the chord

This type of analysis will help establish the harmonic relationship between the melody and the chords, which is necessary to explore the different chord colors, and play specific chords.

Answers, p. 32

❺ Answers

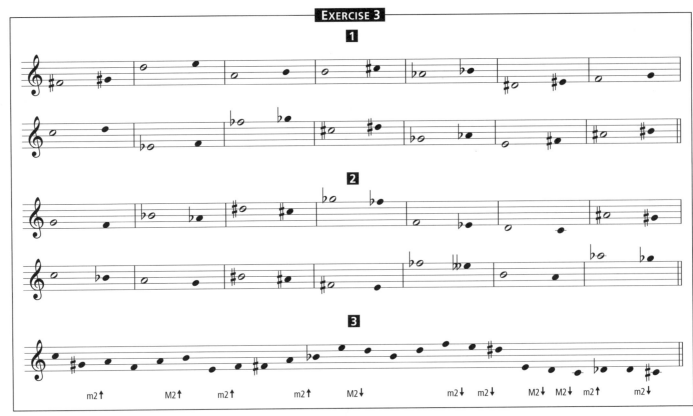

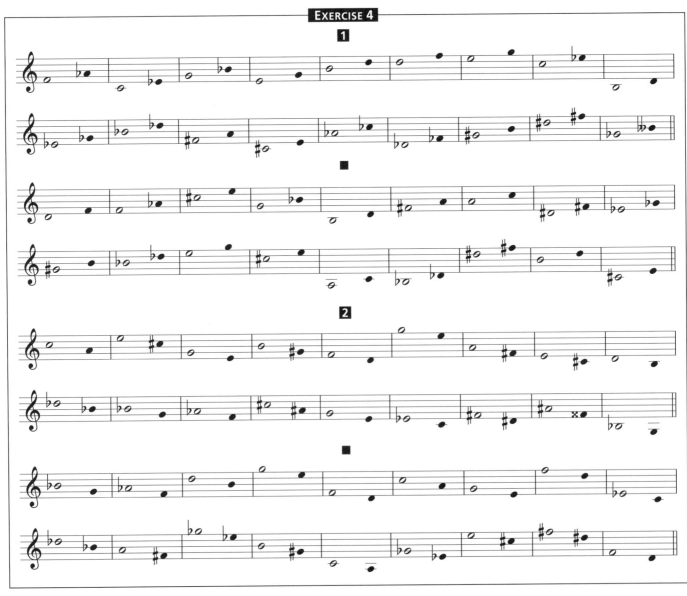

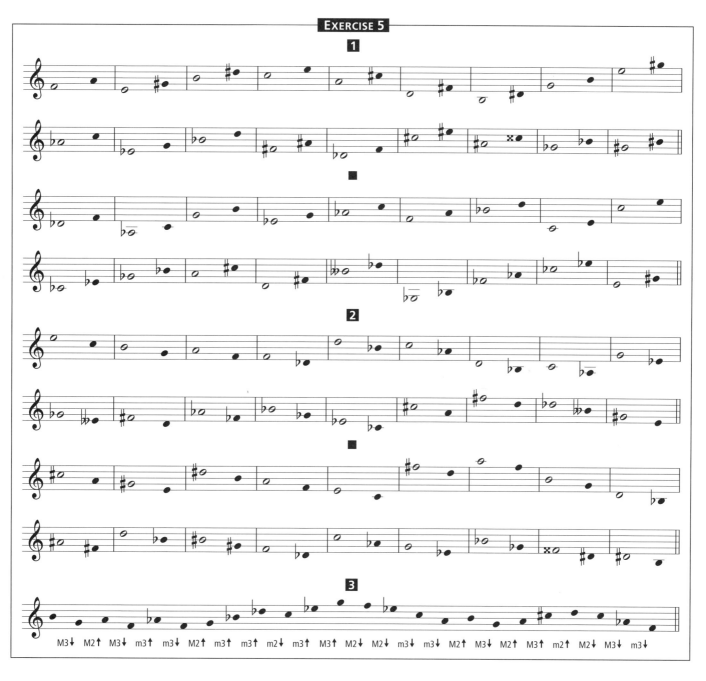

EXERCISE 7

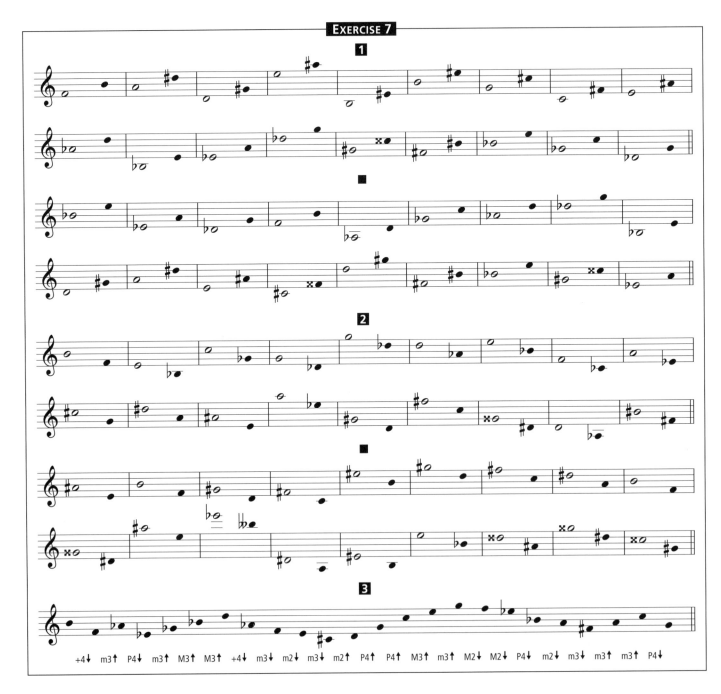

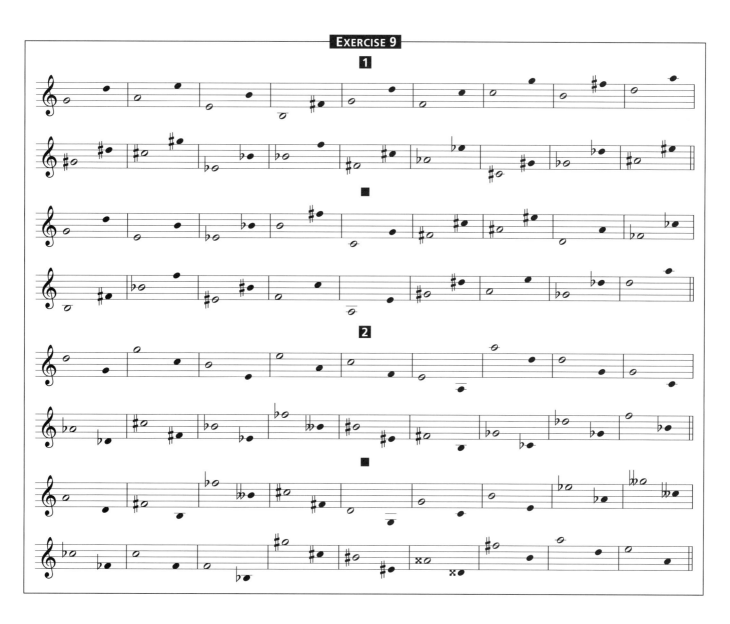

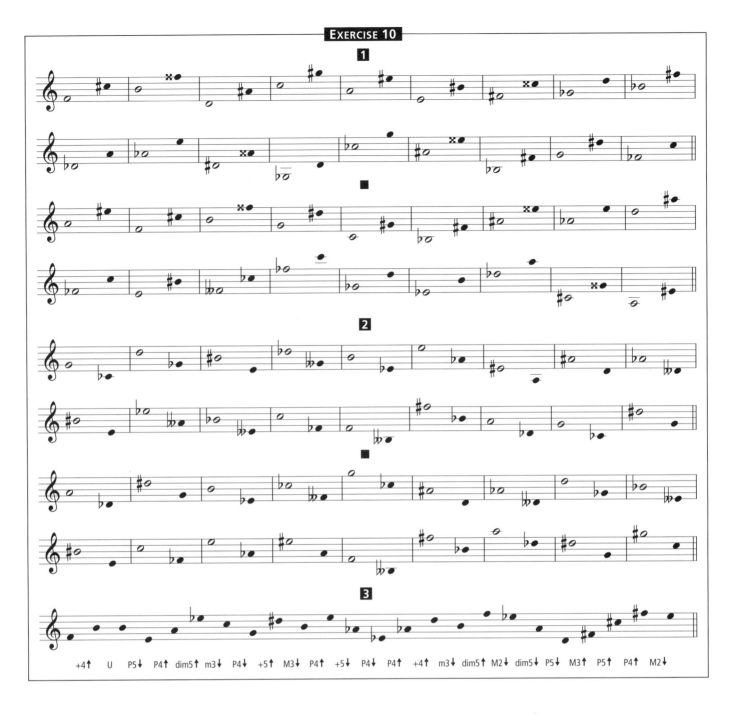

+4↑ U P5↓ P4↑ dim5↑ m3↓ P4↓ +5↑ M3↓ P4↑ +5↓ P4↓ P4↑ +4↑ m3↓ dim5↑ M2↓ dim5↓ P5↓ M3↓ P5↑ P4↑ M2↓

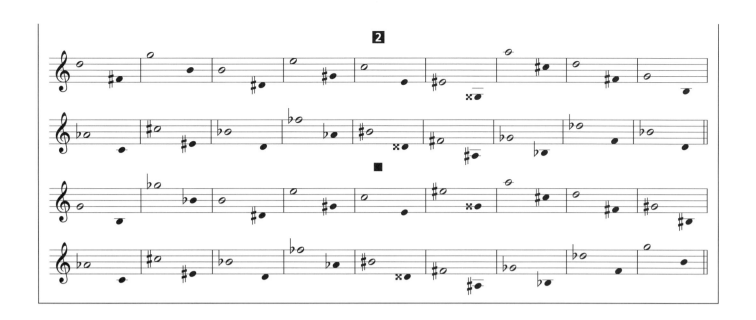

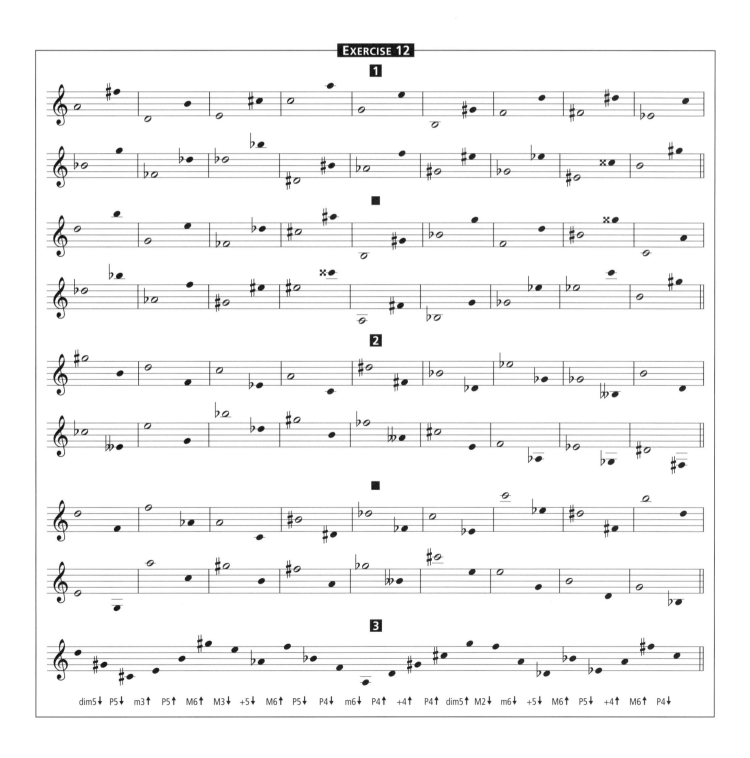

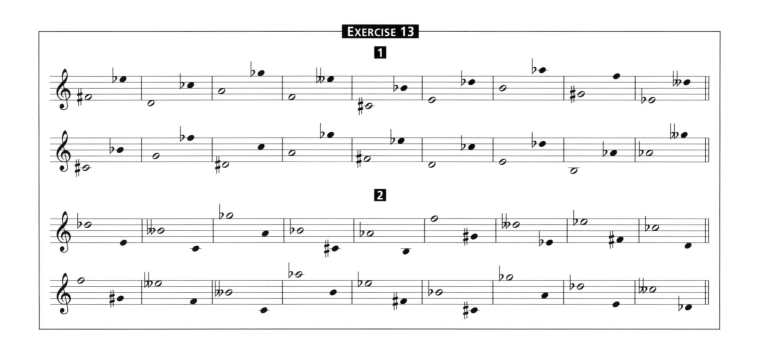

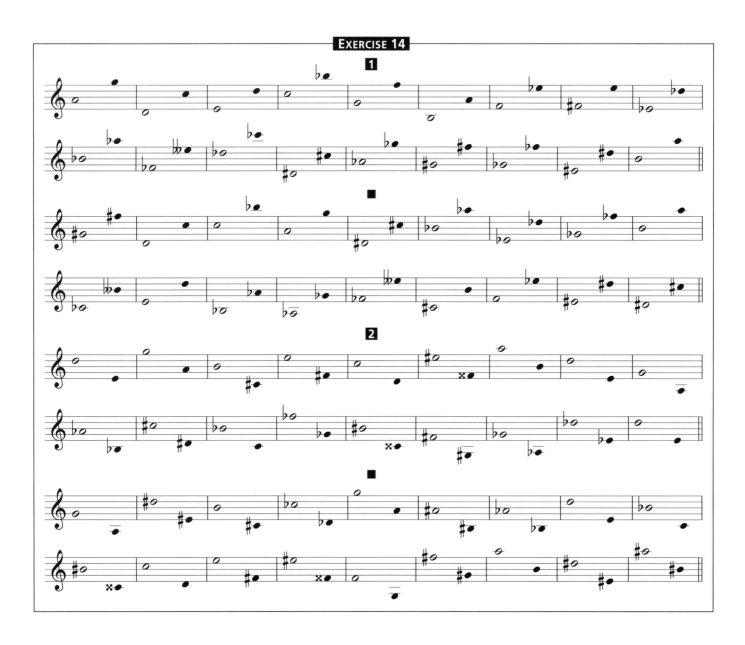

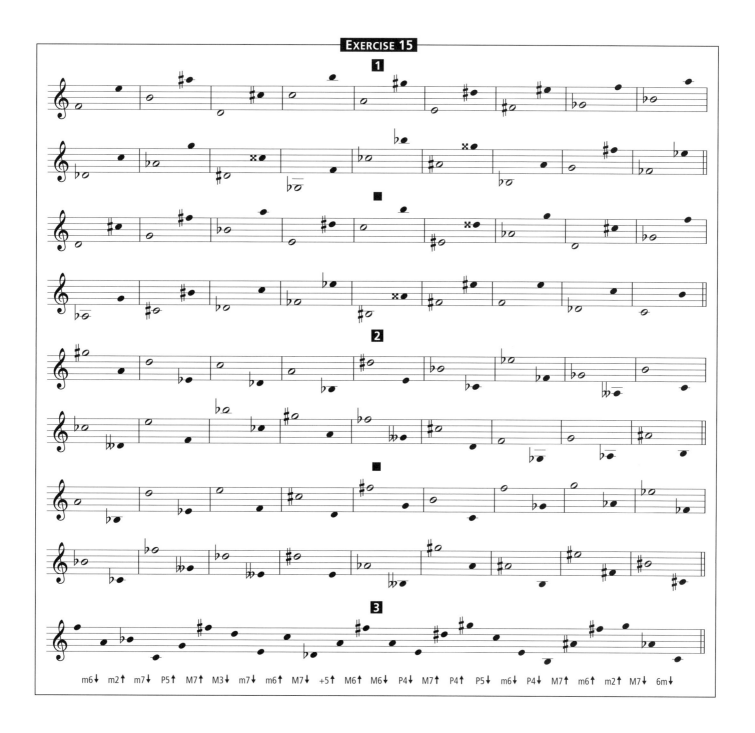

m6↓ m2↑ m7↓ P5↑ M7↑ M3↓ m7↓ m6↑ M7↓ +5↑ M6↑ M6↓ P4↓ M7↑ P4↑ P5↓ m6↓ P4↓ M7↑ m6↑ m2↑ M7↓ 6m↓

CHAPTER 2
THREE-NOTE CHORDS: TRIADS

In the first chapter, we saw that being able to analyze intervals makes it possible to qualify the melodic and harmonic relationships between any two given notes. In this chapter, we will be focusing on the construction of major, minor, diminished, and augmented three-note **chords** (collectively referred to as triads).

In this book, we use the notion of triad to refer to:

- three different pitches sounded simultaneously or played in an arpeggio, and
- the stacking of two 3rds.

Definitions

The **root** of a triad is the note upon which the rest of the chord is built. Intervals are always determined on the basis of their relationship to the root, which is the first degree of the chord and whose quality never changes.

The **natural tonic** is the first degree of the relative major or minor parent scale of each mode. For example, the natural tonic of E Phrygian[1] is C major.

The **modal tonic** is the starting note upon which the mode is built. In this case, E is the modal tonic of E Phrygian. Each degree of the parent scale may serve as the modal tonic of a mode.

The **parent scale** is a major or minor scale upon which seven modes are derived.

The **standard scale** is the reference scale used to analyze the intervals of each mode. The standard scale used throughout this book is the major scale.

A **scale** is an ordered succession of a certain number of degrees spanning from the tonic to the octave above, or below.

A **mode** is the succession of seven degrees derived from a parent scale. Every mode has a distinctive color. Note that, in a tonal system, we also refer to major and minor modes depending on the quality of the 3rd degree of the scale.

A **symmetrical succession of pitches** is a series of equidistant pitches that create equal divisions of the octave and where each note may act as the tonic.

Clusters[2] are types of chords that cannot be represented by chord symbols and which comprise a succession of neighboring major and/or minor seconds. These are not covered in this book.

The term **triad** is most appropriate for three-note chords obtained by stacking two sets of 3rds. While major and minor chords are triads, they can also be completed by the addition of other notes (6th, 7th, 9th, 11th, and 13th).

---

1 Phrygian mode = natural mode derived from the IIIrd degree of the major parent scale (See Natural Diatonic Modes, Chapter 12, p. 185).
2 These chords have a compact sound formed by stacking several major and/or minor seconds.

Work plan

For all the chords presented in this chapter, we have used the same four-step work plan, comprising:

- a definition of the chord in question;
- the various symbols used to identify the chord;
- the chord-voicing possibilities;
- a set of exercises.

❶ Major and minor triads

Major triads and **minor triads** comprise a root, a major (or minor) 3rd, and a perfect 5th. The 3rd is the only note in the chord that indicates whether the triad is minor or major.

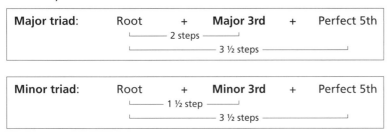

1.1 Music notation principles

When writing chords, two mistakes are common, notably:

- enharmonic errors (such as writing D♭ instead of C♯), and
- interval miscalculation.

To avoid making these types of mistakes, proceed as follows, using the A major triad as an example:

1. Identify the names of the notes (but not the quality of the intervals in the chord), which in this case are A-C-E. This will prevent making enharmonic errors, such as confusing C♯ and D♭ (which are both two tones above A), or E and F♭ (both three-and-a-half tones above A).

2. Determine the quality of the intervals by calculating the number of steps involved:

   - the major 3rd = two whole steps, which gives C♯;
   - the perfect 5th = three-and-a-half steps, which gives E.

The notes of an A major triad are therefore A-C♯-E:

Different ways to name triads

Taking X as the root of any given triad, several symbols are used to designate three-note chords. In the case of:

- major 3rd triads; three possibilities: namely, X (the notation symbol used in this book), as well as Xmaj and XM;
- minor 3rd triads; three possibilities: namely, Xm (notation symbol used in this book), as well as Xmin and X-.

1.2 Basic chord positions

When referring to chords, the terms "position" and "voicing" can cause some confusion. The **position** of a chord indicates which chord tone is the bass (or bottom) note.

There are three positions for three-note chords:

- root position (when the root is in the bass);
- first inversion (3rd in the bass);
- second inversion (5th in the bass).

The **voicing** of a chord indicates the order of the notes from the lowest to the highest. Depending on the position of a chord, several voicings are possible. In this chapter, we will examine three of these:

- **close-position voicings:** the distance between two adjacent intervals in the chord cannot be greater than a 3rd. There is only one possible close-position voicing for a chord in root position;
- **open-position voicings:** contain at least one adjacent interval in the chord that is larger than a 3rd. This provides several open-position voicing possibilities in root and chord-inversion positions;
- **doubled-note voicings:** one or more notes of the chord must be doubled. This provides several doubled-note voicing possibilities in root and chord-inversion positions.

For example, the three voicings of the A major triad in root position are:

Close-position voicing   **Open-position voicing**   **Doubled-note voicing**

Important

The root and the bass note of a chord are often confused; these two concepts are nevertheless quite different and should be clearly defined:

- the **root** is the note upon which a chord is built (the root of A major = A). This note may be sounded in any voice of the chord (first, second, or third voice, etc.)
- the **bass note** is always the lowest note of the chord; it can be the root, 3rd, 5th, 7th, etc. of the chord or even a note that is not part of the chord at all.

Also, avoid systematically associating the root position of a chord with its close-position voicing.

1.3 Types of inversions

A chord is **inverted** when its root is not voiced in the bass. Three-note chords have two inversions:

- **first inversion:** with the 3rd of the chord in the bass;

- **second inversion:** with the 5th of the chord in the bass.

Inverted-chord symbols

Slash-chord symbols are used to represent inverted chords. These symbols comprise the name of the chord and the bass note separated by a slash, with the chord name on the left and the bass note on the right. For example:

- A/C♯ represents the A major chord with a C♯ played in the bass (= first inversion of A);
- A/E represents the A major chord with an E played in the bass (= second inversion of A).

Although chord symbols indicate the position of chords, they do not specify how they are voiced. As we have seen, chords can be voiced in several positions (root position and inversions). Being able to indicate and follow **chord voicings** is therefore an indispensable skill requiring the ability to master intervals and, consequently, to read and write the order of notes, from the lowest to the highest degrees.

Every note is designated a number (Arabic numeral) that represents its scale-tone degree:

- 1 for the root;
- 3 for the 3rd;
- 5 for the 5th.

Examples in A major

It is extremely important to master the notation of chord voicings, not only to tackle the chapters ahead, but also for voicing notes in the precise order of the chord. The A major chord shown above sounds quite different depending on whether it is voiced in position 1-3-5 or 1-5-3. This is particularly important when working with four-, five-, and six-note chords.

Identifying chord names

Being able to name a chord, regardless of its position (root position, first and second inversions, etc.) or voicing (close/open) is essential. To do this, arrange the notes of the chords in their closest position to obtain two sets of stacked 3rds.

EXAMPLES

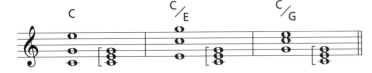

Reminder

The 3rd is the only note in a triad that determines whether the chord is major or minor; the difference between a major and minor 3rd being a half step:

- major triad = root + major 3rd + perfect 5th;
- minor triad = root + minor 3rd + perfect 5th.

This study of major and minor triads also covers altered 5th triads.

1 Write the names of the major and minor triads in close root position

2 Write the names of the major and minor triads in open root position

3 Write in the notes of the chords in close root position

G   Em   Cm   G♭   E♭m   D   F♯   B   A♭m   C♯

4 On the staff, write the notes of the chords in close voicing

C/E   Dm/A   Gm/B♭   B♭/D   Am/E   A/E   C♯m/G♯   E♭m/G♭   Gm/D   D♭/F

5 Write the names and voicings of the chords

B♭/F

6 On the staff, write the notes of the chords according to their respective voicings and complete the chord symbol if necessary

Fm   B♭m   G   A♭m   C♯   E♭m   F♯m   D   A   G♭

Answers, p. 39

② Altered 5th triads

There are two types of altered 5th chords: diminished 5th chords and augmented 5th chords, which respectively form a diminished and an augmented triad.[3]

2.1 Diminished triads

Diminished triads comprise a root, a minor 3rd, and a diminished 5th, as follows:

Diminished triad:	Root	+	Minor 3rd	+	Diminished 5th
	└── 1 ½ step ──┘				
	└────────── 3 steps ──────────┘				

---
3   We will examine X7sus4 triads in greater depth in Chapter 3, p. 52.

Ddim triad

Chord symbols

Diminished triads can be symbolized in several ways: Xdim (notation symbol used in this book), as well as Xm(♭5), Xmin(♭5), X°, and X-(♭5).

2.2 Augmented triads

Augmented triads comprise a root, a major 3rd, and an augmented 5th, as follows:

Example

Gaug triad

Chord symbols

Augmented triads can be symbolized in several ways: Xaug (notation symbol used in this book), as well as X(♯5), XM(♯5), Xaug, Xmaj(♯5), and X+.

Reminder

- diminished triads in root position are built by stacking two minor 3rds: in Ddim, for example, these are D-F and F-A♭;
- augmented triads in root position are built by stacking two major 3rds: in Gaug, for example, these are G-B and B-D♯.

This study of diminished and augmented triads also covers altered 5th triads.

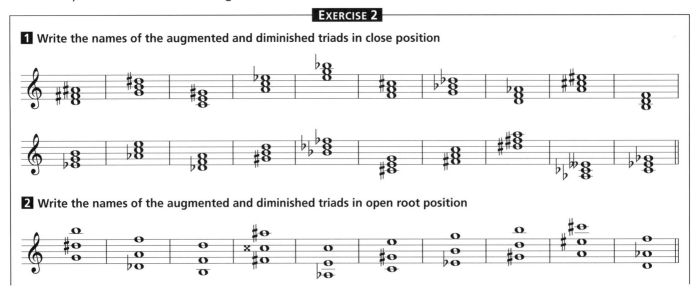

3 On the staff, write the notes of the chords in close root position

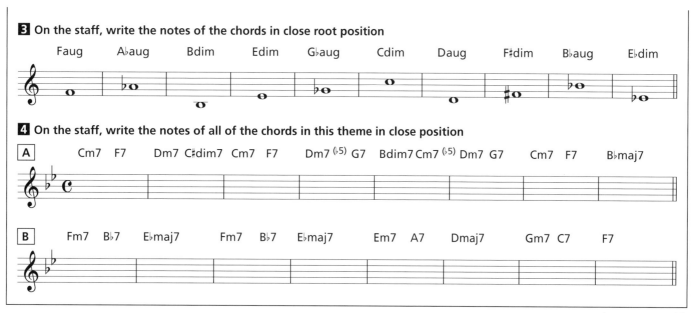

| Faug | A♭aug | Bdim | Edim | G♭aug | Cdim | Daug | F#dim | B♭aug | E♭dim |

4 On the staff, write the notes of all of the chords in this theme in close position

A Cm7 F7   Dm7 C#dim7 Cm7 F7   Dm7 (♭5) G7   Bdim7 Cm7 (♭5) Dm7 G7   Cm7 F7   B♭maj7

B Fm7 B♭7 E♭maj7   Fm7 B♭7 E♭maj7   Em7 A7   Dmaj7   Gm7 C7   F7

Answers, p. 40

❸ Answers

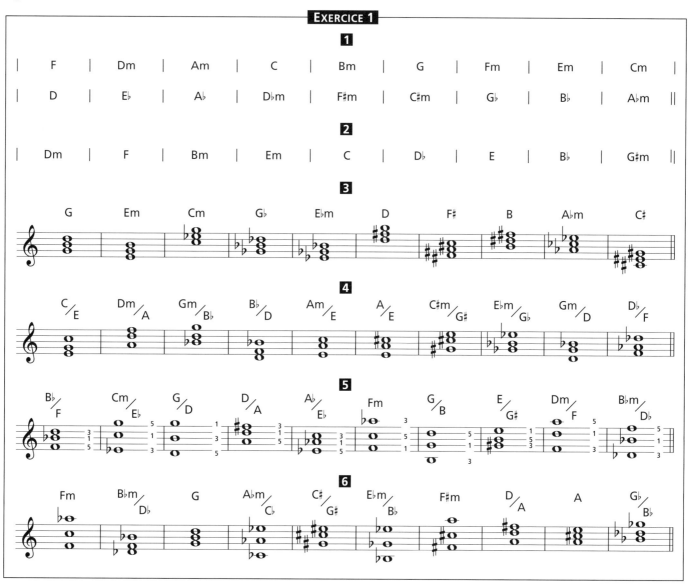

1

Daug	Gaug	Caug	Adim	Edim	Faug	Gdim	Ddim	Aaug	Bdim
E♭aug	A♭aug	D♭aug	G♯dim	B♭dim	C♯dim	F♯dim	D♯dim	A♭dim	Cdim

2

| Gaug | D♭aug | Bdim | F♯aug | A♭aug | Caug | E♭aug | G♯dim | Aaug | Ddim |

3

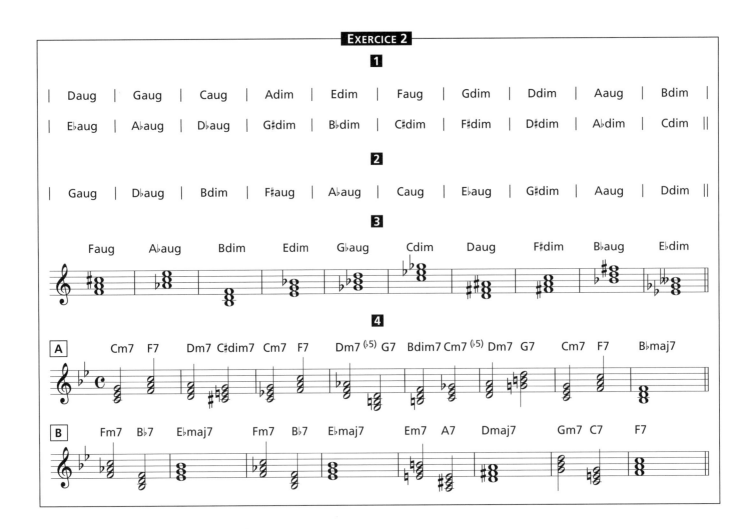

CHAPTER 3
FOUR-NOTE CHORDS: TETRADS

❶ The five qualities of the main chords

All the triads we have studied so far may be enriched by adding a 6th or a 7th to create a four-note chord, called a **tetrad**.

To help you memorize and use these four-note chords, we will present their related chord qualities progressively, by focusing on the:

- two qualities of major chords with an added 7th: Xmaj7 and X7;
- three qualities of minor and diminished chords with an added 7th: Xm7, Xm7(♭5), and Xdim7.

1.1 Major 7th chords: Xmaj7

Major 7th chords[1] contain a major triad plus a major 7th. Note that the name of this chord specifies that the 7th is major. It comprises the following intervals:

Major 7th chord:	Root	+	Major 3rd	+	Perfect 5th	+	Major 7th
	└── 2 steps ──┘						
	└──────── 3 ½ steps ────────┘						
	└──────────────── 5 ½ steps ────────────────┘						

> **Useful tip**
>
> A quick way to calculate the major 7th is to think of it as being a half step below the root.

EXAMPLE   the major 7th above C:

To build a Bmaj7 chord (following the musical notation principles on page 5):

1. Find the names of the notes (without determining the quality of the intervals in the chord). In this case, the notes are B, D, F, A.

2. Determine the quality of the intervals relative to the root:
    - major 3rd = two whole steps above the root (B) = D♯;
    - perfect 5th = three-and-a-half steps above the root = F♯;
    - major 7th = five-and-a-half steps above the root = A♯ (one half step below the root).

EXAMPLE

Bmaj7

---

1 To specify that the 7th in this chord is major, the chord could be defined as being "major with a major 7th." However, to comply with conventional musical nomenclature, we refer to it here as the major 7th chord.

With the exception of X7sus4, triads that have an added 7th and are in root position are built by stacking a series of 3rds. Understanding this characteristic is useful when trying to find the root position of an inverted chord.

Chord symbols

Several symbols are used to designate major 7th chords, namely Xmaj7 (notation symbol used in this book), XΔ, XΔ7, Xma7, XM7, and X7M.

1.2 Seventh chord: X7

Seventh chords comprise a major 3rd, a perfect 5th, and a minor 7th, as follows:

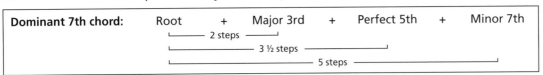

Dominant 7th chord:	Root	+	Major 3rd	+	Perfect 5th	+	Minor 7th
		2 steps					
			3 ½ steps				
				5 steps			

> ## Useful tip
>
> A quick way to calculate the minor 7th is to think of it as being one whole step below the root.
>
> For example, the minor 7th above C:

Chord symbols

The X7 chord symbol is always used to symbolize 7th chords. While "dominant 7ths" may also be referred to as "dominant" and "dominant 7th" chords, this nomenclature may not be specific enough to convey the different ways this chord is used. Although the "dominant 7th" usually refers to 7th chords with a dominant function, we will see that, in certain contexts, it can also designate 7th chords with a tonic function, such as in the blues.

EXAMPLE

1.3 Minor 7th chords: Xm7

Minor 7th chords comprise a minor 3rd, a perfect 5th, and a minor 7th, as follows:

Minor 7th chord:	Root	+	Minor 3rd	+	Perfect 5th	+	Minor 7th
		1 ½ step					
			3 ½ steps				
				5 steps			

EXAMPLE

Chord symbols

Several symbols are used to designate minor 7th chords, namely: Xm7 (notation symbol used in this book), Xmin7, Xmi7, and X-7.

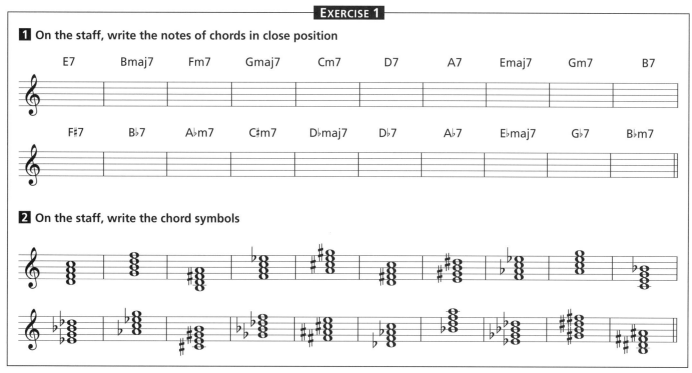

EXERCISE 1

1 On the staff, write the notes of chords in close position

| E7 | Bmaj7 | Fm7 | Gmaj7 | Cm7 | D7 | A7 | Emaj7 | Gm7 | B7 |

| F#7 | Bb7 | Abm7 | C#m7 | Dbmaj7 | Db7 | Ab7 | Ebmaj7 | Gb7 | Bbm7 |

2 On the staff, write the chord symbols

Answers, p. 57

1.4 Minor-seven flat-five chords: Xm7(b5)

Minor-seven flat-five chords comprise a diminished triad (two minor 3rds) and a minor 7th, as follows:

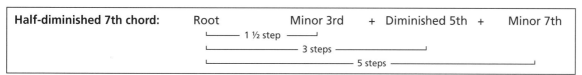

Half-diminished 7th chord:	Root	Minor 3rd	+ Diminished 5th +	Minor 7th
	⌐— 1 ½ step —⌐			
	⌐——— 3 steps ———⌐			
	⌐————— 5 steps —————⌐			

Important

This chord may be referred to as a:

- minor-seven flat-five (name used in this book);
- half-diminished;
- minor 7th diminished 5.

EXAMPLE

Chord symbols

Several symbols are used to designate minor-seven flat-five chords, namely: Xm7(b5) (notation symbol used in this book), Xmin7(b5), X-7b5), X⌀, and X⌀7.

1.5 Diminished chords: Xdim7

Diminished chords comprise a diminished triad and a diminished 7th, as follows:

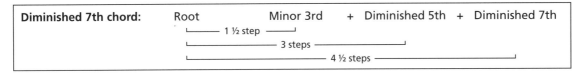

Diminished 7th chord:	Root	Minor 3rd	+	Diminished 5th	+	Diminished 7th
	└── 1 ½ step ──┘					
	└────── 3 steps ──────┘					
	└────────── 4 ½ steps ──────────┘					

When writing "diminished chord" symbols, some musicians make no distinction between the diminished tetrad (Xdim7) and the diminished triad (Xdim). This inattention to detail often leads to confusion and chord-symbol misinterpretation. To avoid this, the 7th must always be mentioned in the chord symbol if it is to be played.

It is important that the diminished 7th be written correctly without confusing it with its enharmonic equivalent, the major 6th (for example, writing A instead of B♭♭). Enharmonic errors of this kind are extremely common.

As illustrated below, a diminished chord voiced in close root position is in fact a series of stacked minor 3rds.

EXAMPLE

Chord symbols

Several symbols are used to designate diminished 7th chords: Xdim7 (notation symbol used in this book), Xdim (which can cause confusion with the diminished triad), and X°7.

EXERCISE 2

1 On the staff, write the notes of the chords in close position

Bm7 (♭5)　Gm7 (♭5)　Adim7　Dm7 (♭5)　Edim7　Gdim7　Cm7 (♭5)　Ddim7　Cdim7　Fm7 (♭5)

C♯m7 (♭5)　E♭m7 (♭5)　F♯dim7　B♭dim7　F♯m7 (♭5)　G♯dim7　B♭m7 (♭5)　D♯dim7　E♭dim7　A♭m7 (♭5)

2 Write the symbols above each chord

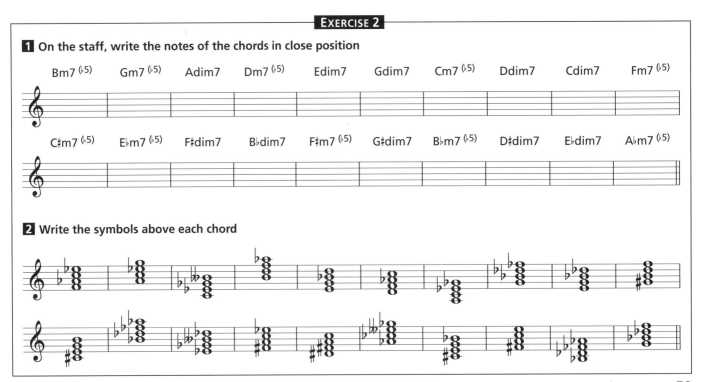

Answers, p. 58

---

❷ Different root positions

As in the case of triads, four-note chords in root position can be voiced in close position, as well as in open and doubled-note positions. Two examples of open and doubled-note position voicings of the chords Bmaj7 and E7 in root position are given below:

EXAMPLES

Bmaj7 and E7: open position (1-5-3-7)

 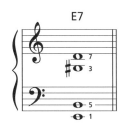

Bmaj7 and E7: doubled-note voicing (1-5-3-7-3)

 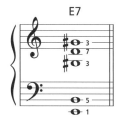

These examples show that it is more difficult to identify the root in a chord comprised of four notes rather than three. To identify the root, find the note upon which it is possible to stack a succession of 3rds.

❸ Types of inversions

Because four-note chords contain one note more than triads, they offer an additional inversion possibility. Tetrads may therefore be expressed in their root position, as well as their first, second, and third inversions, and can be voiced in various ways. The following examples can be applied to all four-note chords:

First inversion (3rd in the bass): in Bmaj7, the bass note is D♯, and in E7 it is G♯: 3-1-5-7.

Second inversion (5th in the bass): in Bmaj7, the bass note is F♯ and in E7 it is B: 5-3-7-1.

 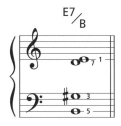

Third inversion (7th in the bass): in Bmaj7, the bass note is A♯ and in E7 it is D: 7-5-1-3.

Identifying chords

When the notes of a chord are not in close root position, identifying the name of the chord can be quite tricky. So, how does one know what the chord is and whether it is in root or inverted position? As we have seen, chords built on a triad with an added 7th must contain a series of stacked 3rds when the chord is in root position. This is the easiest position to identify the name of a chord.

EXAMPLES

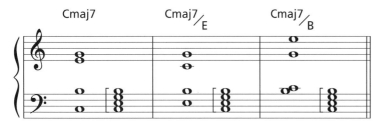

Those new to the study of harmony often tend to think of chords as being a group of notes (chord tones) played simultaneously on a polyphonic instrument.[2] Chords, however, may be voiced and heard in several other ways, such as in piano scores or different instrumental arrangements of musical works, where each instrument plays a specific note of the chord.

Take, for example, Prelude No. 1 from Johann Sebastian Bach's *Well-Tempered Clavier.* Although none of the chord tones in this piece are played simultaneously as vertical chords, the chord structure of each measure can be determined by analyzing the horizontal succession of notes.

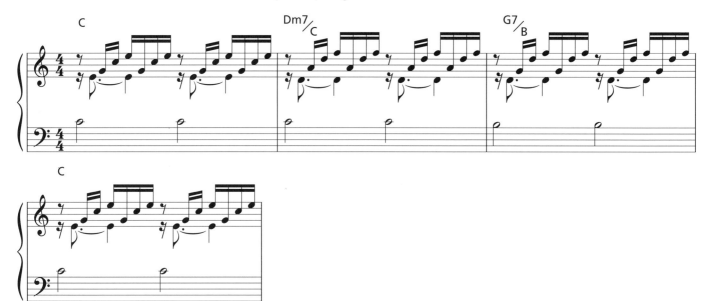

The following excerpt from Franz Schubert's String Quartet No. 14 ("Death and the Maiden") can also be analyzed by examining its chord structure and applying the chord symbols.

---

2 Instruments, such as the piano, guitar, and vibraphone where several voices can be played at the same time.

Second movement; measures 10-17:

Reminder

The three 7th chords comprising a triad and a perfect 5th are listed in the table below:

Chord symbol	Triad	Seventh	Interval combination
Xmaj7	major	major	All major (major 3rd and major 7th)
X7	major	minor	Mixed (major 3rd and minor 7th)
Xm7	minor	minor	All minor (minor 3rd and minor 7th)

Xm7($\flat$5) and the Xdim7 are 7th chords built upon a diminished triad. The only difference between these two chords is the quality of their respective 7ths:

Chord symbol	Triad	Seventh
Xm7 ($\flat$5)	diminished	minor
Xdim7	diminished	diminished

The five main chord qualities used in functional harmony are listed in the table below (Xmaj7, X7, Xm7, Xm7(♭5), and Xdim7). Note that all these chords are built upon a series of alternating minor and major 3rds:

Xmaj7	Root	Major 3rd	Perfect 5th	Major 7th
X7	Root	Major 3rd	Perfect 5th	**Minor 7th**
Xm7	Root	**Minor 3rd**	Perfect 5th	Minor 7th
Xm7 (♭5)	Root	Minor 3rd	**Diminished 5th**	Minor 7th
Xdim7	Root	Minor 3rd	Diminished 5th	**Diminished 7th**

EXAMPLES

EXERCISE 3

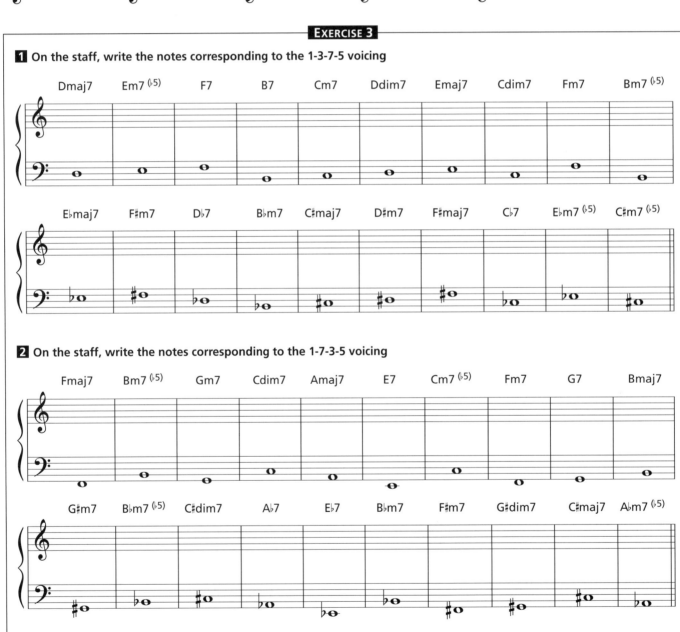

3 Write the names of the chords and indicate their voicings

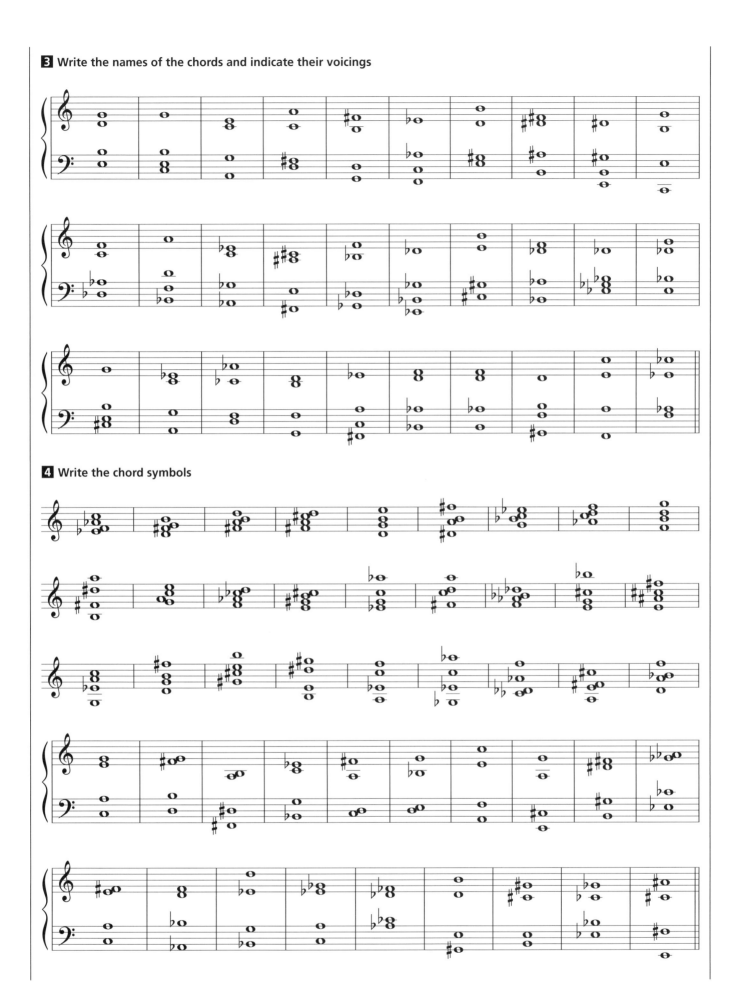

4 Write the chord symbols

5 Write the chord symbols based on the melody and piano accompaniment

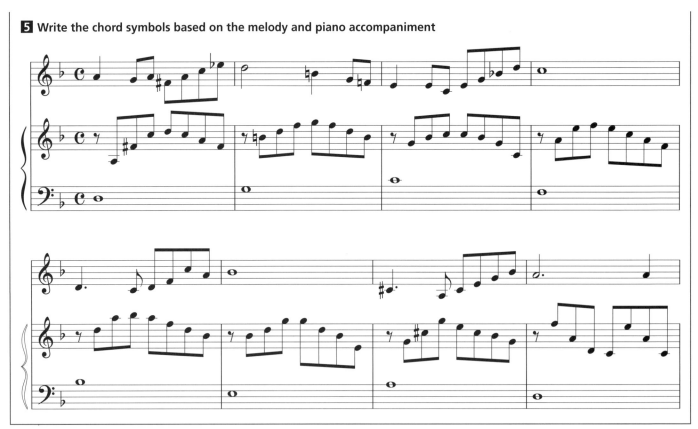

Answers, p. 58-59

❹ Other four-note chords

4.1 Triads with added 6ths: X6 and Xm6

The major 6th can be added to major and minor triads. This gives another two four-note chords, namely:

- **the major 6th chord** (or 6th chord) = a major triad + a major 6th, as follows;

Major 6th chord:	Root	+	Major 3rd	+	Perfect 5th	+	Major 6th
	└─ 2 steps ─┘						
	└─── 3 ½ steps ───┘						
	└──── 4 ½ steps ────┘						

- **the minor 6th chord** = a minor triad + major 6th, as follows;

Minor 6th chord:	Root	+	Minor 3rd	+	Perfect 5th	+	Major 6th
	└─ 1 ½ step ─┘						
	└─── 3 ½ steps ───┘						
	└──── 4 ½ steps ────┘						

Useful tip

A quick way to calculate the major 6th is to think of it as being one whole step above the perfect 5th.

Close and open root voicings of B♭6 and Am6:

Close root voicing   **Open root voicing**

B♭6

Am6

B♭6

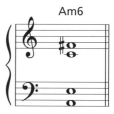
Am6

Chord symbols

Several symbols are used to designate major and minor 6th chords. Depending on the lead sheet, these include X6 for the major and Xm6 for the minor (symbols used in this book), as well as Xmaj6 and XM6, and Xmin6 and X-6, respectively.

Important

These two new chord qualities (X6 and Xm6) are the first examples of chords whose construction is not based on the stacking of 3rds principle. The interval between the 5th and the 6th is a major 2nd. When writing these chords, therefore, it is important not to stack the notes as if they were 3rds. In the following example, the D must be written to the side of, not above, the C, as follows:

F6

When you come across an X chord symbol with no other specification (as is often the case in *Real Book* lead sheets, for example), you can play a straightforward major triad (with no additions) or a major 6th (X6).

In the case of Xm chords, these may be played as straightforward minor triads (with no additions), or as an Xm(maj7), an Xm7, or an Xm6. (See examples, p. 118.)

Inversions

Although inversions of X6 and Xm6 chords are rare, they follow the same rules and principles as other four-note chords.

The only difference between X6 and Xm6 chords is the quality of their respective 3rds:

- X6 = root + major 3rd + perfect 5th + major 6th;
- Xm6 = root + minor 3rd + perfect 5th + major 6th.

We will look at other major and minor chords containing a minor 6th in the chapters on modes.

4.2 Minor-major 7th chords: Xm(maj7)

Minor-major 7th chords comprise a minor 3rd, a perfect 5th, and a major 7th, as follows:

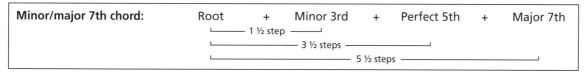

Minor/major 7th chord:	Root	+	Minor 3rd	+	Perfect 5th	+	Major 7th

Close and open root voicings of Em (maj7):

Close root voicing   **Open root voicing**

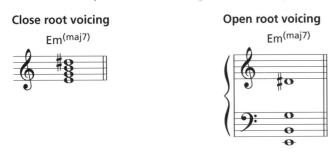

Chord symbols

Several symbols are used to designate minor-major 7th chords: Xm(maj7) (symbol used in this book), Xmin(M7), Xm(M7), X-(M7), Xm(Δ), Xm(Δ7), Xmin(Δ), and X-(Δ).

EXERCISE 4

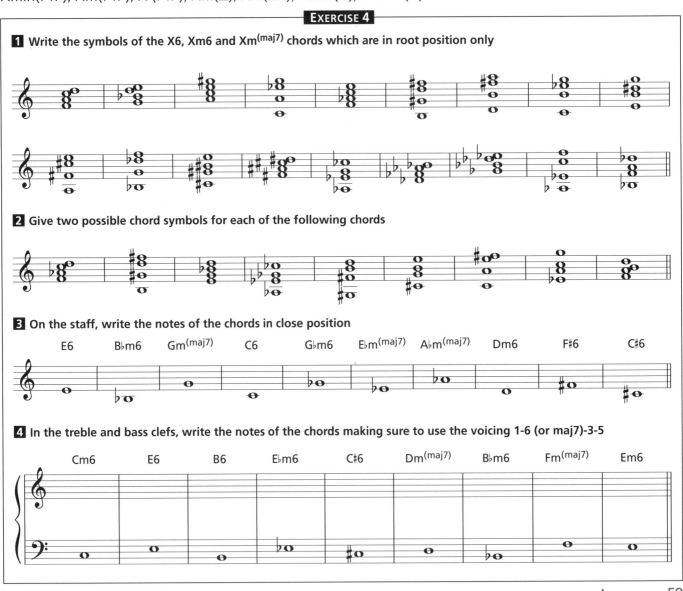

1 Write the symbols of the X6, Xm6 and Xm^(maj7) chords which are in root position only

2 Give two possible chord symbols for each of the following chords

3 On the staff, write the notes of the chords in close position

E6   B♭m6   Gm^(maj7)   C6   G♭m6   E♭m^(maj7)   A♭m^(maj7)   Dm6   F♯6   C♯6

4 In the treble and bass clefs, write the notes of the chords making sure to use the voicing 1-6 (or maj7)-3-5

Cm6   E6   B6   E♭m6   C♯6   Dm^(maj7)   B♭m6   Fm^(maj7)   Em6

Answers, p. 59

4.3 Sus4 chords: X7sus4

Sus4 chords differ from the other chords we have studied so far in that the second chord tone in root position is not a major or minor 3rd, but a perfect 4th. As indicated in the chord symbol, the X7sus4 is a chord with a "suspended" 4th. Sus4 chords therefore comprise a perfect 4th, a perfect 5th, and a minor 7th, as follows:

Suspended dominant 7th chord:	Root	+	Perfect 4th	+	Perfect 5th	+	Minor 7th
	└─ 2 ½ steps ─┘						
	└──── 3 ½ steps ────┘					
	└───────── 5 steps ─────────┘				

EXAMPLES

Close and open root voicings of G7sus4:

Close root voicing **Open root voicing**

Originally, the sole function of the X7sus4 was to delay the arrival of the X7 chord. The example below traces the "journey" of C, which is:

- prepared as the 7th of Dm7 in measure 1, then;

- delayed by the G7sus4 on beat 1 of measure 2 (where it becomes the 4th), before;

- resolving down, on beat 3 of measure 2, to B, which is the 3rd of G7.

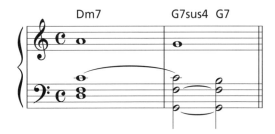

Depending on the musical style, the X7sus4 may be used for its chord quality (i.e., its sound), without having to resolve to the dominant, which is its function. On page 147, we will discover other ways this chord can be used.

Chord symbols

Several symbols are used to designate this chord: X7sus4 (notation symbol used in this book), X(sus4)7 and X7sus, and sometimes a IIm7/V slash chord, such as Dm7/G.

Note that X7sus4 chord inversions are rare. This chord is almost always used in root position.

> ### Reminder
>
> X7 and X7sus4 chords are differentiated by one note (the 3rd in X7 and the 4th in X7sus4):
> - X7: root + major 3rd + perfect 5th + minor 7th;
> - X7sus4: root + perfect 4th + perfect 5th + minor 7th.

4.4 Augmented major 7th chords:[3] Xmaj7(♯5)

Augmented major 7th chords comprise an augmented triad and a major 7th, as follows:

Augmented major 7th chord:	Root	+	Major 3rd	+	Augmented 5th	+	Major 7th
	└─ 2 steps ─┘						
	└──── 4 steps ────┘					
	└───────── 5 ½ steps ─────────┘				

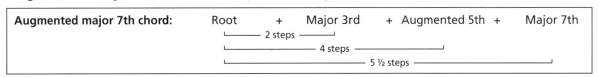

─────────

3 Also known as major-seven sharp-five chords.

Close and open root voicings of Fmaj7(♯5):

Close root voicing

Fmaj7 (♯5)

Open root voicing

Fmaj7 (♯5)

Chord symbols

Several symbols are used to designate this chord: Xmaj7(♯5) (symbol used in this book), X+M7, XΔ(♯5), and X+Δ. It may also be referred to as the major-seven sharp-five, the augmented major 7th, and the major 7+5, etc.

Different inversions

While Xmaj7(♯5) chord inversions are rare, they are subject to the same construction and chord-symbol rules as other chords.

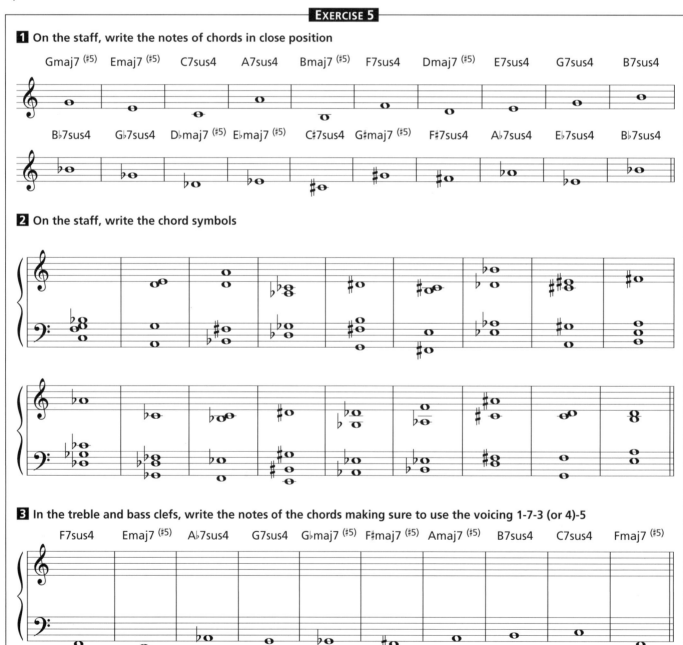

EXERCISE 5

1 On the staff, write the notes of chords in close position

Gmaj7 (♯5)   Emaj7 (♯5)   C7sus4   A7sus4   Bmaj7 (♯5)   F7sus4   Dmaj7 (♯5)   E7sus4   G7sus4   B7sus4

B♭7sus4   G♭7sus4   D♭maj7 (♯5)   E♭maj7 (♯5)   C♯7sus4   G♯maj7 (♯5)   F♯7sus4   A♭7sus4   E♭7sus4   B♭7sus4

2 On the staff, write the chord symbols

3 In the treble and bass clefs, write the notes of the chords making sure to use the voicing 1-7-3 (or 4)-5

F7sus4   Emaj7 (♯5)   A♭7sus4   G7sus4   G♭maj7 (♯5)   F♯maj7 (♯5)   Amaj7 (♯5)   B7sus4   C7sus4   Fmaj7 (♯5)

Answers, p. 60

❺ Using chord inversions

Regardless of a chord's position,[4] its function remains the same. The fact that the root of a chord is not voiced in the bass changes its sound and opens up other bass-note possibilities. In the example below, the Cmaj7/E in measure 3 creates an ascending diatonic movement in the bass line.

Chord inversions may exist in the original composition, or be introduced in the interpreter's arrangement or improvisation. In the two examples below, the chord inversions are part of the original compositions.

EXAMPLE 1

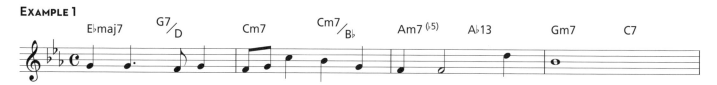

EXAMPLE 2

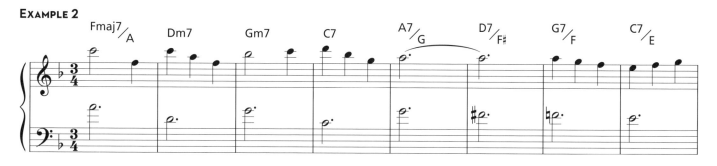

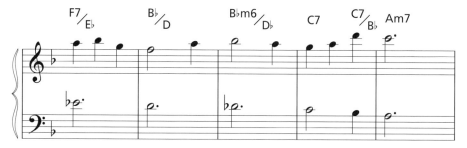

The chords in the following chart were modified by the arranger.

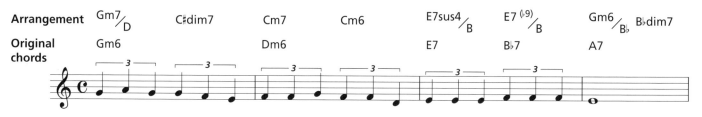

---

4 This study does not cover inversion possibilities generated by bass players' improvised bass lines.

6 General review

1 In the treble and bass clefs, write the notes of each chord in close position

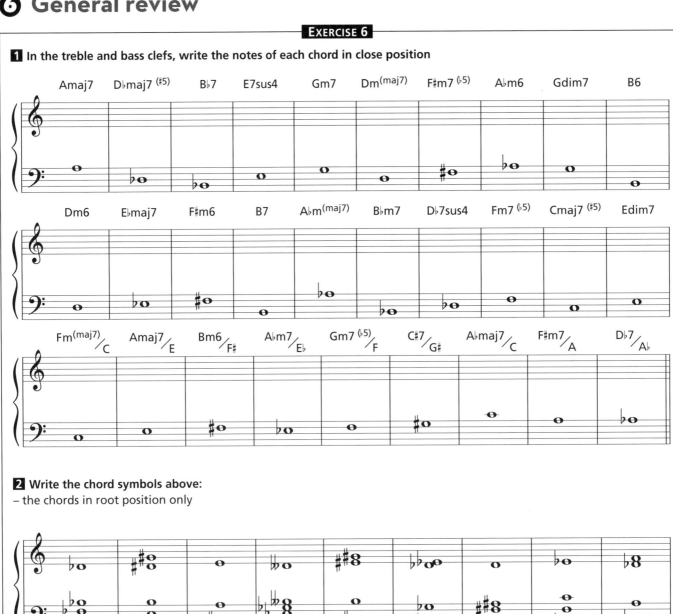

2 Write the chord symbols above:
– the chords in root position only

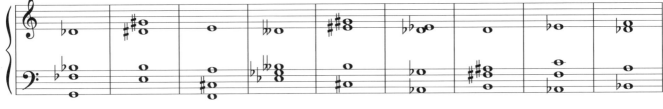

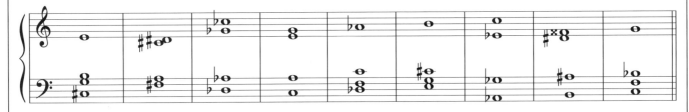

– the inverted chords

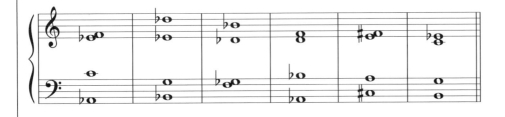

Write the chord symbols of the first four measures of Johann Sebastian Bach's *Chorale BWV 342*

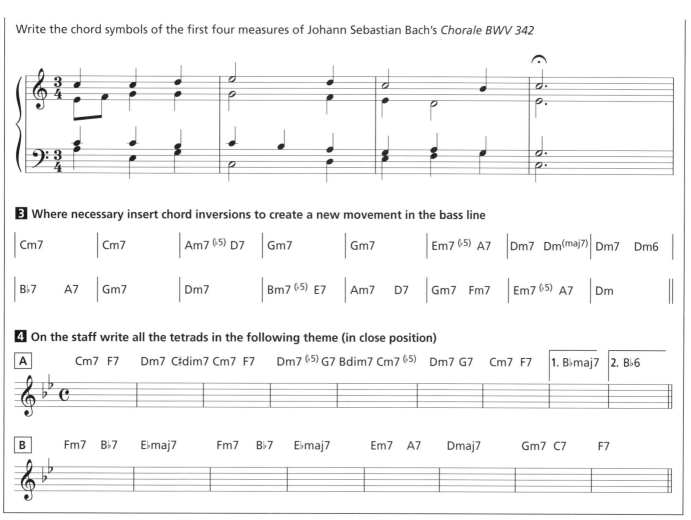

3 Where necessary insert chord inversions to create a new movement in the bass line

| Cm7 | Cm7 | Am7 (♭5) D7 | Gm7 | Gm7 | Em7 (♭5) A7 | Dm7 Dm(maj7) | Dm7 Dm6 |

| B♭7 A7 | Gm7 | Dm7 | Bm7 (♭5) E7 | Am7 D7 | Gm7 Fm7 | Em7 (♭5) A7 | Dm |

4 On the staff write all the tetrads in the following theme (in close position)

A   Cm7 F7   Dm7 C♯dim7 Cm7 F7   Dm7 (♭5) G7 Bdim7 Cm7 (♭5)   Dm7 G7   Cm7 F7   1. B♭maj7   2. B♭6

B   Fm7   B♭7   E♭maj7   Fm7   B♭7   E♭maj7   Em7   A7   Dmaj7   Gm7 C7   F7

Answers, p. 60-61

⑦ Answers

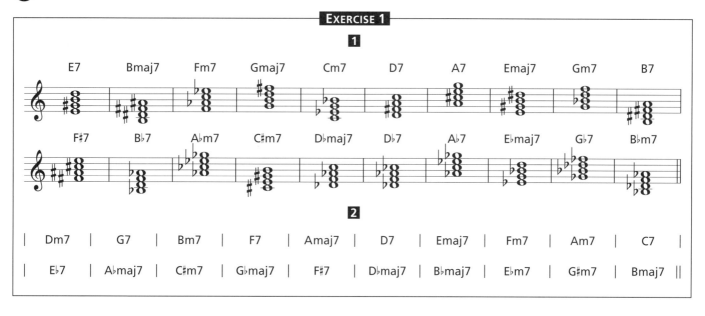

1

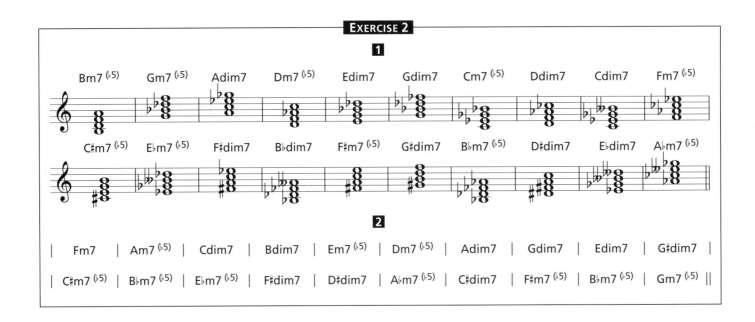

2

| Fm7 | Am7 (♭5) | Cdim7 | Bdim7 | Em7 (♭5) | Dm7 (♭5) | Adim7 | Gdim7 | Edim7 | G#dim7 |
| C#m7 (♭5) | B♭m7 (♭5) | E♭m7 (♭5) | F#dim7 | D#dim7 | A♭m7 (♭5) | C#dim7 | F#m7 (♭5) | B♭m7 (♭5) | Gm7 (♭5) ||

EXERCISE 3

1

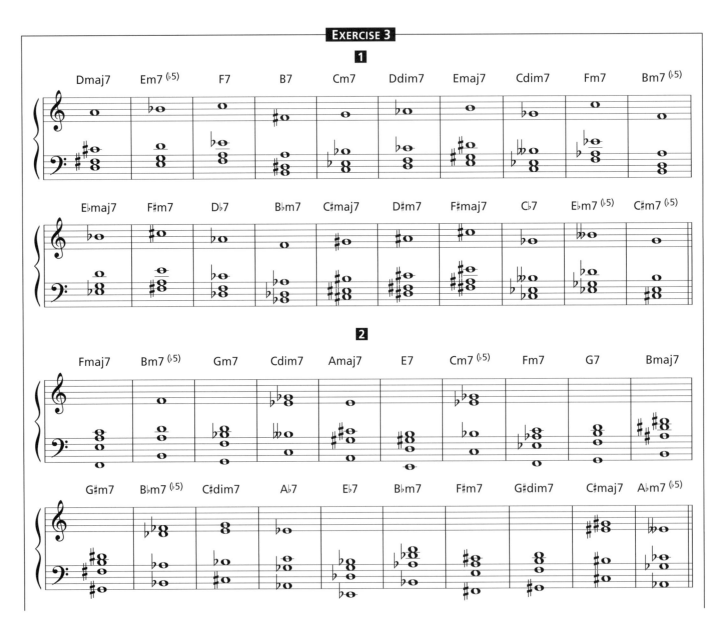

2

3

| Em7 $\frac{3}{7}\frac{5}{1}$ | Cmaj7 $\frac{5}{7}\frac{3}{1}$ | Am7 $\frac{5}{3}\frac{7}{1}$ | D7 $\frac{5}{7}\frac{3}{1}$ | Gmaj7 $\frac{7}{3}\frac{5}{1}$ | Fm7 $\frac{7}{3}\frac{5}{1}$ | E7 $\frac{5}{7}\frac{3}{1}$ | Bmaj7 $\frac{5}{7}\frac{3}{1}$ | Emaj7 $\frac{7}{3}\frac{5}{1}$ | Cmaj7 $\frac{5}{7}\frac{3}{1}$ |

| D♭maj7 $\frac{3}{7}\frac{5}{1}$ | B♭maj7 $\frac{7}{5}\frac{3}{1}$ | A♭7 $\frac{5}{3}\frac{7}{1}$ | F♯7 $\frac{5}{3}\frac{7}{1}$ | G♭maj7 $\frac{7}{3}\frac{5}{1}$ | E♭m7 $\frac{7}{3}\frac{5}{1}$ | C♯m7 $\frac{7}{3}\frac{5}{1}$ | B♭m7 $\frac{5}{7}\frac{3}{1}$ | E♭m7 $\frac{7}{3}\frac{5}{1}$ | Edim7 $\frac{3}{7}\frac{5}{1}$ |

| C♯m7 (♭5) $\frac{5}{7}\frac{3}{1}$ | Am7 (♭5) $\frac{5}{3}\frac{7}{1}$ | Ddim7 $\frac{5}{7}\frac{3}{1}$ | G7 $\frac{5}{3}\frac{7}{1}$ | F♯dim7 $\frac{7}{3}\frac{5}{1}$ | B♭7 $\frac{5}{7}\frac{3}{1}$ | Bdim7 $\frac{5}{7}\frac{3}{1}$ | G♯dim7 $\frac{5}{7}\frac{3}{1}$ | Fmaj7 $\frac{5}{7}\frac{3}{1}$ | Fm7 (♭5) $\frac{5}{7}\frac{3}{1}$ |

4

| Fm7/E♭ | Gmaj7/D | Bm7/F♯ | Dmaj7/F♯ | Em7/D | B7/D♯ | Cm7/G | Dm7(♭5)/A♭ | G7/F |

| B7 | Am7/G | Ddim7/F | C♯m7/E | A♭maj7/E♭ | D7/F♯ | B♭m7/F | C♯dim7/E | F♯7/E |

| Am7(♭5)/G | Gmaj7/D | C♯m7/G♯ | Emaj7/B | F7/A | A♭7/G♭ | D♭7/C♭ | F♯m7/A | B♭maj7/D |

| Am7/C | Gmaj7/D | B7/F♯ | Cm7/B♭ | D7/C | Em7(♭5)/D | Fmaj7/A | A7/E | G♯m7/B | A♭m7/E♭ |

| F♯m7(♭5)/C | B♭7/A♭ | E♭maj7/B♭ | Adim7/C | D♭m7/A♭ | E7/G♯ | C♯m7/B | C♭maj7/E♭ | F♯7/E |

5

| D7 | G7 | C7 | Fmaj7 | B♭maj7 | Em7 (♭5) | A7 | Dm7 |

1

| F6 | Gm6 | Am(maj7) | Cm6 | Fm(maj7) | Bm6 | D6 | Cm(maj7) | Em(maj7) |

| A6 | B♭m6 | C♯m(maj7) | F♯6 | A♭m(maj7) | D♭m6 | G♭6 | A♭6 | B♭m(maj7) |

2

| Fm6 | Bm6 | Em7 (♭5) | A♭m7 | G♯m7 (♭5) | C♯m7 (♭5) | Am6/C | Am7 (♭5)/E♭ | Bm7 (♭5)/F |

| Dm7 (♭5)/F | G♯m7 (♭5)/B | Gm6/E | C♭6/A♭ | Bm6/G♯ | Em6/C♯ | F♯m7 (♭5)/C | Cm6/E♭ | Dm6/F |

3

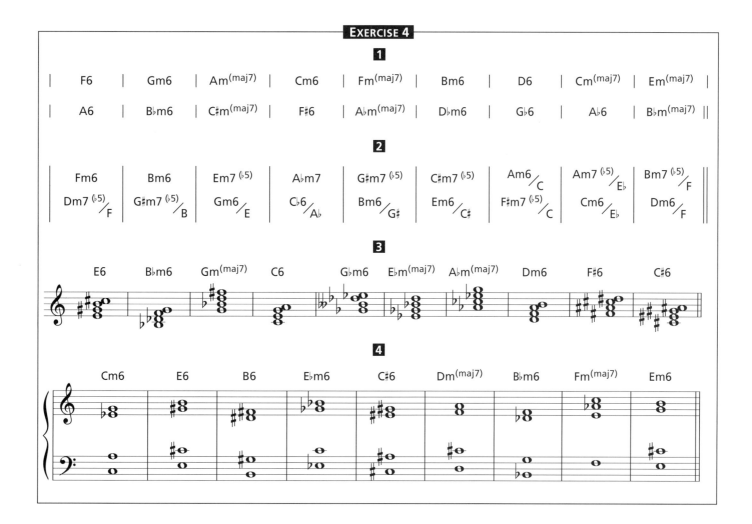

4

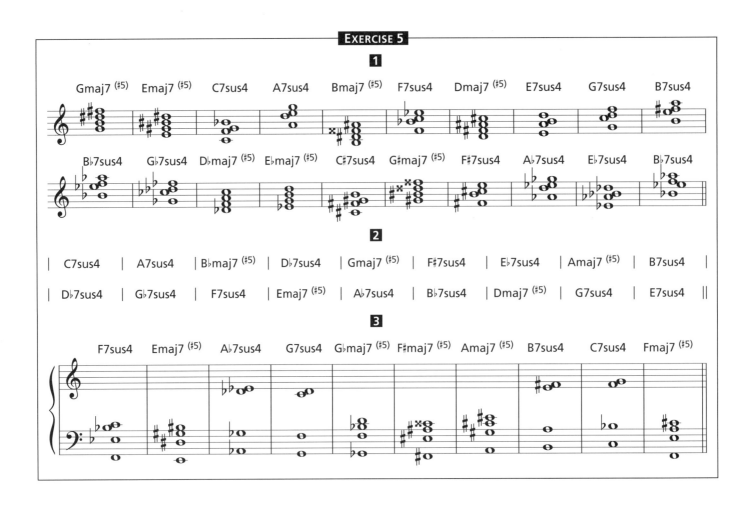

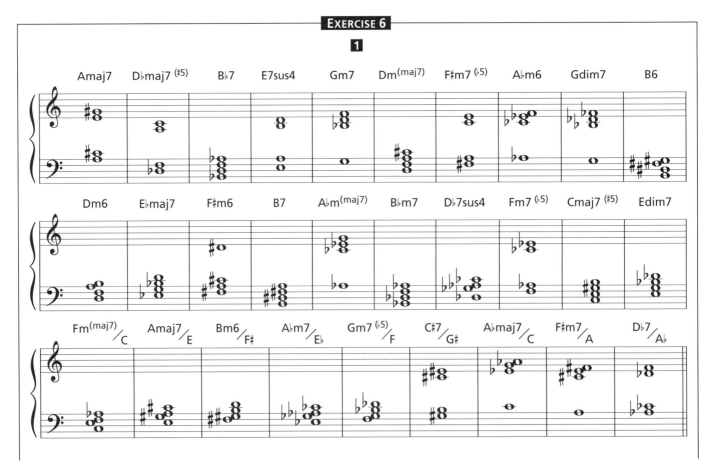

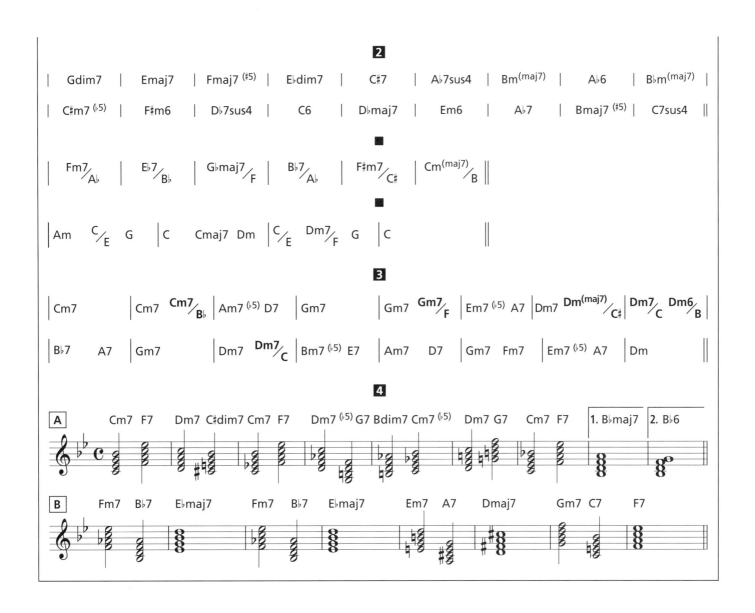

CHAPTER 4
FOUR-NOTE CHORD EXTENSIONS

❶ The harmonic density of chords[1]

In the previous chapters, we saw that stacking:

- two notes forms intervals;
- three notes forms major, minor, diminished, and augmented triads (harmonic density 3);
- four notes forms the tetrads Xmaj7, X7, Xm7, Xm7(♭5), Xdim7, X6, Xm6, Xm(maj7), X7sus4, and Xmaj7(♯5) (harmonic density 4).

Depending on the musical context, you can add one or more notes to four-note chords, such as the 9th, the 11th, or the 13th. These notes have no predetermined place in the chord. For example, a 9th does not have to be voiced above the 7th; it can be voiced anywhere in the chord from the bass to the soprano.

These **extension notes** (also known as color notes or superstructure notes) serve to produce different sonorities and to enrich chords. Found in the music of many classical composers — such as Wagner, Debussy, Ravel, Bartók, Shostakovich, et al. — these extension notes have gradually become integrated into the harmonic and melodic vocabulary of jazz.

> **Important**
>
> While many jazz students are tempted by extension notes, these are often used incorrectly. The decision to employ an extension note is often guided by the simple desire to play a note in particular without there being a logical reason for this choice or a contextual need. However, before looking into all the possible advantages extension notes may have to offer, we must ask ourselves why we want to add one or more notes to any given chord: To create a dissonance? To prepare a modulation, or maybe to express the colors of a mode? We will address these questions in greater depth when we study the modes in Chapters 12 and 13. For the time being, however, let's focus on the different extension possibilities available.

❷ Three extension notes

2.1 Ninths

The 9th interval has three qualities (major, minor, and augmented).

Interval quality	Extension symbol
Major ninth	9
Minor ninth	♭9
Augmented ninth	♯9

---

1 The harmonic density of a chord indicates the number of sounds actually contained within the chord.

The 9th is equivalent to the 2nd, the only difference between the two intervals being their functions.

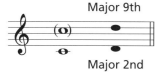

The #9 interval is often confused with its enharmonic equivalents, the minor 3rd and minor 10th. While all these notes have the same sound, their functions and names are quite different. It is the harmonic context that determines the name of the interval.

When speaking, we often refer to:

- the "9th" to designate a major 9th;
- the "flat nine" to designate a minor 9th;
- the "sharp nine" to designate an augmented 9th.

Useful tip

A minor 9th is equivalent to a minor 2nd, one octave higher (one half step above the root).

A major 9th is equivalent to a major 2nd, one octave higher (one whole step above the root).

An augmented 9th is equivalent to an augmented 2nd, one octave higher (one and a half steps above the root).

The minor 10th is equivalent to the minor 3rd, one octave higher.

2.2 Elevenths

The 11th interval has two qualities, perfect and augmented.

Interval quality	Symbol
Perfect 11th	11
Augmented 11th	#11

The 11th is equivalent to the 4th.

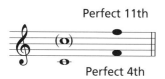

When speaking, we often refer to:

- the "11th" to designate a perfect 11th;
- the "sharp 11" to designate an augmented 11th.

Be careful not to confuse the #11 with its enharmonic equivalent, the ♭5; both notes have the same sound, but different names and functions.

2.3 Thirteenths

The 13th interval has two qualities (major and minor).

Interval quality	Symbol
Major 13th	13
Minor 13th	♭13

The 13th is equivalent to the 6th.

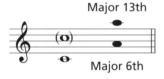

When speaking, we often refer to:

- the "13th" to designate a major 13th;
- the "flat 13th" to designate a minor 13th.

Extension notes and modes

The following example summarizes the different harmonic extensions (vertical) and melodic extensions (horizontal).

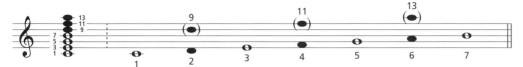

❸ Most common extension-note applications

In this section, we will explore the extension-note possibilities offered by the different chord qualities. First, let's look at the recommended and most frequently used extensions.

Note that the presence of:

- **add** followed by a scale degree in a chord symbol indicates that the specified scale degree should be the only note added to the chord. For example, X(add 9) specifies that the 9th should be played with the triad, without the 7th, while X7(add ♯11) specifies that the dominant 7th should be played with the addition of only one extension note, the augmented 11th.

- **omit** followed by a scale degree in a chord symbol indicates that the specified scale degree should be omitted from the chord. For example, in Xmaj9(omit 5), only the 7th and 9th are included in the chord, and the 5th is omitted.

- **N.C.** (no chord) indicates that the section in question should not be harmonized.

These three options are nevertheless quite rare in lead sheets. Only the specific chord symbols we have retained will be used to designate the chords (and their extensions) cited in this book.

3.1 Xmaj7 chords

The most common extensions are:

- the major 9th;
- augmented 11th;
- the major 13th.

While it is common practice to play a major 9th in an augmented 11th chord, this is not obligatory.

Chord symbols

Xmaj7(9) – or its abbreviated form, Xmaj9; Xmaj7(9, ♯11) or Xmaj9(♯11); Xmaj7(9, 13) or Xmaj(13); Xmaj7(9, ♯11, 13) or Xmaj13(♯11).

EXAMPLES

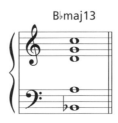

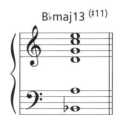

3.2 X7 chords

X7 chords offer the greatest choice in terms of extension notes (and their multiple combinations). It is possible to enrich a dominant chord by adding its:

- major 9th, minor 9th, and/or augmented 9th;
- flat 10th;
- augmented 11th;
- major and minor 13ths.

Chord symbols

There are numerous chord symbol possibilities, depending on the different combinations and abbreviations. The main chord symbols are:

- X7(9) = X9;
- X7(♭9), X7(♯9);
- X7(9, ♯11) = X9(♯11);
- X7(9, 13) = X13 (Note that since the ♯11 must always be indicated, it is not always played in an X13 chord);
- X7(♭9, 13): abbreviation = X13(♭9);
- X7alt: all extension notes (except the unaltered 9th, 11th, and 13th) can be added. This means that all added notes in an "altered" X7 should be altered, although the chord symbol does not specify what the extension notes are.

EXAMPLES

Close and open root voicings of C7 chords with extensions:

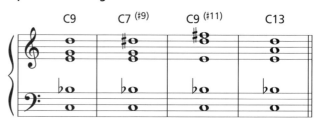

Note that, in the case of certain X7 chord voicings with extensions, such as C9(♯11) or C13, the 5th is left out to lighten the harmonic density of the chord. The 5th can be omitted here because it is heard in the natural harmonics.

The ♭10 may be found in an X7 chord symbol if it has a melodic and harmonic function. We will study this feature in greater depth in the chapters on modes. The ♭10 may also be used as a blues note.

X13 and X6

Although the 6th and the 13th are the same notes, applying the wrong chord symbol can lead to confusion. Compare the following chord symbols:

- X13 comprises a major 3rd + a minor 7th + a major 9th + a major 13th (implying an X7 chord + a major 9th + a major 13th);
- X6 comprises a major 3rd + a major 6th (i.e., an Xmaj + major 6th).

The main X7 altered-note extensions are: X7(♭9, ♯9); X7(♭9, ♯11); X7(♭9, ♭13); X7(9, ♭13); and X7(♭9, 13).

Attention

Many music books and lead sheets incorrectly use X7(♯5) to designate X7(♭13) chords. This is usually due to an enharmonic mistake stemming from the confusion between the augmented 5th and the minor 13th. Two examples of this common error are given below.

Example 1

In measure 2 above, given the presence of B♭ in the melody (the minor 13th of D7), the chord symbol should be D7(♭13). Also, in measures 4 and 6, since the tonal context of C minor suggests E♭, the chord symbol should be G7(♭13).

Example 2

In the above example, the G7(♯5) chord in measure 3 implies an augmented 5th (D♯). In the melody, however, the presence of E♭ (the enharmonic equivalent of D♯) is a minor 13th. The chord symbol indicated is therefore incorrect. It should be G7(♭13).

This type of mistake also creates problems when writing the modes related to chords. We will examine the question of chord-symbol incoherence in greater depth in Chapter 11.

3.3 Xm7 chords

We can enrich Xm7 chords by adding one or several of the following notes:

- the major 9th;
- the perfect 11th;
- the major 13th.

Chord symbols

Xm7(9) or Xm9, Xm7(9, 11) or Xm11, and Xm7(9, 13) or Xm13.

Examples

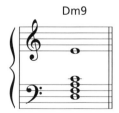
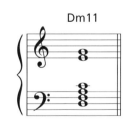
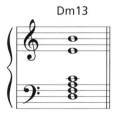

3.4 Xm7(♭5) chords

We can enrich Xm7(♭5) chords by adding one or both of the following notes:

- the major 9th;
- the perfect 11th.

Chord symbols

Xm9(♭5), Xm11(♭5).

EXAMPLES

3.5 Xdim7 chords

We can enrich X dim7 chords by adding one or several of the following notes:

- the major 9th;
- the perfect 11th;
- the minor 13th;
- the major 7th.

Useful tip

These four extension notes form a diminished chord located one whole step above the root of the main chord. Each note located one whole step above a chord tone is a potential extension. The following example shows the Bdim7 chord and its four extension notes (C♯, E, G, and B♭). The extension notes form the C♯dim7 chord:

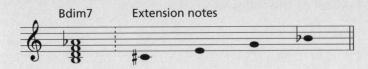

Chord symbols

Extension notes are rarely indicated in Xdim7 chords. If they were indicated, we would obtain the following chord symbols: Xdim7(9); Xdim7(11); Xdim7(♭13), and Xdim7(maj7).

EXAMPLES

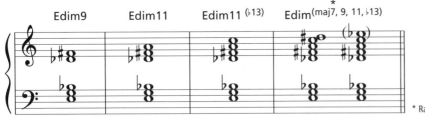

* Rarely indicated.

1 Write the names of the extension notes beside the chord names

♭9 of	C7:	F7:	A♭7:	F♯7:	C♯7:
9 of	Dmaj7:	B♭m7:	F♯m7 ^(♭5):	Bm6:	E7sus4:
♯9 of	E♭7:	A7:	C7:	F♯7:	D♭7:
11 of	Fm7:	B♭m^(maj7):	Am7:	C♯m7 ^(♭5):	Ddim7:
♯11 of	E♭maj7:	A7:	B♭7:	Dmaj7:	C♯7:
♭13 of	G7:	A♭7:	B7:	F♯7:	E♭7:
13 of	D♭7:	F7:	B♭7:	G♭7:	C♯7:

2 Write the names of the extension notes that can be played on the following chords

B♭maj7:   D7:   Gm7:   F♯m7 ^(♭5):

Edim7:   A♭6:   Dm6:   A♭m^(maj7):

C7sus4:

3 In the treble clef, write the extention notes of the chords

Emaj9 ^(♯11)   Gm13   D9 ^(♭13)   B♭7 ^(♭9, 13)   E♭maj13   Fm11 ^(♭5)   Cmaj9 ^(♯11)   G9 ^(♭13)

4 Write the chord symbols

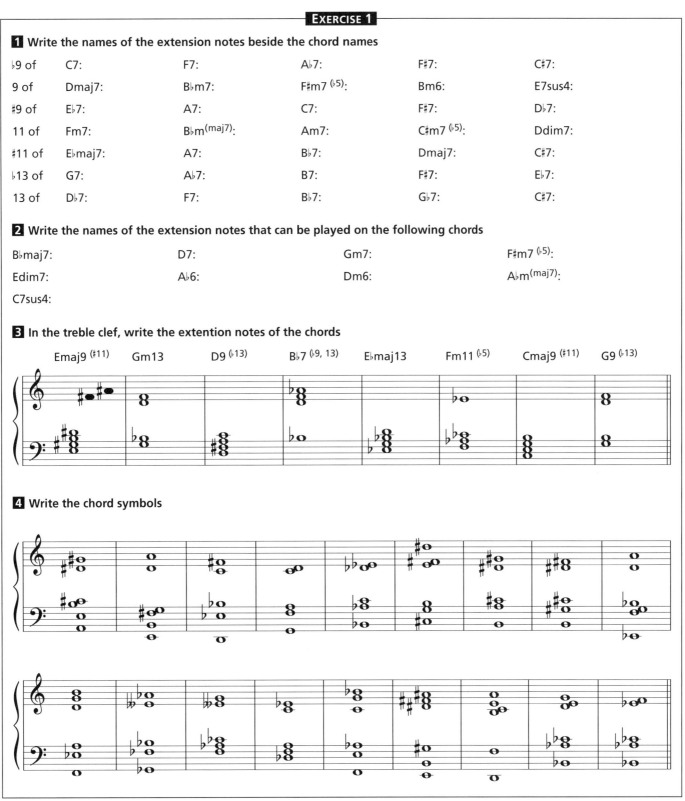

Answers, p. 72-73

④ Using extensions with other chords

4.1 X6 chords

We can enrich X6 chords by adding one or both of the following notes:

- the major 9th;
- the augmented 11th.

Chord symbols

X6/9; X6/9(♯11).

EXAMPLES

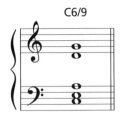

The C6/9 above is also an example of a **quartal chord** formed by stacking a series of perfect 4ths (in this case, E-A-D-G).

4.2 Xm6 chords

We can enrich Xm6 chords by adding one or both of the following notes:

- the major 9th;
- the perfect 11th.

Chord symbols

Xm6/9, Xm6/9(11).

EXAMPLES

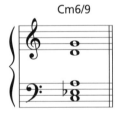

4.3 Xm(maj7) chords

We can enrich Xm(maj7) chords by adding one or several of the following notes:

- the major 9th;
- the perfect 11th;
- the major 13th.

Chord symbols

Xm(maj9), Xm11(maj7), and Xm13(maj7).

EXAMPLES

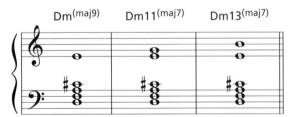

4.4 X7sus4 chords

We can enrich this chord by adding one or several of the following notes:
- the major or minor 9th;
- the major 10th;
- the major 13th.

Chord symbols

X9sus4 and X7sus4(♭9).

EXAMPLES

Close root voicings

C9sus4

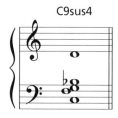

C7sus4 (♭9)

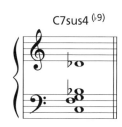

*
C13sus4

* Note that in this voicing (used notably by Bill Evans) the 3rd and the 4th of chord are sounded simultaneously. Use the Mixolydian mode.

4.5 Xmaj7(♯5) chords

We can enrich Xmaj7(♯5) chords by adding one or both of the following notes:
- the major 9th;
- the augmented 11th.

Chord symbols

Xmaj7(♯5, 9) or Xmaj9(♯5), Xmaj7(♯5, ♯11) or Xmaj9(♯5, ♯11).

EXAMPLES

Close root voicings

Dmaj9 (♯5)

Dmaj9 (♯5, ♯11)

EXERCISE 2

1 In the treble and bass clefs, write the notes of the chords

Emaj9 (♯5, ♯11) A9sus4 E♭m11(maj7) Fm6/9 E♭6/9 (♯11) B7sus4 (♭9) Gm11(maj9) C♯m6/9 E6/9 (♯11)

2 Write the chord symbols

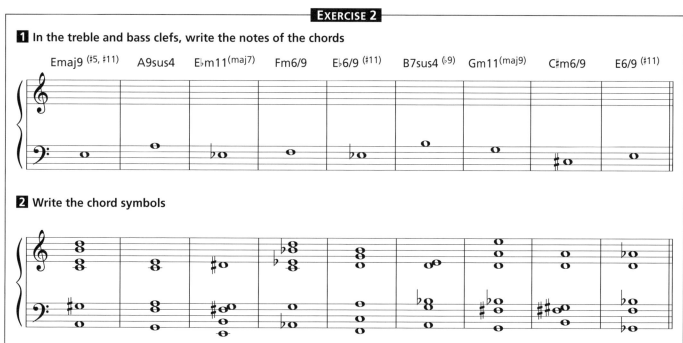

Answers, p. 73

❺ Summary table

Extension notes can be added to chords for several reasons: to enrich their texture, emphasize a particular color, or prepare a modulation, etc. Whatever the reason, all notes added to triads and tetrads create a dissonance. Without necessarily associating dissonance with instability, the decision to create dissonance should always be based on the musical context.

There are two types of extension notes, namely those which:

- belong to the tonality. For example, in measure 2 below, the 9th and the 13th of G7 are extension notes belonging to the tonality of the cadence (C major);

|Dm7 |G7 (9, 13) |C | ℅ |

- do not belong to the tonality. The ♭9 and ♭13 extension notes in G7 below do not belong to the tonality, and therefore create greater instability.

|Dm7 |G7 (♭9, ♭13) |C | ℅ |

Chord quality	Common extensions used	Example in C
Xmaj7	9, #11, 13	D, F#, A
X7	♭9, 9, #9, #11, ♭13, 13	D♭, D, D#, F#, A♭, A
Xm7	9, 11, 13	D, F, A
Xm7 (♭5)	9, 11	D, F
Xdim7	maj7, 9, 11, ♭13	B, D, F, A♭
X6	9, #11	D, F#
Xm6	9, 11	D, F
Xm(maj7)	9, 11, 13	D, F, A
X7sus4	♭9, 9, 13	D♭, D, A
Xmaj7 (#5)	9, #11	D, F#

❻ Answers

EXERCISE 1

1

♭9 of	C7: D♭	F7: G♭	A♭7: B♭♭	F#7: G	C#7: D
9 of	Dmaj7: E	B♭m7: C	F#m7 (♭5): G#	Bm6: C#	E7sus4: F#
#9 of	E♭7: F#	A7: B#	C7: D#	F#7: G𝄪	D♭7: E
11 of	Fm7: B♭	B♭m(maj7): E♭	Am7: D	C#m7 (♭5): F#	Ddim7: G
#11 of	E♭maj7: A	A7: D#	B♭7: E	Dmaj7: G#	C#7: F𝄪
♭13 of	G7: E♭	A♭7: F♭	B7: G	F#7: D	E♭7: C♭
13 of	D♭7: B♭	F7: D	B♭7: G	G♭7: E♭	C#7: A#

2

B♭maj7: C, E, G	D7: E♭, E, E#, G#, B♭, B	Gm7: A, C, E	F#m7 (♭5): G#, B
Edim7: F#, A, C, D#	A♭6: B♭, D	Dm6: E, G	A♭m(maj7): B♭, D♭, F
C7sus4: D♭, D, A			

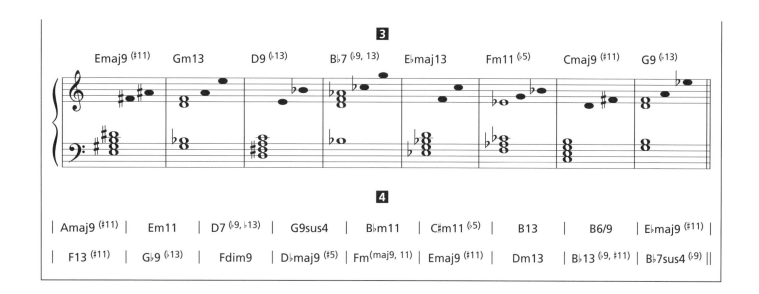

3

Emaj9 (#11)　　Gm13　　D9 (♭13)　　B♭7 (♭9, 13)　　E♭maj13　　Fm11 (♭5)　　Cmaj9 (#11)　　G9 (♭13)

4

| Amaj9 (#11) | Em11 | D7 (♭9, ♭13) | G9sus4 | B♭m11 | C#m11 (♭5) | B13 | B6/9 | E♭maj9 (#11) |

| F13 (#11) | G♭9 (♭13) | Fdim9 | D♭maj9 (#5) | Fm(maj9, 11) | Emaj9 (#11) | Dm13 | B♭13 (♭9, #11) | B♭7sus4 (♭9) ||

EXERCISE 2

1

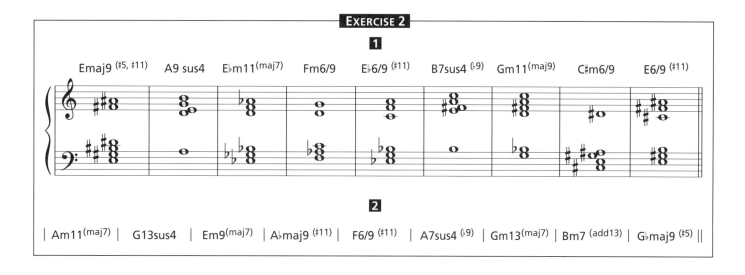

Emaj9 (#5, #11)　　A9 sus4　　E♭m11(maj7)　　Fm6/9　　E♭6/9 (#11)　　B7sus4 (♭9)　　Gm11(maj9)　　C#m6/9　　E6/9 (#11)

2

| Am11(maj7) | G13sus4 | Em9(maj7) | A♭maj9 (#11) | F6/9 (#11) | A7sus4 (♭9) | Gm13(maj7) | Bm7 (add13) | G♭maj9 (#5) ||

CHAPTER 5
THE MAJOR SCALE

The **diatonic major scale** (commonly referred to as the **major scale**) is the reference scale used to draw comparisons throughout this book. In Chapter 13, we will look at two other major scales: the harmonic major and the double harmonic major.

As we saw in the previous chapters, Arabic numerals are used to designate chord voicings. To represent the degrees of scales and modes, however, we use Roman numerals, in keeping with the generally accepted rules of harmony. This system is used, among other things, to analyze different chord progressions, as well as to prioritize the scale degrees according to the musical context and for transposing.

❶ The major scale

1.1 Definition

The **major scale** must respect three conditions, namely that:

- it comprises seven conjunct notes;
- these notes have different pitch names;
- it follows a specific order of whole-step (W) and half-step (H) intervals.

Applying these conditions to the major scale gives the following W/H interval structure:

Degrees	I	II	III	IV	V	VI	VII	(VIII)
Intervals	W	W	H	W	W	W	H	

Writing principles

When analyzing scales and modes, you will notice that these are composed of an ordered series of half steps, whole steps, and, in some cases, one-and-a-half or two steps. Because using "0.5" or "1/2" is not a practical system to designate half-step intervals in scale and mode analysis, we prefer to use:

- 1 for a half step;
- 2 for a whole step;
- 3 for 1-1/2 steps;
- 4 for two whole steps.

Applying this whole-step/half-step numbering system to the above major-scale structure gives the following scale-tone progression.

Degrees	I	II	III	IV	V	VI	VII	(VIII)
Intervals	2	2	1	2	2	2	1	

The major scale, therefore, comprises two half-step intervals (1) between degrees III—IV, and VII—VIII, and five whole-step intervals (2).

Taking D as the starting note (i.e., the tonic) and adding seven conjunct notes, each with a different name, gives the following sequence of notes (before the addition of any accidentals):

To respect the order of whole steps and half steps, we raise the F and the C, as follows:

> **Important**
>
> The major scale is one of the five **heptatonic scales** (comprising seven pitches), and a parent scale. Each degree of a parent scale may serve as the modal tonic of a mode.

1.2 Melodic analysis

The intervals and scale-tone degrees corresponding to the scale of D major are listed in the following table. Note that the intervals comprising the major scale are either major or perfect.

Notes	Intervals	Degrees
D	Tonic	I
D - E	Major second	II
D - F♯	Major third	III
D - G	Perfect fourth	IV
D - A	Perfect fifth	V
D - B	Major sixth	VI
D - C♯	Major seventh	VII

1.3 Tetrachords

A **tetrachord** is a succession of four conjunct pitches used to construct scales and modes. All scales and modes comprise a lower and an upper tetrachord. In the case of the major scale, the two tetrachords are separated by a "connector interval" of one whole step (2), represented here by the symbol {i}. Note that, analyzing the interval-sequence composition of tetrachords makes it possible to identify the specific characteristics and differentiate the types of tetrachords used in the various scales/modes.

EXAMPLE

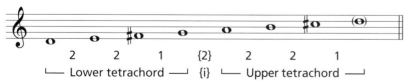

These two tetrachords are separated by a connector interval of one whole step {i} = 2.

Lower tetrachord	2 2 1	Major tetrachord
Upper tetrachord	2 2 1	Major tetrachord

1.4 Scale degree names

Every note of a major or minor scale corresponds to a **degree** represented by a Roman numeral and is allocated a specific name: I = Tonic, II = Supertonic, III = Mediant, IV = Subdominant, V = Dominant, VI = Submediant, and VII = Leading Tone. This nomenclature makes it possible to analyze, understand, and memorize chord functions. Take the scale of C major, for example:

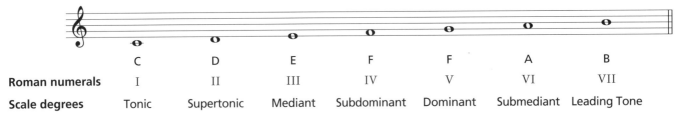

C	D	E	F	F	A	B
Roman numerals I	II	III	IV	V	VI	VII
Scale degrees Tonic	Supertonic	Mediant	Subdominant	Dominant	Submediant	Leading Tone

❷ Major key signatures

All major and minor scales are defined according to the number or, in the case of C major and A minor, the lack of sharps and flats in their **key signature**. The number of flats or sharps corresponding to the tonality of a piece of music are featured in the key signature at the beginning of each staff immediately after the treble and/or bass clef(s) and written in their corresponding note positions on the staff (F♯ on the fifth line and C♯ in the third space of the treble clef, etc.). It is important to memorize the order of sharps and flats so you can identify the tonality and respect the accidentals required in any given key signature.

> **Important**
>
> Order of sharps (ascending Circle of Fifths): F♯, C♯, G♯, D♯, A♯, E♯, and B♯.
> Order of flats (descending Circle of Fifths): B♭, E♭, A♭, D♭, G♭, C♭, and F♭.

EXAMPLE
The D major key signature contains two sharps (F♯ and C♯).

2.1 Sharp key signatures

As we have just seen, placing the sharps in the key signature after the treble (and/or bass) clef(s) greatly simplifies the musical notation. The number of sharps specified in the key signature always follows the order of sharps in the ascending Circle of Fifths. For example, one sharp in the key signature is always F♯, while two sharps are always F♯ and C♯, and three sharps, F♯, C♯, and G♯, etc.

2.2 Identifying scales by the number of sharps in the key signature

To identify the major scale corresponding to the number of sharps, look at the last sharp in the key signature and go up a half step.

Examples

- two sharps in the key signature: last sharp = C♯; go up a half step = D major.
- four sharps in the key signature: last sharp = D♯; go up a half step = E major.

Another way to determine the key signature is to go through the order of sharps while counting the number of associated sharps on your fingers, starting from the key of G (with 1 sharp = F♯) .

(F   C)   G   D   A   E   B   F♯   C♯   Scale
            1   2   3   4   5   6   7   Number of sharps

2.3 Finding the number of sharps in any given scale

Here, the objective is to find the number of sharps contained in any given major scale. To do this, take the sharp situated one half step below the tonic (I) of the scale. In G major, for example, this is F♯, which is the last (and, in this case, the only) sharp in the key signature.

Examples

- the scale of E major: one half-step below E = D♯, which is the last sharp in the key signature (and the fourth sharp in the ascending Circle of Fifths). This tells us that the scale of E has four sharps: F♯, C♯, G♯, and D♯;
- the scale of A major: one half-step below A = G♯, which is the last sharp in the key signature (and the third sharp in the ascending Circle of Fifths). As such, the scale of A has three sharps: F♯, C♯, and G♯.

2.4 Flat key signatures

Flats, like sharps, are also placed in the key signature, but in the order of the descending Circle of Fifths.

2.5 Identifying scales by the number of flats in the key signature

To identify the scale corresponding to the number of flats, take the second-to-last flat in the key signature; this indicates the major tonality of the scale.

Examples

- three-flat key signature (B♭, E♭, and A♭); the second-to-last flat indicates that the tonality is E♭;
- five-flat key signature (B♭, E♭, A♭, D♭, and G♭); the second-to-last flat indicates that the tonality is D♭ major.

2.6 Finding the number of flats in any given scale

The name of a major flat-key scale is indicated by the second-to-last flat in the key signature. To identify all the flats in the key, recite the order of flats until you reach the name of the scale, then add a flat.

EXAMPLES

- scale of B♭ major: Since B♭ is the second-to-last flat, there are two flats in the key signature, B♭ and E♭;

- scale of A♭ major: Since A♭ is the second-to-last flat, there are four flats in the key signature, B♭, E♭, A♭ and D♭.

You have to memorize the key signature of F (one flat); the second-to-last flat reference does not apply here, because F contains only one flat (B♭).

Another way to determine flat key signatures is to go through the order of flats while counting the number of associated flats on your fingers, until you reach the name of the scale, and then add a flat.

(F)	B♭	E♭	A♭	D♭	G♭	C♭	Scale
1	2	3	4	5	6	7	Number of flats

Important

With the exception of F, the notion of "flat" is mentioned in the names of all other flat keys (B♭, E♭, A♭ major, etc.).

EXERCISE 1

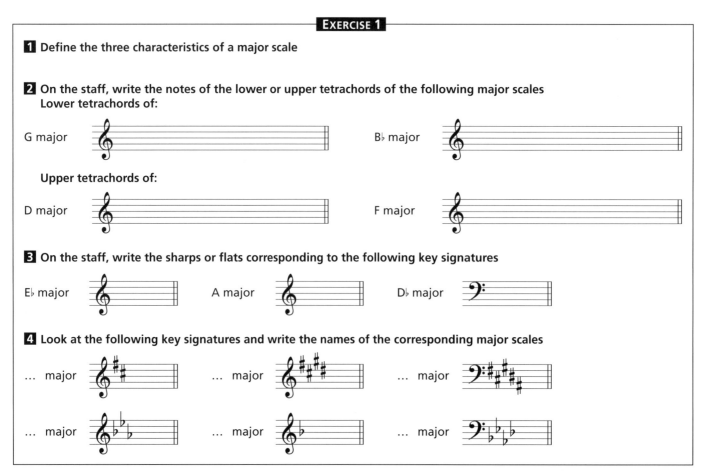

1 Define the three characteristics of a major scale

2 On the staff, write the notes of the lower or upper tetrachords of the following major scales
Lower tetrachords of:

G major

B♭ major

Upper tetrachords of:

D major

F major

3 On the staff, write the sharps or flats corresponding to the following key signatures

E♭ major   A major   D♭ major

4 Look at the following key signatures and write the names of the corresponding major scales

... major   ... major   ... major

... major   ... major   ... major

Answers, p. 80

❸ Harmonizing the major scale

3.1 Harmonization based on triads

All seven degrees of the scale can be harmonized with triads, based on the scale degree in question, and formed exclusively from notes in the scale. The triads built on the degrees of the scale of D major, for example, are:

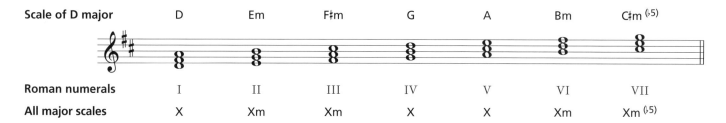

Scale of D major	D	Em	F#m	G	A	Bm	C#m (♭5)
Roman numerals	I	II	III	IV	V	VI	VII
All major scales	X	Xm	Xm	X	X	Xm	Xm (♭5)

3.2 Harmonization based on tetrads

Now let's harmonize the degrees of the major scale using tetrads.

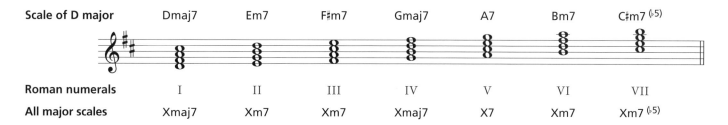

Scale of D major	Dmaj7	Em7	F#m7	Gmaj7	A7	Bm7	C#m7 (♭5)
Roman numerals	I	II	III	IV	V	VI	VII
All major scales	Xmaj7	Xm7	Xm7	Xmaj7	X7	Xm7	Xm7 (♭5)

3.3 Summary table

The four chord qualities encountered in major scales, and their respective scale-tone degrees, are listed in the table below.

Chord quality	Degrees of the major scale
Xmaj7	I, IV
Xm7	II, III, VI
X7	V
Xm7 (♭5)	VII

In a major scale, therefore:

- an Xmaj7 can be played on degrees I or IV: a Dmaj7, with no other specification, can therefore be I in D major or IV in A major;

- an Xm7 can be played on degrees II, III, and VI: an Em7 can be II of D major, III of C major, or VI degree of G major;

- an X7 chord can be played only on a V degree: A7 is V7 of D major;

- an Xm7(♭5) chord can be played only on a VII degree: C#m7(♭5) is VII of D major.

> **Important**
>
> X7 is the only chord restricted to one degree of the scale, the V (dominant). For analysis purposes, it is therefore important to find the corresponding scale. Xm7(♭5) chords are rarely used on the VII degree of a major scale. This chord is usually encountered as a II in a minor key.

1 Using tetrads, harmonize the major scales corresponding to the following key signatures

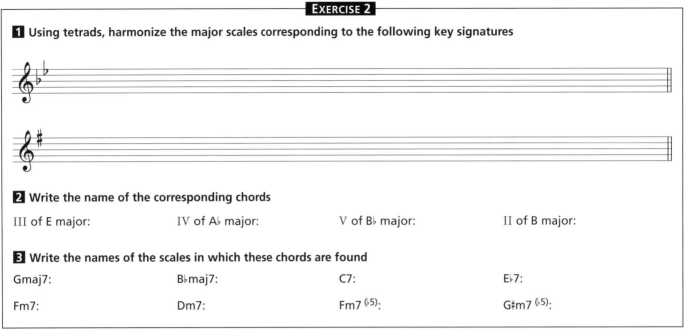

2 Write the name of the corresponding chords

III of E major: IV of A♭ major: V of B♭ major: II of B major:

3 Write the names of the scales in which these chords are found

Gmaj7:   B♭maj7:   C7:   E♭7:

Fm7:   Dm7:   Fm7 (♭5):   G♯m7 (♭5):

Answers, p. 80

④ Answers

EXERCISE 1

1. Seven conjunct notes   2. Seven different pitches   3. Respect the 2 / 2 / 1 / 2 / 2 / 2 / 1 interval sequence

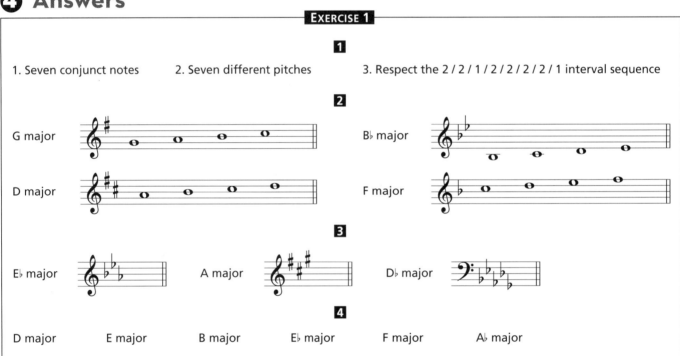

EXERCISE 2

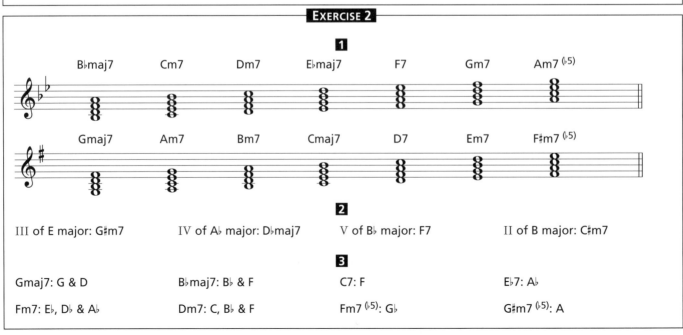

III of E major: G♯m7   IV of A♭ major: D♭maj7   V of B♭ major: F7   II of B major: C♯m7

3

Gmaj7: G & D   B♭maj7: B♭ & F   C7: F   E♭7: A♭

Fm7: E♭, D♭ & A♭   Dm7: C, B♭ & F   Fm7 (♭5): G♭   G♯m7 (♭5): A

Chapter 6
THE HARMONIC MINOR SCALE

Despite their name, **minor scales** are not inferior to major scales. Every minor scale is derived from its relative major scale. As we will see, there are several types of minor scales, a fact that complicates its relationship with respect to the major mode. Pieces written in the tonal minor rarely use one type of minor scale.

❶ The natural minor scale: relative minor

The natural minor scale is most often used in a modal context where it is referred to as the **Aeolian mode**.[1] It also serves as a basis to construct the two main minor scales, namely:

- the harmonic minor and
- the melodic minor.

To find the **relative minor** of a major scale, count down a minor 3rd from the major tonic to the VIth degree. For example:

- F major: a minor 3rd below the F major tonic gives the minor tonic of D;
- D minor is, therefore, the relative minor of F major. Both scales contain exactly the same notes and share the same key signature. The only difference between them is the order of whole-step (2) and half-step (1) intervals.

D minor scale:

> ### Important
>
> Since the natural minor is itself derived from the VIth degree of the major scale, **it is not a parent scale**, and, as such, cannot generate a series of modes. Also, because the natural minor lacks a **leading tone**[2] (i.e., the VIIth degree, a half-step below the tonic), it is mainly used in a modal context.

❷ The harmonic minor scale

To compensate for the absence of a leading tone in the natural minor scale, and to comply with the harmonic requirements of the tonal system, the VIIth degree of the natural minor scale is raised a half step to create the **harmonic minor**, a scale that makes it possible to harmonize minor melodies in accordance with the same principles applied to cadences in major tonalities. For this reason, this scale is called the harmonic minor.

---

1 See Aeolian mode, Chapter 12, p. 187.
2 The 7th degree of a scale is a major 7th relative to the tonic, which is a weak degree with a strong pull toward the tonic.

2.1 Definition

The harmonic minor scale must fulfill the same three requirements as the major scale, namely that:

- it comprises seven conjunct notes;
- these notes have different pitch names;
- it follows a specific order of whole-step (2) and half-step (1) intervals.

Degrees	I	II	III	IV	V	VI	VII	(VIII)
Intervals		2	1	2	2	1	3	1

EXAMPLE

Taking D as the starting note (tonic minor):

- add seven conjunct notes, each with a different name.

- to respect the correct order of whole and half steps, we lower the B and raise the C:

Important

All minor scales (in their natural, harmonic, and melodic forms) have the same key signature as their relative major. The only difference is the addition of accidentals required to alter the specific degrees of each scale type.

To respect the correct order of intervals required in the D harmonic minor scale, for example, we lower the B and raise the C. This gives a scale containing one flat and one sharp. Only B♭ is featured in the key signature, while every C encountered in the piece is raised to C♯.

The harmonic minor scale is a parent scale from which seven modes can be derived.

2.2 Melodic analysis

An analysis of the intervals in the harmonic minor scale shows that, in addition to major, minor, and perfect intervals, this system also contains an augmented 2nd interval between the VIth and VIIth degrees (B♭-C♯). In early Western music, this interval was perceived as a dissonance, and therefore rarely used in melodies. As we will see in the next chapter, this interval was subsequently altered to form the melodic minor scale.

The intervals and scale-tone degrees corresponding to the D harmonic minor scale are listed in the following table:

Notes	Intervals	Degrees
D	Tonic	I
D - E	Major second	II
D - F	Minor third	III
D - G	Perfect fourth	IV
D - A	Perfect fifth	V
D - B♭	**Minor sixth**	VI
D - C♯	**Major seventh**	VII

2.3 Tetrachords

The two tetrachords forming the D harmonic minor scale are:

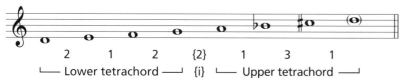

| 2 | 1 | 2 | {2} | 1 | 3 | 1 |
| Lower tetrachord | | | {i} | Upper tetrachord | | |

Lower tetrachord	2 1 2	Minor tetrachord
Upper tetrachord	1 3 1	Harmonic tetrachord

Reminder

So far, we have encountered three types of tetrachords:

Major tetrachord	2 2 1
Minor tetrachord	2 1 2
Harmonic tetrachord	1 3 1

2.4 Key signatures

All minor scales (in their natural, harmonic, and melodic forms) have the same key signature as their relative major. To find the relative major of a minor scale, count up a minor 3rd from the minor tonic.

Example

To find the relative major of D minor, count up a minor 3rd from D to obtain the relative major tonic: F. These two related scales share the same key signature: one flat (B♭).

D minor, therefore, always has one flat (B♭) in its key signature and one accidental (C♯).[3] While some scales and chords call for the combination of flats and sharps, these are never featured together in key signatures.

> **Important**
>
> Every key signature has two tonal possibilities: a major and its relative minor. For example, the tonality of a piece with one sharp in its key signature (F♯) could be G major or, counting down a minor 3rd from the G tonic, E minor. Later, we will see how to determine whether the tonality of a piece is major or minor.[4]

---

3 An accidental is typically a sharp or a flat that is not present in the key signature, or a natural that cancels sharps and flats in the key signature.
4 Determining tonality, p. 93.

1 What is the difference between the natural and the harmonic minor?

2 On the staff, write the notes of the lower or upper tetrachords of the following scales:
– lower tetrachords of:

F natural minor

B harmonic minor

– upper tetrachords of:

G natural minor

A harmonic minor

3 What are the key signatures of the following scales?

D harmonic minor: A natural minor: A harmonic minor: C# harmonic minor:

4 On the staff, write the key signatures and the notes of the following scales

B natural minor

C harmonic minor

F# natural minor

E harmonic minor

5 Write the names of the corresponding minor scales

...

...

...

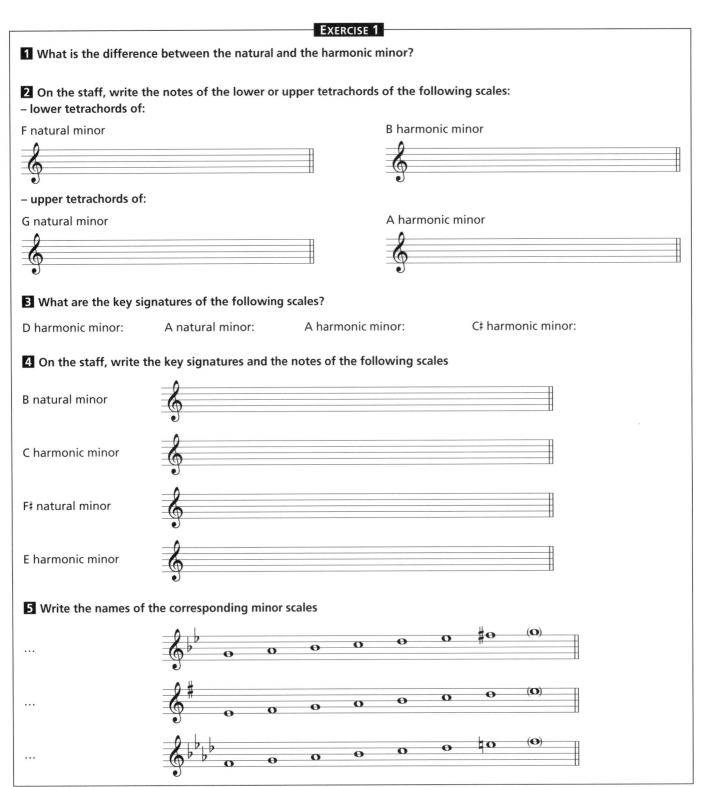

Answers, p. 86

❸ Harmonization of harmonic minor scales

3.1 Harmonization based on tetrads

Like the major scale, it is possible to harmonize minor scales using triads and tetrads. Here, we are going to focus directly on tetrad harmonization. For example, the tetrads built on the degrees of the D harmonic minor scale are:

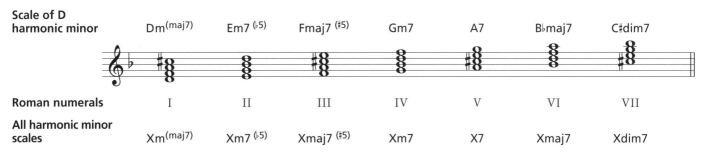

Scale of D harmonic minor	Dm(maj7)	Em7 (♭5)	Fmaj7 (♯5)	Gm7	A7	B♭maj7	C♯dim7
Roman numerals	I	II	III	IV	V	VI	VII
All harmonic minor scales	Xm(maj7)	Xm7 (♭5)	Xmaj7 (♯5)	Xm7	X7	Xmaj7	Xdim7

3.2 Summary table: harmonic minor scale

The summary table below shows the richness of the harmonic minor scale in terms of chord qualities. Indeed, every degree of this scale has its own specific chord quality. Note that the harmonic minor chord presents two new chords, Xmaj7(♯5) and Xdim7.

Chord quality	Degree of the harmonic minor scale
Xm(maj7)	I
Xm7 (♭5)	II
Xmaj7 (♯5)	III
Xm7	IV
X7	V
Xmaj7	VI
Xdim7	VII

EXERCISE 2

1 Using tetrads, harmonize the following minor scales

E♭ natural minor

A harmonic minor

2 Write the name of the corresponding chords

II of E♭ harmonic minor: III of F harmonic minor: IV of G♯ natural minor:

V of D♭ harmonic minor: VII of C natural minor: I of B♭ harmonic minor:

3 Write the names of the natural and harmonic scales in which these chords are found

A♭maj7:   Cmaj7 (♯5):

D7:   F♯dim7:

Fm(maj7):   A♭m7:

Bm7 (♭5):   Gmaj7:

Answers, p. 86

❹ Answers

1

The natural minor has a minor 7th and the harmonic minor a major 7th.

2

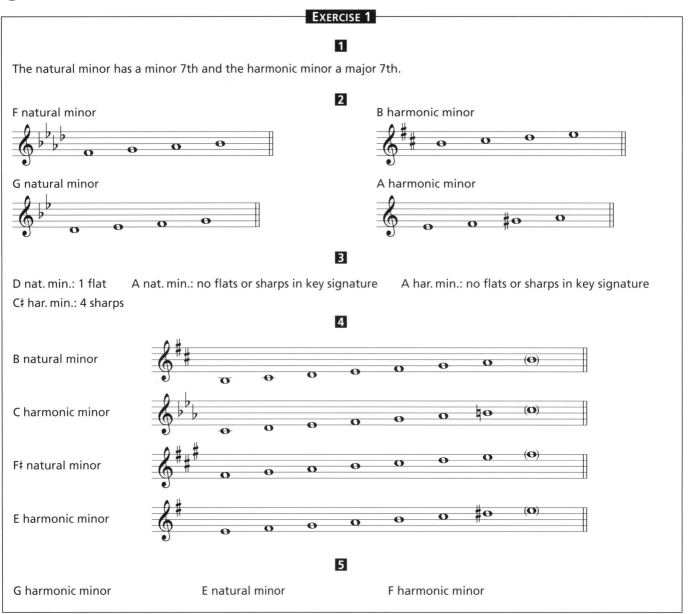

F natural minor

G natural minor

B harmonic minor

A harmonic minor

3

D nat. min.: 1 flat   A nat. min.: no flats or sharps in key signature   A har. min.: no flats or sharps in key signature

C♯ har. min.: 4 sharps

4

B natural minor

C harmonic minor

F♯ natural minor

E harmonic minor

5

G harmonic minor   E natural minor   F harmonic minor

1

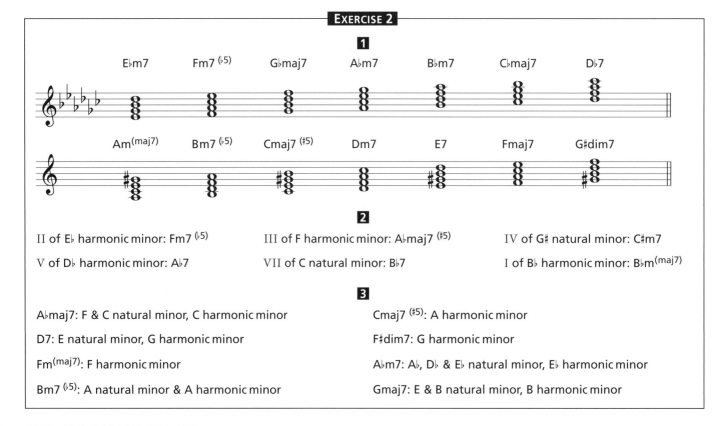

E♭m7   Fm7 ⁽♭5⁾   G♭maj7   A♭m7   B♭m7   C♭maj7   D♭7

Am⁽maj7⁾   Bm7 ⁽♭5⁾   Cmaj7 ⁽♯5⁾   Dm7   E7   Fmaj7   G♯dim7

2

II of E♭ harmonic minor: Fm7 ⁽♭5⁾   III of F harmonic minor: A♭maj7 ⁽♯5⁾   IV of G♯ natural minor: C♯m7

V of D♭ harmonic minor: A♭7   VII of C natural minor: B♭7   I of B♭ harmonic minor: B♭m⁽maj7⁾

3

A♭maj7: F & C natural minor, C harmonic minor   Cmaj7 ⁽♯5⁾: A harmonic minor

D7: E natural minor, G harmonic minor   F♯dim7: G harmonic minor

Fm⁽maj7⁾: F harmonic minor   A♭m7: A♭, D♭ & E♭ natural minor, E♭ harmonic minor

Bm7 ⁽♭5⁾: A natural minor & A harmonic minor   Gmaj7: E & B natural minor, B harmonic minor

CHAPTER 7
THE MELODIC MINOR SCALE

As we saw in Chapter 6, the harmonic minor scale contains a leading tone, introduced so the scale can be used to harmonize cadences. This modification made to the natural minor creates an augmented 2nd interval between the VIth and VIIth degrees of the scale. Although this interval is quite familiar to our ears today, it posed melodic problems in pre-Romantic music. For melodic purposes, therefore, to eliminate the augmented 2nd between the VIth and VIIth degrees, the VIth degree was raised a half step to form the melodic minor scale.

❶ The melodic minor scale

The **melodic minor scale** must fulfill the same three requirements as all other diatonic scales; namely, that:

- it is comprised of seven conjunct notes;
- these notes have different pitch names;
- it respects the following order of whole-step (2) and half-step (1) intervals.

Degrees	I	II	III	IV	V	VI	VII	(VIII)
Intervals		2	1	2	2	2	2	1

EXAMPLE

Taking D as the starting note (tonic minor):

- add seven conjunct notes, each with a different name. This results in the following sequence of notes (before the addition of any accidentals):

- to respect the correct order of whole and half steps, we raise the B♭ to B♮ and the C to C♯:

> **Important**
>
> The melodic minor is a parent scale from which seven modes can be derived.
>
> Comparing the interval structures of melodic minor and major scales shows that the only difference between the two is the quality of their respective 3rds.

1.1 Melodic analysis

The intervals and corresponding scale-tone degrees in the D melodic minor scale are presented in the table below:

Notes	Intervals	Degrees
D	Tonic	I
D - E	Major second	II
D - F	Minor third	III
D - G	Perfect fourth	IV
D - A	Perfect fifth	V
D - B	**Major sixth**	VI
D - C♯	**Major seventh**	VII

1.2 Tetrachords

The two tetrachords that form the melodic minor scale (based on D melodic minor) are:

Lower tetrachord	2 1 2	Minor tetrachord
Upper tetrachord	2 2 1	Major tetrachord

These two tetrachords are separated by a connector interval of one whole step {i} = 2.

> **Important**
>
> The only difference between a melodic minor and its relative major is the quality of their respective 3rds:
> - D major: D   E   **F♯**   G   A   B   C♯   (D)
> - D melodic minor: D   E   **F**   G   A   B   C♯   (D)

1.3 Key signatures

Note that there is a certain incoherence in the key signatures of melodic minor scales. In the case of D minor, for example, the last (and in this case, the only) flat in the key signature is B♭. Being the VIth degree of the scale, the B♭ should always be raised a half tone (to become B♮) and all VIIth degrees, sharpened (C♯).

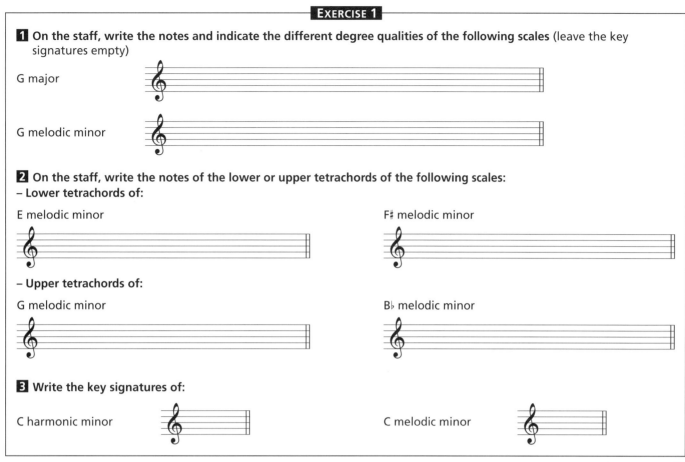

1 On the staff, write the notes and indicate the different degree qualities of the following scales (leave the key signatures empty)

G major

G melodic minor

2 On the staff, write the notes of the lower or upper tetrachords of the following scales:
– Lower tetrachords of:

E melodic minor

F♯ melodic minor

– Upper tetrachords of:

G melodic minor

B♭ melodic minor

3 Write the key signatures of:

C harmonic minor

C melodic minor

Answers, p. 91

❷ Harmonization of melodic minor scales

The tetrad harmonization of each degree of the D melodic minor scale is as follows:

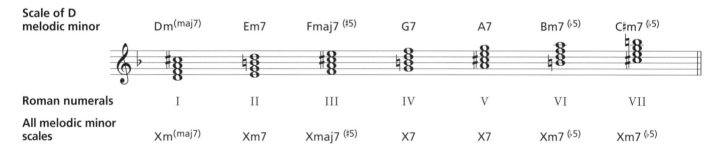

Scale of D melodic minor	Dm(maj7)	Em7	Fmaj7 (♯5)	G7	A7	Bm7 (♭5)	C♯m7 (♭5)
Roman numerals	I	II	III	IV	V	VI	VII
All melodic minor scales	Xm(maj7)	Xm7	Xmaj7 (♯5)	X7	X7	Xm7 (♭5)	Xm7 (♭5)

Unlike the harmonic minor, the harmonization of the melodic minor scale creates no new types of chords. It does, however, contain two X7 and two Xm7(♭5) chords.

❸ Summary table: melodic minor scale

3.1 Chords of the melodic minor scale

Chord quality	Degree of melodic minor
Xm(maj7)	I
Xm7	II
Xmaj7 (♯5)	III
X7	IV, V
Xm7 (♭5)	VI, VII

3.2 Minor scale comparisons

A summary of the notes in the three minor scales (in D) is given in the table below:

Aeolian mode (natural minor)	D	E	F	G	A	B♭	C
Harmonic minor	D	E	F	G	A	B♭	C♯
Melodic minor	D	E	F	G	A	B	C♯
Degrees	I	II	III	IV	V	VI	VII

└──── Pentachord ────┘

3.3 Pentachords

As the table above shows, the notes of first five degrees (pentachord) of the natural, harmonic, and minor scales are always the same; only the VIth and VIIth degrees are different:

Aeolian mode (natural minor)	Minor 6th	Minor 7th
Harmonic minor	Minor 6th	Major 7th
Melodic minor	Major 6th	Major 7th

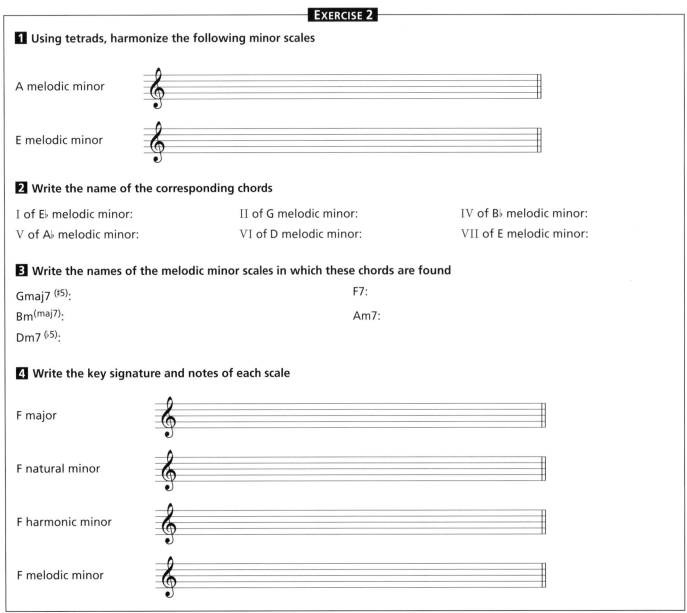

EXERCISE 2

1 Using tetrads, harmonize the following minor scales

A melodic minor

E melodic minor

2 Write the name of the corresponding chords

I of E♭ melodic minor: II of G melodic minor: IV of B♭ melodic minor:

V of A♭ melodic minor: VI of D melodic minor: VII of E melodic minor:

3 Write the names of the melodic minor scales in which these chords are found

Gmaj7 (♯5): F7:

Bm(maj7): Am7:

Dm7 (♭5):

4 Write the key signature and notes of each scale

F major

F natural minor

F harmonic minor

F melodic minor

Answers, p. 91

❹ Answers

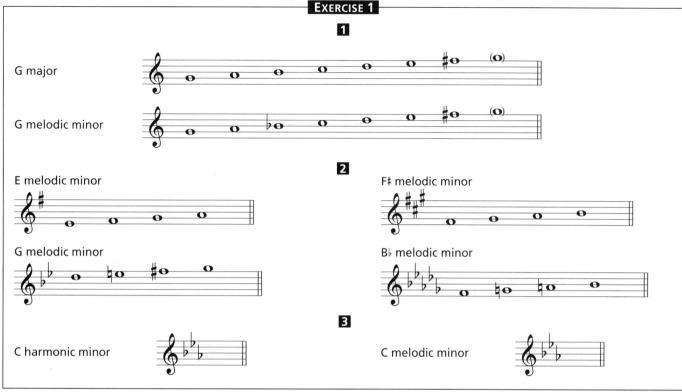

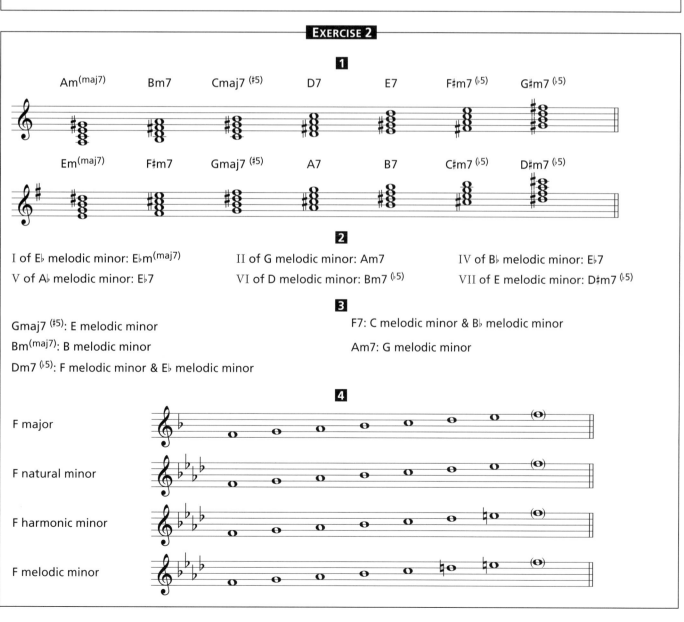

2

I of E♭ melodic minor: E♭m(maj7)   II of G melodic minor: Am7   IV of B♭ melodic minor: E♭7

V of A♭ melodic minor: E♭7   VI of D melodic minor: Bm7 (♭5)   VII of E melodic minor: D♯m7 (♭5)

3

Gmaj7 (♯5): E melodic minor   F7: C melodic minor & B♭ melodic minor

Bm(maj7): B melodic minor   Am7: G melodic minor

Dm7 (♭5): F melodic minor & E♭ melodic minor

CHAPTER 8
CHORD FUNCTIONS

❶ Scales and tonality

The concepts of tonality and scales can be confusing. In this chapter, we will endeavor to shed some light on the subject by providing simple explanations and limiting the exploration of more advanced concepts, which we will examine later.[1]

For instance, take the scale and tonality of C major. While these concepts share many similarities, the differences between them are made apparent when it comes to their respective definitions and functions. As we have seen, all major (and minor) scales must consist of seven conjunct notes, each with a different name, and respect a specific order of whole- and half-step intervals. In these scales, we noted the presence of certain chords and melodic intervals that determine the tonality of the scale in question.

Major and minor **tonalities** determine the use of different chords according to their specific function. This is notably the case for the tonic (I), the chord with the strongest gravitational pull.

Because of the tonal attraction that exists around the first degree (I), it is possible to play chord progressions that move relatively far away from this tonal center, which creates a sensation of "tension and release," one of the fundamental principles of tonal music.

The resolution chord, or target chord, must belong to the scale of the tonality in question. This gives three main chord choices, which, in the case of C major in the example below, are Cmaj7 and its diatonic substitutes, Am7 and Em7. The tension chords (V), however, can be derived from the C major scale or "borrowed" from other scales. "Borrowed"[2] chords give the cadence a different color without modifying the fundamental tonality. To express a tonality, strong chords, such as those built on degrees I and V, must be used, although chords borrowed from other scales may also be used, as shown below.

EXAMPLES in the key of C major

The following progression contains chords derived exclusively from the scale of C major:

|Cmaj7 |Am7 |Dm7 |G7 |

The next progression contains chords derived from C major, as well as two chords borrowed from other tonalities:

|Cmaj7 |A7 (♭9) |Dm7 |D♭9 |
              Borrowed chord   **Borrowed chord**

> **Important**
>
> In examples 1 and 2 above, we stay in the tonality of C major. All the chords in example 1 are derived from the scale of C major and form a diatonic cadence. In example 2, chords A7(♭9) and D♭9 do not belong to the tonality of C, but are borrowed from other tonalities. However, they do not alter the fundamental tonality.

---

1   See Chapter 12, p. 169, for a comparative study of scales, modes and tonalities.
2   Using borrowed chords makes it possible to choose one or several chords from another tonality without modulating.

1.1 Closely-related keys

Closely-related keys are tonalities that have six notes in common and one that is different. Because of their proximity to each other, closely-related keys are often used to modulate[3] without creating a significant tonal contrast.

EXAMPLE

The table below lists the closely-related keys of the C major scale:

C major (no flats or sharps in key signature)	A minor (no flats or sharps in key signature)
F major (1 flat)	D minor (1 flat)
G major (1 sharp)	E minor (1 sharp)

All scales have five closely-related keys. Tonalities containing more than one note that differs from the original scale are called distantly-related keys.

1.2 Determining the key of a piece of music

The tonality of a piece of music can be determined by analyzing its key signature, and then its chords. Every key signature is associated with a major and a minor tonality. The function of the tonic chord defines whether the mode is major or minor.

EXAMPLES

All three musical excerpts below have three flats in their key signature, implying the keys of either E♭ major or C minor. The tonality of each excerpt (major or minor) is determined by analyzing the functions of its chords.

Excerpt 1: The first and last chords are E♭, which confirms the tonality of E♭ major.

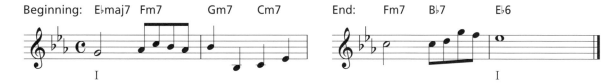

Excerpt 2: The first and last chords are Cm, which confirms the tonality of C minor. Here, we simply refer to the tonality as C minor, without specifying whether the minor is natural, harmonic, or melodic.

Excerpt 3: The first chord is Cm (the tonic minor), and the last chord is E♭ (the tonic major). The tonality is therefore determined by the predominance of one tonality over the other throughout the piece, which, in this case, is C minor.

---

3 Change the tonal center.

Key signatures with no sharps or flats

The key signature in the following musical excerpt contains no sharps or flats; the tonality could therefore be C major, A minor, or an undefined tonality.

Here, there is no tonality due to the absence of a sufficiently defined tonal center. As such, no chord performs the tonic function. This music is not atonal; it is modal.

1.3 Parallel scales

Parallel scales and modes share the same tonic and have at least one note that is different. B♭ major and B♭ melodic minor are parallel scales with only one different note, their respective 3rds. Because of the specific relationship and proximity between parallel scales, each scale can borrow chords from the other and modulate from one tonality to the other.

EXAMPLES

The following theme starts in C minor...

... then modulates to C major.

❷ Tonal functions

All chords can belong to several different tonalities. Dm7, for example, can be a II chord in C major, a VI chord in F major, or a IV chord in A minor. The Dm7 chord itself does not change; it is the harmonic context that indicates its **tonal function.** As we saw in our study of major and minor scales, every scale tone is assigned a chord and a function, according to the tonality in question, in accordance with the principles of functional harmony.

Unlike modal harmony, **functional harmony** attributes a more or less important function to each degree of the scale, according to the chord's relationship with the tonic (the strongest scale-tone degree). There are two categories of degrees, namely:

- **strong degrees** (or tonal degrees): I, IV, and V;
- **weak degrees** (or modal degrees): II, III, VI, and VII.

It is important to note that, in functional harmony, weak degrees are drawn to their neighboring strong degrees. This tonal attraction is present in both the melody and the chords. The **leading tone** (VII) is the weakest degree of the scale. Because of this, it has the greatest tonal attraction to the tonic (the strongest degree), and, as such, provides a particularly important melodic and harmonic function.

2.1 Tonic function

The **tonic** exercises the main diatonic function, because it indicates the tonality of — and generates a sense of resolution, rest, and stability in — a musical phrase. This function essentially concerns the chord built upon the Ist degree (I), which exerts the strongest gravitational pull over the other chords. The I chord may sometimes be replaced by, or substituted with, chords III and VI, which also create a sensation of rest.

The tonic chord, be it an Xmaj7 (in the major) or an Xm7 (in the minor), never contains the IVth degree of the scale.

EXAMPLE

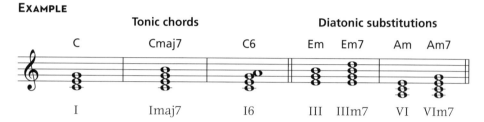

As the above example shows, the tonic chord may take the form of a triad or a tetrad.

The use of **diatonic substitution** makes it possible to replace one chord with another that belongs to the same tonality and has the same function. Note that these chords are similar, the only difference being their respective roots.

EXAMPLES

2.2 Dominant function

The **dominant chord** also exercises an essential diatonic function because it creates a sensation of instability and tension.

Dominant chords typically concern the Vth degree of the scale, and in particular the V7 chord. The particularity of the V7 chord is that it contains a tritone (an unstable interval between the 3rd and the 7th) and includes the leading tone, which has a strong pull toward the tonic. The presence of the tritone and the leading tone create a sensation of instability in the V chord. As we have seen, V7 offers a wide range of extension possibilities because of its tension-creating function. In Chapter 9, we will discover that this chord also offers many substitution possibilities.

2.3 Subdominant function

The function of **subdominant chords** (also known as pre-dominants) is to create tension. There are two types of subdominant chords, those built on the supertonic (II) and on the subdominant (IV). Both chords feature the IVth degree and do not contain the leading tone. These two chords are similar in that they share many common chord tones.

In C major:

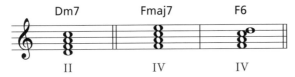

In general, the supertonic (II) is the most frequently used subdominant chord in jazz standard II–V chord progressions, while the subdominant (IV) is more commonly used in IV–I plagal cadences.

EXERCISE 1

1 Write the closely-related tonalities of the following keys

G major			B♭ major	

2 Indicate the tonality of the following jazz themes

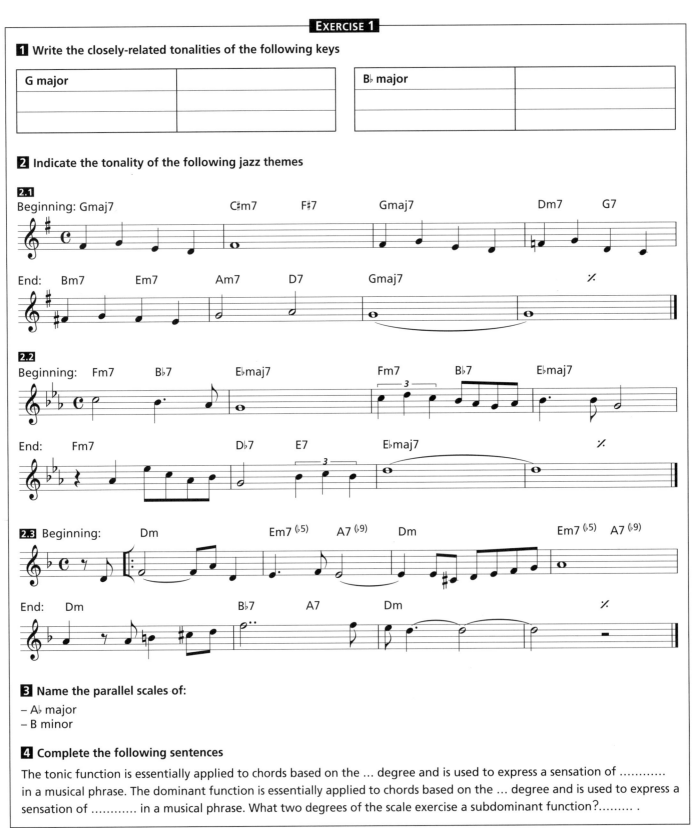

3 Name the parallel scales of:

– A♭ major
– B minor

4 Complete the following sentences

The tonic function is essentially applied to chords based on the … degree and is used to express a sensation of …………
in a musical phrase. The dominant function is essentially applied to chords based on the … degree and is used to express a sensation of ………… in a musical phrase. What two degrees of the scale exercise a subdominant function?……… .

Answers, p. 122

❸ Tonal cadences

We will now examine the different chord relationships, functions, and progressions. In functional harmony, the tonality must be clearly established and confirmed in the melody and harmony by organizing specific chord progressions in **cadences.**[4]

A **harmonic cadence** is a characteristic progression of chords that marks the passage of one musical phrase to another while establishing the tonality. In music, this chord progression serves the same purpose as punctuation in written and spoken language.

> **Important**
>
> To gain a better understanding of chord progressions, and to be able to analyze and transpose them in all keys, we assign Roman numerals to chords used in cadences. Depending on the tonality, we then attribute the chord quality that corresponds to the degree of the scale.

EXAMPLES

III of B♭ major:	B♭maj7 I	Cm7 II	**Dm7** III	
IV of D melodic minor:	Dm(maj7) I	Em7 II	Fmaj7 (♯5) III	**G7** IV

3.1 Two-chord cadences

To facilitate the comparison of the following chord cadences, all the chord-cadence examples are in the key of F (major or minor). The musical excerpts, however, are in their original keys.

Perfect authentic cadences: V–I

The **perfect authentic cadence** is the progression of dominant to tonic chords (tension–release) in root position. This cadence expresses a moment of release or definitive closure and, as such, is often encountered at the end of a piece, section, or musical phrase.

EXAMPLES

|C7 |Fmaj7 |
 V   I

---

4 From the Italian cadere, "to fall."

Imperfect authentic cadences: **V–I** (requiring the presence of at least one inverted chord)

The **imperfect authentic cadence** is similar to the perfect cadence in that it also includes a dominant-to-tonic chord progression. The difference here is that at least one of the two chords must be inverted, as illustrated in the two examples below:

EXAMPLES

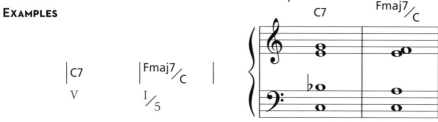

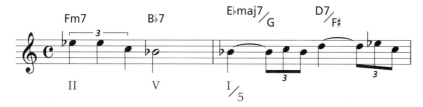

While the notion of resolution is still present, it is less pronounced than in the perfect cadence and has a function similar to a semicolon between two musical phrases.

Half cadences: ...–V

The **half cadence**[5] is the progression from one chord to another chord that has a dominant function (for example, I resolving to V).

EXAMPLES

Fmaj7	C7	
I	V	

This type of suspended cadence ends on an unresolved tension chord, which has a function similar to that of a question mark at the end of a sentence.

Deceptive cadences: V–...

The **deceptive cadence**[6] is generally used in modulating passages and involves a progression from the dominant to any chord other than the tonic, to create an element of surprise (for example, V resolving to VI).

EXAMPLES

	C7	Dm7	
	V	VI	

---

5 Also known as the semi-cadence.
6 Also known as the interrupted cadence.

Plagal cadences: IV—I

The **plagal cadence** involves the progression of the subdominant chord (IV) to the tonic (I). Frequently used in jazz standards, this cadence offers several variants, depending on the quality of the IV chord.

EXAMPLES
• IV and I: belonging to F major

• IV7: borrowed from F melodic minor

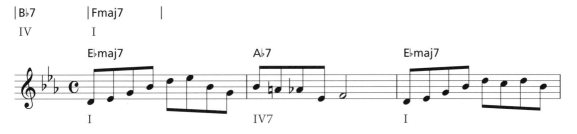

In the following musical excerpt, the tonic (E♭) begins in the major mode and, via a plagal cadence (A♭9(♯11)—E♭m9), moves to the minor mode by measure 3.

In the next example, the original Imaj7 chord (Gmaj7) has been replaced by I7 (G7) to create a bluesier feel.

• IVm7: borrowed from F harmonic minor

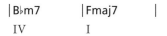

• IV7 and Im: belonging to F melodic minor

• IVm (maj7): borrowed from F harmonic major

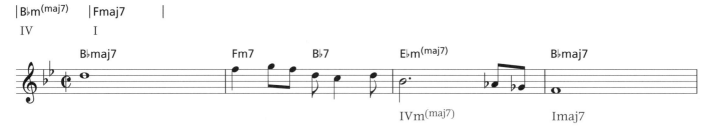

• IV—IVm—I: combination of major and minor modes

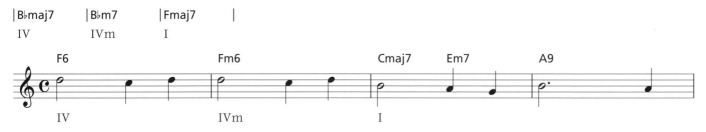

• #IVm7(♭5)—I or #IVdim7—I

EXAMPLES

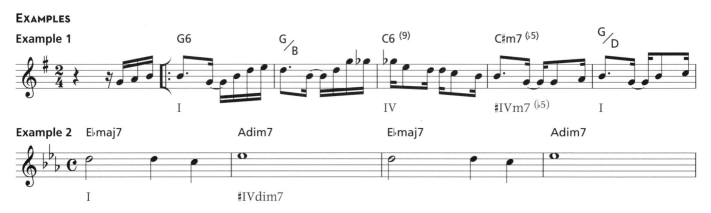

All the examples above illustrate the main two-chord cadences. Although this list is not exhaustive, it is sufficiently complete to enable a preliminary analysis of jazz cadences.

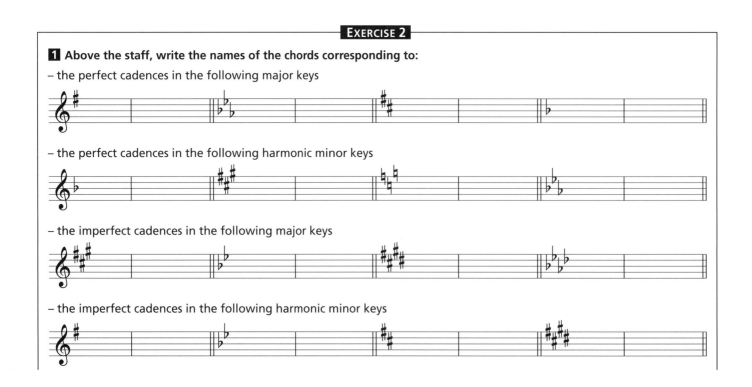

2 Write the names of the following cadences

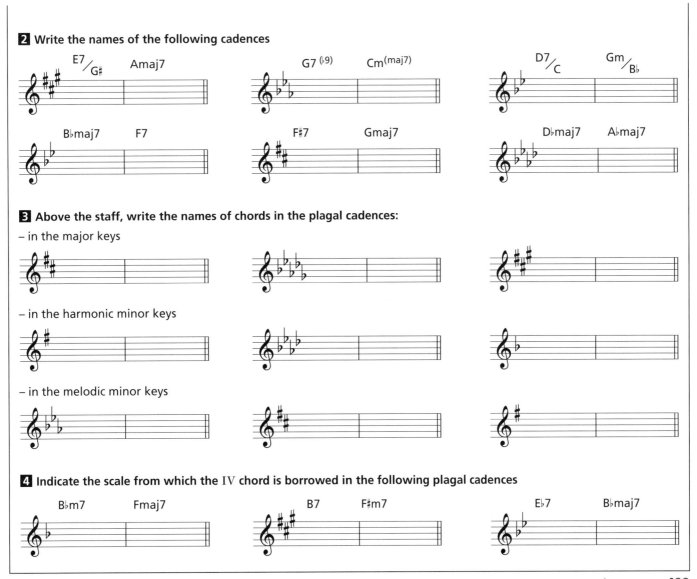

3 Above the staff, write the names of chords in the plagal cadences:

– in the major keys

– in the harmonic minor keys

– in the melodic minor keys

4 Indicate the scale from which the IV chord is borrowed in the following plagal cadences

Answers, p. 122

3.2 Three-chord cadences

The most common chord progression used in jazz is the **two-five-one**, which derives its name directly from its chord structure (II–V–I).

II–V–I major cadences

So far, we have studied cadences built solely on two-chord, tension-release progressions. Now let's look at complete three-chord cadences built on subdominant (II or IV)–dominant (V)–tonic (I) progressions (tension preparation–tension–release). As we have seen, the II (supertonic) and IV (subdominant) chords both exercise a subdominant function. In jazz, the supertonic (II) is the most common subdominant chord used to prepare the dominant (V) tension chord.

EXAMPLE

|Gm7 |C13 |Fmaj7 |
  II   V   I

To improvise over, or enrich, a melody built on a II–V–I chord progression in the key of F major, use the scale of F major, since there are no non-diatonic notes in the cadence. All the extension notes that can be applied to the C7 chord belong to the key of F (in this example, 9, 11, and 13).

As we will see in the II–V–I cadences that follow, and more particularly when we study modes, it is not always possible to find a common scale that applies to all three chords.

II–V–I minor cadences

The quality of the II chord, and the extensions used with the V chord, determine whether a minor II–V–I chord progression is in the harmonic minor or the melodic minor.

• In the harmonic minor

The II chord is an Xm7(♭5) and the V chord, an X7(♭9, ♭13).

EXAMPLE 1

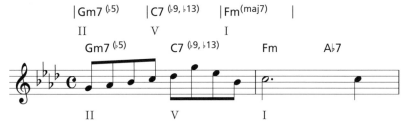

• In the melodic minor

The II chord is an Xm7 and the V chord, an X7(9, ♭13).

EXAMPLE 2

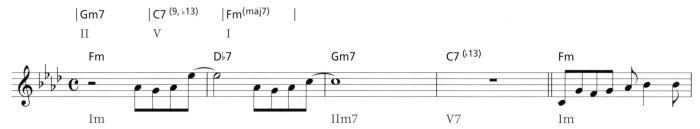

Reminder

These II–V–I progressions further illustrate the difference between tonality and scales. While both examples are in the key of F minor, they use chords borrowed from other scales (F harmonic minor and F melodic minor).

II–V–I minor/major cadences

As in the case of plagal cadences, the II–V–I cadence offers several chord combinations. These are derived from elements borrowed from parallel modes, and offer an interesting mixture that plays on major/minor mode ambiguity.

• IIm7(♭5)–V7(♭9, ♭13)–Imaj7

Here, the II–V–I progression begins in the minor and ends in the parallel tonic major. The fact that the cadence resolves to an Xmaj7 chord (rather than an Xm) creates an element of surprise, since the minor tonality was clearly installed with IIm7(♭5) and V7(♭9, ♭13), suggesting a resolution on the tonic minor.

EXAMPLE

• IIm7–V7(♭9, ♭13)–Imaj7

Borrowing the V7 chord from a parallel mode is common in this type of cadence. In Chapter 4 on chord extensions, we saw that all non-diatonic notes added to chords create a dissonance considerably greater than diatonic-note extensions. Here, we amplify the tension function of V7 by adding dissonances (such as ♭9 and ♭13, which do not belong to the tonality of F major, but rather to F minor), to create greater tension halfway through the cadence, and heighten the "need" for resolution.

EXAMPLES

Because Gm7 and Fmaj7 in this example belong to the tonality of F major, we can improvise over the F major scale.

In addition, since the notes comprising C7(♭9, ♭13) – C, D♭, E, F, G, A♭, B♭ – belong to the tonality of **F harmonic minor**, we can use this scale to improvise over this chord. We will later see that other scale choices are also possible.

The next two cadences are less frequent, in the major and the minor modes.

• IIm7–V7–Im

EXAMPLES

|Gm7	|C13	|Fm7		
II	V	I

While the II–V at the beginning of this cadence implies a resolution to the major, the passage ends on the 1st degree of the parallel minor mode.

• IIm7(♭5)–V7(9, 13)–Imaj7

EXAMPLES

|Gm7 (♭5)	|C13	|Fmaj7		
II	V	I

Likewise, although the IIm7(♭5) in this example suggests the beginning of a minor cadence, the color of the V7 chord implies the major mode (with the inclusion of the major 9th and 13th extensions).

Analyzing II–V–I progressions in a complete theme

The following theme contains three types of II–V–I chord progressions, notably:

- in the minor (measures 1-4, 9-12, and 25-28): the tonality of F harmonic minor is used for the chords Gm7(♭5) and C7. Fm offers the possibility of remaining in F harmonic minor, as well as moving into F Aeolian or melodic minor, since the chord built on the first degree of the minor may be Im(maj7), Im6, or Im7;

- in the major (measures 17-20): the tonality of B♭ major is used for the three chords;

- a combination of minor and major cadences (measures 5-8, 13-15, and 29-31): the tonality is C harmonic minor for the chords Dm7(♭5) and G7, then moves into C major on the Cmaj7 chord.

* See p. 113 for instructions on how to use this degree.

Important

It is vitally important to be able to visualize, hear, and memorize II–V–I cadences, since these are used frequently in jazz standards:

- in the major: IIm7–V7–Imaj7;
- in the minor: IIm7(♭5)–V7-Im.

The Xm7(♭5) chord is regularly used in II–V minor cadences, and, as such, serves as a reference.

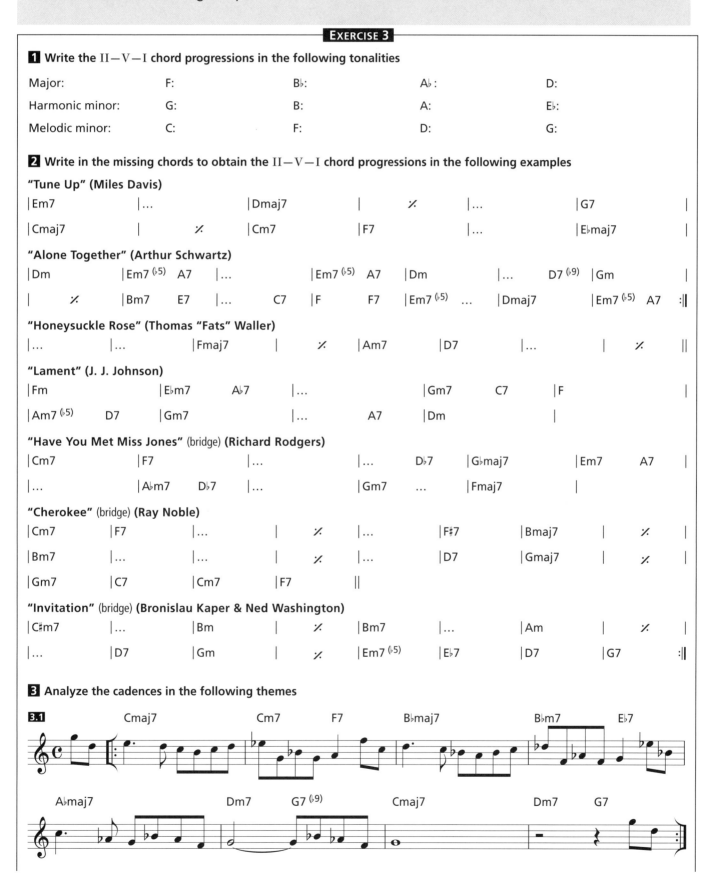

EXERCISE 3

1 Write the II – V – I chord progressions in the following tonalities

Major:	F:	B♭:	A♭:	D:
Harmonic minor:	G:	B:	A:	E♭:
Melodic minor:	C:	F:	D:	G:

2 Write in the missing chords to obtain the II – V – I chord progressions in the following examples

"Tune Up" (Miles Davis)

|Em7 |... |Dmaj7 | ⁄ |... |G7 |
|Cmaj7 | ⁄ |Cm7 |F7 |... |E♭maj7 |

"Alone Together" (Arthur Schwartz)

|Dm |Em7 (♭5) A7 |... |Em7 (♭5) A7 |Dm |...   D7 (♭9) |Gm |
| ⁄ |Bm7   E7 |...   C7 |F   F7 |Em7 (♭5) ... |Dmaj7 |Em7 (♭5) A7 :‖|

"Honeysuckle Rose" (Thomas "Fats" Waller)

|... |... |Fmaj7 | ⁄ |Am7 |D7 |... | ⁄   ‖|

"Lament" (J. J. Johnson)

|Fm |E♭m7   A♭7 |... |Gm7   C7 |F |
|Am7 (♭5) D7 |Gm7 |...   A7 |Dm | |

"Have You Met Miss Jones" (bridge) **(Richard Rodgers)**

|Cm7 |F7 |... |...   D♭7 |G♭maj7 |Em7   A7 |
|... |A♭m7   D♭7 |... |Gm7   ... |Fmaj7 | |

"Cherokee" (bridge) **(Ray Noble)**

Cm7	F7	...	⁄	...	F♯7	Bmaj7	⁄
Bm7	...	...	⁄	...	D7	Gmaj7	⁄
Gm7	C7	Cm7	F7 ‖

"Invitation" (bridge) **(Bronislau Kaper & Ned Washington)**

|C♯m7 |... |Bm | ⁄ |Bm7 |... |Am | ⁄ |
|... |D7 |Gm | ⁄ |Em7 (♭5) |E♭7 |D7 |G7   :‖|

3 Analyze the cadences in the following themes

3.1

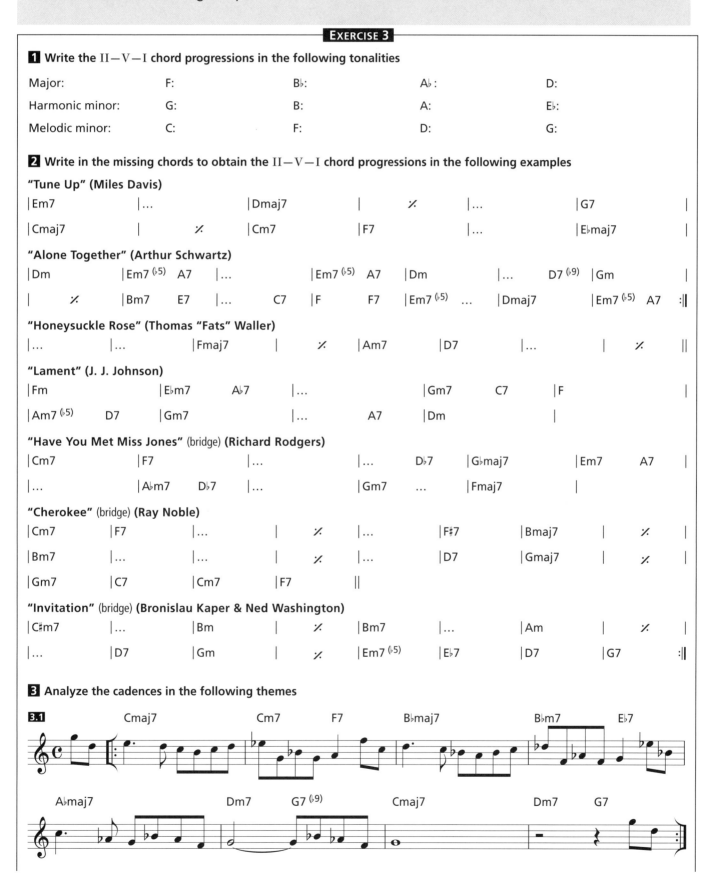

4 Complete (......) the II—V—I cadence table
As in the example in G, all V chords include 9/13 extensions.

Tonalities	II		V			I		
	Major	Har. min.	Major	Har. min.	Mel. min.	Major	Nat. min.	Mel. min.
G	Am7			D7 (♭9, ♭13)		Gmaj9		
A		......		......		......		
E♭	......		......			......		
D		......		......		......		
A♭	......				......		......	
C		......		......				......
B♭	......		......			......		
F	......			......				......

Answers, p. 123-124

IV—V—I major cadences

While the use of the subdominant (IV) is less common than the supertonic (II) as a dominant preparatory chord, its presence in complete cadences creates different movements in the bass, and new chord qualities. This cadence is often used in rhythm and blues, as well as gospel music.

The three chords in the following IV—V—I cadence are derived from the same major scale (F major).

EXAMPLES

| B♭maj7 | C13 | Fmaj7 | |
| IV | V | I | |

IV–V–I minor cadences

As in the plagal IV–I cadence, the IVth degree offers several possibilities, depending on the minor mode from which the chord is derived.

• Harmonic minor: IVm7–V7–Im

In the harmonic minor, the qualities of the chords attributed to the IVth and Vth degrees are always Xm7–X7, as in the IIm7–V7–I cadence. The only difference between IVm7 and IIm7 is their respective bass notes.

EXAMPLES

|B♭m7 |C7 (♭9, ♭13) |Fm |
  IV   V   I

• Melodic minor: IV7–V7–Im

Here, the subdominant chord is an X7 chord, which produces a progression of two X7 chords leading to a Im. Complete cadences in the melodic minor are rare, since IV7(13) is more frequently encountered as a borrowed chord used in major tonalities.

EXAMPLE

|B♭13 |C7 (9, ♭13) |Fm |
  IV   V   I

IV–V–I minor/major mixed cadences

As in IV–I and II–V–I cadences, there are several ways to combine major and parallel minor modes. Some examples are given below:

EXAMPLE 1
Chords IV and V are derived from the harmonic minor mode, and chord I from the major mode.
|B♭m7 |C7 (♭9, ♭13) |Fmaj7 |
  IV   V   I

EXAMPLE 2
Chords IV and I are derived from the major mode, and chord V is borrowed from the harmonic minor.
|B♭maj7 |C7 (♭9, ♭13) |Fmaj7 |
  IV   V   I

EXAMPLE 3
Chord IV is borrowed from the melodic minor, and chords V and I are derived from the major mode.
|B♭13 |C13 |Fmaj7 |
  IV   V   I

VI–V–I cadences

In this cadence, the VI chord serves to prepare the arrival of the dominant (V). Although VI–V–I is less common than IV–V or II–V chord progressions, it is sometimes used. Unlike cadences comprising chords built on II or IV chords, the absence of the IVth degree in the preparatory VI chord in this cadence is more or less offset by the movement in the bass, and the complete or partial parallel motion between the VI and V chords.

• In the major: VIm7–V7–Imaj7

EXAMPLE

|Dm7 |C7 |Fmaj7 |
  VI   V   I

This cadence is theoretically possible, but rarely used.

• In the harmonic minor: VImaj7–V7–Im

EXAMPLES

|D♭maj7 |C7 |Fm |
  VI   V   I

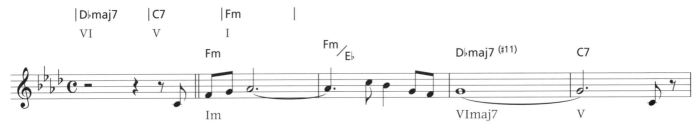

• In the melodic minor: VIm7(♭5)–V7–Im

This progression is most frequently encountered in cadences where VI7 or ♭VI7 are used to prepare V7.

EXAMPLES

|Dm7 (♭5) |C7 |Fm |
  VI   V   I

|D♭7 |C7 |Fm |
  VI   V   I

• In the natural minor

The VIth degree of the natural minor (Xmaj7) can be altered to become an X7 in a VI–V–I chord progression. In this type of cadence, the VIth chord is close to that of a chromatic dominant. (See p. 135.)

EXAMPLES

|D♭7 |C7 |Fm |
  VI   V   I

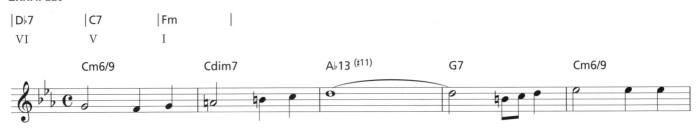

1 Complete the IV—V—I cadence table. Write the chord symbols on the dotted lines.

Tonality	IV Major	IV Har. minor	IV Mel. minor	V Major	V Har. minor	V Mel. minor	I Major	I Nat. minor	I Mel. minor
G	Cmaj9				D7 $^{(\flat 9, \flat 13)}$		Gmaj9		
F		......				......			......
A♭	......			......			......		
C			......		......			......	
A		......			......		......		
E			......		......				......
B♭		......		......				......	
E♭	......			......					......

2 Complete the VI—V—I cadence table. Write the chord symbols on the dotted lines.

Tonality	VI Major	VI Har. minor	VI Mel. minor	V Major	V Har. minor	V Mel. minor	I Major	I Nat. minor	I Mel. minor
G	Em9				D7 $^{(\flat 9, \flat 13)}$		Gmaj9		
B		......				......			......
D		......			......			......	
C	......			......					......
A♭			......		......	......			
E			......		......	......			
B♭	......				......				......
E♭		......			......			......	

Answers, p. 124-125

3.3 Common chord progressions

II—V chord progressions

II—V chord progressions that do not resolve on a strong degree are often encountered. Progressions involving a subdominant chord (II or IV) moving to the dominant (V) in a given tonality, and that do not resolve, create a feeling of unresolved tension. This is further amplified when the progression is followed by another II (or IV)—V chord sequence. This intensifies the need for resolution and creates a harmonic and melodic "rebound" from one cadence to the next. This type of progression is particularly pervasive in bebop.

• Sequential II—V progressions descending or ascending by half-step

The half-step difference from one II—V sequence to the next is present either in the first or the second chords of each II—V progression.

EXAMPLES

|Dm7   G7 |E♭m7   A♭7 |

|Dm7   G7 |D♭m7   G♭7 |

|Dm7   **G7** |F♯m7   B7 |B♭m7   E♭7 |

|Dm7   **G7** |A♭m7   D♭7 |

• Sequential II–V progressions descending or ascending by one whole step

The whole-step difference from one II–V sequence to the next is present either in the first or the second chords of each II–V progression.

EXAMPLES

Dm7	**G7**		**Am7**	D7	
Dm7	**G7**		**Fm7**	B♭7	
Dm7	G7		**Em7**	A7	
Dm7	G7		**Cm7**	F7		(circle of fifths)

Note that in the last cadence example above, the Cm7 chord in measure 2 plays a dual role: that of the final chord in the II–V–I cadence (Dm7–G7–Cm7), as well as the first chord in the new II–V cadence (Cm7–F7). This progression is quite popular in bebop.

• Sequential II–V progressions combining Circle-of-Fifths and half-step progressions

The following example illustrates how a series of consecutive II–Vs moving through the Circle of Fifths and by half-steps can be used to resolve to the final chord (in this case, Cmaj7).

| F♯m7 | **B7** | | Em7 | **A7** | | **A♭m7** | D♭7 | | Cmaj7 | |

└── circle of fifths ──┘
└── half-step ──┘

• Sequential II–V pairs in jazz themes

CONSECUTIVE II–Vs MOVING BY HALF STEP

Example 1

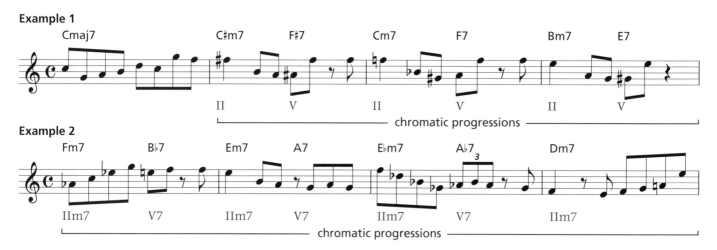

Example 2

CONSECUTIVE II–Vs MOVING BY WHOLE STEPS

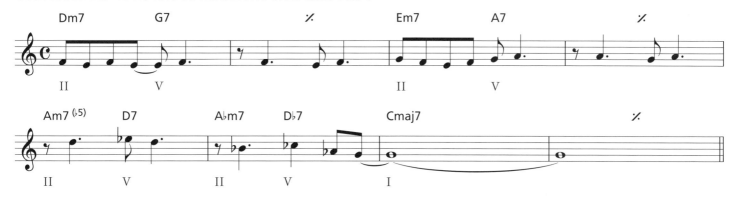

In the excerpt above, the sequence of II–V progressions (Dm7–G7 and Am7(♭5)–D♭7) moving to neighboring tones (Em7–A7 and A♭m7–D♭7, respectively) acts as a series of harmonic blocks. These progressions can also be analyzed by using a diatonic approach. For example, the Em7–A7 (II–V) sequence in measures 3 and 4 can also be defined as a III–VI7 progression (in the key of C). It is important to note that some of these chords are borrowed from other scales and require the application of the appropriate modes, a subject we will examine in greater depth in Chapters 12 and 13.

I–VI–II–V cadences

Also known as the "rhythm changes" chord progression (from George Gershwin's "I Got Rhythm"), this cadence is common in jazz standards, notably from the music-hall and bebop eras.

The main feature of the I–VI–II–V cadence is that it forms a circular movement through the Circle of Fifths, and can therefore be played over sections of undetermined length, such as in introductions or codas. This progression can be used in major and minor tonalities, and offers many variations derived from the use of borrowed chords and substitutions. Several variants of the I–VI–II–V cadence progression are given below:

EXAMPLES

In F major	|Fmaj7	|Dm7	|Gm7	|C7	|
	I	VI	II	V	
In F harmonic minor	|Fm	|D♭maj7	|Gm7 (♭5)	|C7 (♭9)	|
	I	VI	II	V	
In F melodic minor	|Fm	|Dm7 (♭5)	|Gm7	|C7 (♭9)	|
	I	VI	II	V	
In F harmonic and melodic minor	|Fm	|Dm7 (♭5)	|Gm7 (♭5)	|C7 (♭9)	|
	I	VI	II	V	
	|Fm	|D♭maj7	|Gm7 (♭5)	|C7 (♭9)	|
	I	VI	II	V	
In F major and minor	|Fmaj7	|Dm7	|Gm7 (♭5)	|C7 (♭9)	|
	I	VI	II	V	

B♭ major: I–VIm7–IIm7–V

C minor: Im–VIm7(♭5)–IIm7(♭5)–V7

E major/minor: Imaj7–VIm7–II7(♭5)–V7

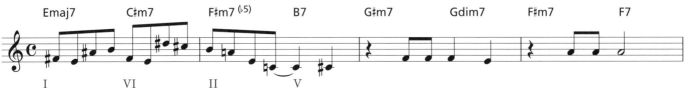

EXERCISE 5

1 Write the I—VI—II—V chord progressions in the following tonalities

In E♭ major | | | | |

In G harmonic minor | | | | |

In C melodic minor | | | | |

In E harmonic minor | | | In E melodic minor | | |

In D melodic minor | | | In D harmonic minor | | |

In B major | | | In B harmonic minor | | |

2 Complete the chord progressions to obtain the diatonic cadences in the following jazz tunes

"In a Sentimental Mood" (bridge in D♭ major) **(Duke Ellington)**

|...   ... |...   ... |...   B♭7 |E♭7   A♭7 |
 I   VI   II   V   I

"Sophisticated Lady" (bridge in G major) **(Duke Ellington)**

|...   ... |...   ... |G7   G♯dim7 |...   ... |
 I   VI   II   V   II   V

"Don't Blame Me" (in C major) **(Jimmy McHugh)**

|...   Fm7 B♭7 |Em7   A7 |...   ... |...   ... |
 I   III   II   V   I   VI

|...   ... |Em7 (♭5)   A7 |...   ... |...   ... :‖
 II   V   II   V   I   V

3 Analyze the cadences in the following theme

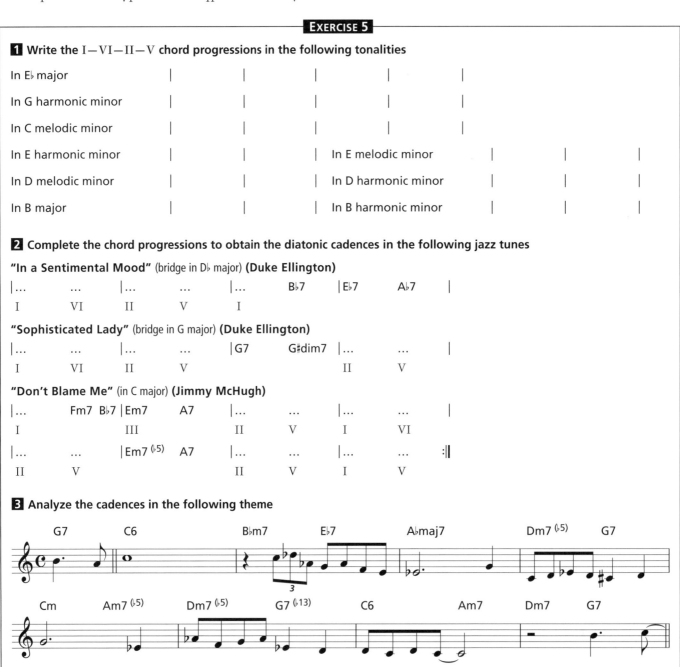

Answers, p. 125

III–VI–II–V–I cadences

This cadence is a simple variant of the rhythm changes chord progression and is often found at the beginning or the end of a tune when the rhythm changes progression is played more than once without repeating the I chord. In this case, III is used to substitute the I chord, as illustrated in measures 3-4 below:

EXAMPLE

|Fmaj7   Dm7 |Gm7   C7 |Am7   Dm7 |Gm7   C7 |
  I   VI   II   V   III   VI   II   V

In the following example, measures 1-4 display a basic rhythm changes cadence (I–VI–II–V), and measures 5-8, the variant (III–VI–II–V).

At the beginning

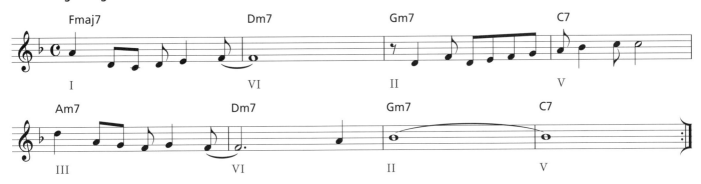

The next example features the rhythm changes variant in the last four measures of a tune. This time, the VI7 chord is major.

At the end

♭VII–I cadences

♭VII–I is considered a modal cadence, since ♭VII is a chord borrowed from a parallel mode. Although we will be looking at modes in detail in Chapters 12 and 13, a cursory modal analysis of this cadence here is helpful to analyze these themes.

The ♭VII chord has three different qualities, depending on its parent scale. For example, in C major, ♭VII may be:

- ♭VII7: the VIIth degree of C Aeolian: B♭7–Cmaj7;
- ♭VIImaj7: the VIIth degree of C Mixolydian:[7] B♭maj7–Cmaj7;
- ♭VIIm7: the IInd degree of C Phrygian[8] (much rarer): B♭m7–Cmaj7.

EXAMPLES

The ♭VII–I sequence above is also called a "backdoor" turnaround.

---

7 Mixolydian mode = natural mode derived from the Vth degree of the major parent scale (See Natural Diatonic Modes, Chapter 12, p. 186).
8 Phrygian mode = natural mode derived from the IIIrd degree of the major parent scale (See Natural Diatonic Modes, Chapter 12, p. 185).

In the next example, the tonic chord is played with an X7 quality to give it a bluesy feel.

• ♭VIImaj7 of F Mixolydian

EXAMPLES

| E♭maj7 | Fmaj7 | |

♭VIImaj7   I

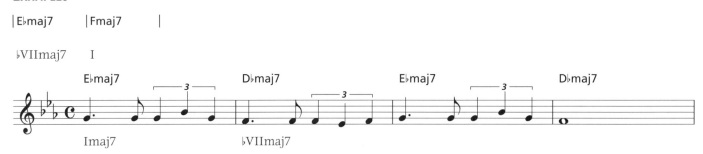

II—♭VII7—I cadences

The II—♭VII—I progression is more elaborate than the ♭VII—I cadence because the ♭VII7 tension chord is prepared by the supertonic (II) to create a subdominant—dominant—tonic chord progression, as illustrated in measures 1 and 2 below:

EXAMPLE

IV—♭VII—I cadences

The IV chord can also perform this subdominant function. As in plagal cadences, this chord can be borrowed from the parallel harmonic and melodic minor scales of the target tonality.   The harmonic rhythm of this cadence usually spans two measures, with the IV and ♭VII7 chords played in the same measure, as illustrated in the examples below.

• IVmaj7: belonging to the major target scale

EXAMPLE

| B♭maj7   E♭7 | Fmaj7 | |
IVmaj7 ♭VII7   I

• IVm7: belonging to the parallel harmonic or melodic minor scale (for example, F harmonic minor)

EXAMPLES

| B♭m7 | E♭7 | Fmaj7 | |
| IVm7 | ♭VII7 | I | |

EXERCISE 6

1 Write the ♭VII7—I chord progressions in the following tonalities

In G major | | | |

In D major | | | |

In B♭ major | | | |

2 Write the IV—♭VII7—I chord progressions in the following tonalities

In A♭ major | | | | |

In E♭ major | | | | |

In B major | | | | |

3 Write the IVm7—♭VII7—I chord progressions in the following tonalities

In E major | | | | |

In G major | | | | |

In E♭ major | | | | |

Answers, p. 126

3.4 Chords built on the first degree of the scale

Chords built on the first degree of the scale (the tonic, or I chord) play a particularly important role in functional harmony, because they determine the tonality. These chords are often voiced in root or inverted position throughout the piece of music. Several functions of Ist degree chords are presented below.

Chords built on the first degree of the major scale: Imaj

In major tonalities, chords built on the first degree can be represented by the Roman numeral I, with no additional precisions. The three main chords built on the Ist degree are:

- the major triad;
- the Imaj7 chord;
- the I6 chord.

Tonic chord triads voiced in root position are rarely used in jazz standard harmonizations. These are generally reserved for creating a sensation of stability and definitive closure, as in the following example.

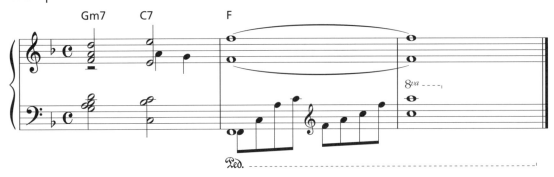

In general, the 6th is added to the triad rather than the major 7th when the notes in the melody and the bass are identical. The presence of the 6th in the chord avoids a clash between the major 7th and the root in the melody. This would be the case for the C6 chord below.

In most cases, the tonic chord is presented as Imaj7, as follows:

In the following excerpt, the B♭maj7–B♭maj7(♯5)–B♭6 chord progression in measures 1 and 2 is an example of **oblique motion**[9] between the root and the fifth degree of the chord. This technique is typically reserved for I minor chords, but in this instance it is used on a I major chord.

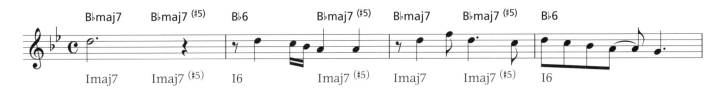

When the tonic chord spans several measures, and if the melody permits, it is possible to modify the color of the chord or add other chords, as long as the tonic chord continues to exercise its main function. Take the following melody, for example:

---

9 In oblique motion, one voice moves while the other remains at the same pitch.

Several reharmonization possibilities are given below:

| |Cmaj7 Fmaj7 | ⁒ | ⁒ |Dm7 G7 |

| |Cmaj7 Fm(maj7) | Cmaj7 Fm6 |Cmaj7 Fm(maj7) |Dm7 G7 |

| |Cmaj7 Fm6/C | ⁒ | ⁒ |Dm7 G7 |

| |Cmaj7 G7sus4 | ⁒ | ⁒ |Dm7 G7 |

| |Cmaj7 B♭7 | ⁒ |Cmaj7 B♭maj7 |Dm7 G7 |

These reharmonizations can also be combined to form new chord progressions. In the following improvisation over the chord changes of Jerome Kern's "All The Things You Are," notice how the original Cmaj7 chords in measures 2 and 3 have been reharmonized with a I–II–III–V chord progression.

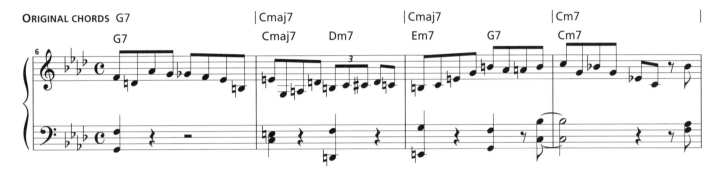

I–I7/3¹⁰–IV–♯IVdim7–I/5 cadences

This chord progression, built around the Ist degree and based on a variant of the plagal IV–I cadence, is notably characterized by the ascending stepwise motion in the bass line. This progression is typically used in gospel music and blues.

EXAMPLE |Fmaj7   F7/A |B♭   Bdim7 |F/C   C7 |

    I   I7/3   IV   ♯IVdim7 I/5   V7

I–I7/7–IV/3–IVm/3–I/5 cadences

This cadence creates another common bass line based on a variant of the plagal cadence. Here, the cadence is characterized by the descending step-wise motion in the bass line.

EXAMPLE |Fmaj7   F7/E♭ |B♭/D   B♭m7/D♭ |F/C   C7 |

    I   I7/7   IV/3   IVm/3   I/5   V7

---

10 I7/3 = first inversion of the tonic chord, with the 3rd played in the bass. See slash chords, Chapter 2, p. 35.

Important

These two plagal-cadence progressions favor a smooth movement in the bass line, achieved by using certain chord inversions. In both cases:

- we begin on the root position of the I chord (Fmaj7), and, after passing through a series of specific chord inversions, reach the second inversion of the I chord;
- the bass line connects the root and second-inversion positions of the I chord with an ascending or descending chromatic line.

Chords built on the first degree of the minor scale: Im

In minor tonalities, chords built on the first degree are generally represented as a Im (with no additional precisions), because when a fourth note is added to the chord, several alterations are possible, depending on which minor mode is used. These include:

- Im(maj7): for the harmonic minor mode;
- Im7: for the Aeolian (or natural minor) mode;
- Im6: for the melodic minor mode.

Whenever the melody permits, therefore, it is possible to reharmonize a Im chord using any one of these chords, as illustrated below:

EXAMPLES

The Im chord can also be harmonized as a triad without the addition of a fourth note, although this is quite rare.

When the Im chord spans two measures, various chromatic movements can be used based on the different minor modes.

EXAMPLES

Chromatic movement descending from the root to the VIth degree:

- in the soprano voice:

|Fm   Fm(maj7) |Fm7   Fm6 |
Im   Im(maj7) Im   Im6

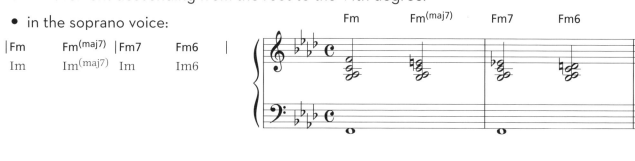

- in the bass line:

|Fm   Fm(maj7)/E |Fm7/Eb   Fm6/D |
Im   Im(maj7)/7 Im7/7   Im6/6

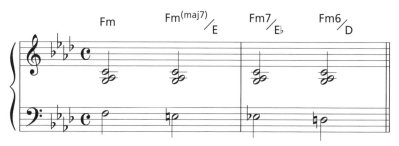

Chromatic movement ascending from the 5th:

|Fm   Fm(b6) |Fm6   Fm7 |
Im   Im(b6) Im6   Im7

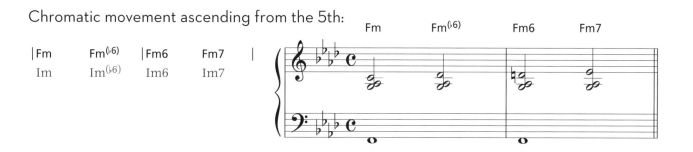

Several examples of chromatic movements are given below:

Example 1

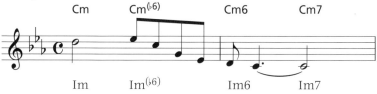

Example 2

Example 3

Example 4

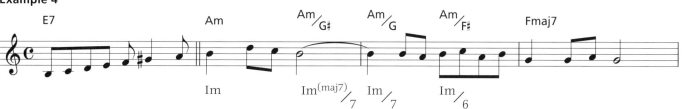

1 On the staff, write in the missing notes to complete the following chords

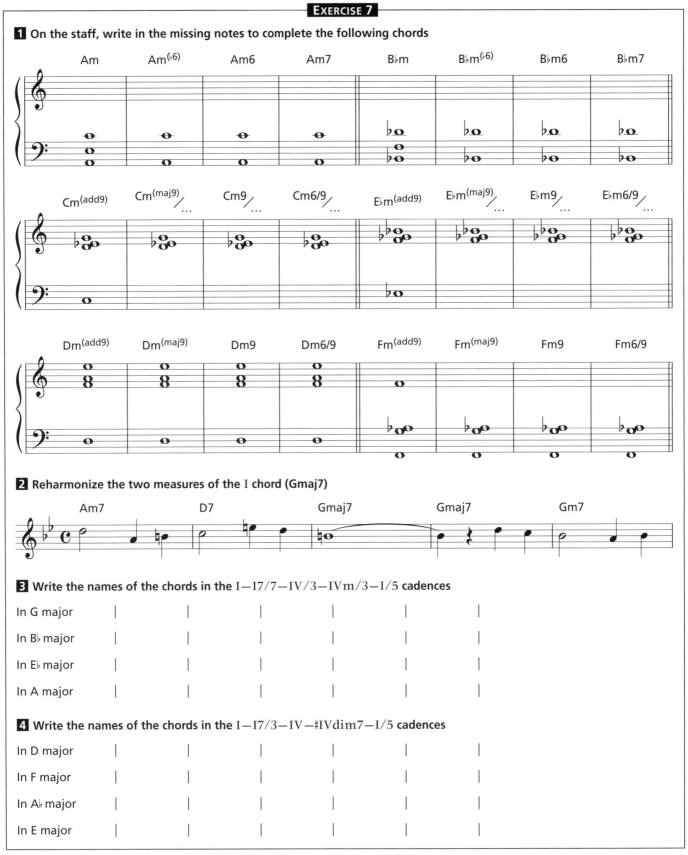

2 Reharmonize the two measures of the I chord (Gmaj7)

3 Write the names of the chords in the I—I7/7—IV/3—IVm/3—I/5 cadences

In G major | | | | | |

In B♭ major | | | | | |

In E♭ major | | | | | |

In A major | | | | | |

4 Write the names of the chords in the I—I7/3—IV—♯IVdim7—I/5 cadences

In D major | | | | | |

In F major | | | | | |

In A♭ major | | | | | |

In E major | | | | | |

Answers, p. 126-127

Tunes ending on the 1st degree: turnarounds or turnbacks

The I chord is often used to end, and confirm the tonality of, a piece of music. This chord is included in **turnaround** (or turnback) cadences in the last measure(s) of tunes to facilitate a return to the beginning of the piece.

Several types of turnarounds exist. All the examples below are in the key of F major:

- **the one-measure turnaround:** here, the most effective lead-in to a I chord is the dominant, which, together, form a perfect cadence. (See Chapter 9 for other chord-preparation possibilities.) Several one-measure turnaround possibilities are given below:

End				Beginning	
|Fmaj7				||Fmaj7	|
|Fmaj7	╱	C7	╱	||Fmaj7	|
|Fmaj7	╱	G♭7	╱	||Fmaj7	|
|Fmaj7	╱	G♭maj7	╱	||Fmaj7	|
|Fmaj7	╱	E♭7	╱	||Fmaj7	|
|Fmaj7	╱	C7 sus4	C7	||Fmaj7	|
|Fmaj7	╱	Gm7	C7	||Fmaj7	|

- **the two-measure turnaround:** several chord progressions may be used at the end of a tune to return to the I chord:

End				Beginning	
|Fmaj7		|Fmaj7		||Fmaj7	|
|Fmaj7		|C7 sus4	C7	||Fmaj7	|
|Fmaj7		|Gm7	C7	||Fmaj7	|
|Fmaj7	Dm7	|Gm7	C7	||Fmaj7	|
|Fmaj7	D7	|Gm7	C7	||Fmaj7	|
|Fmaj7	D7	|G7	C7	||Fmaj7	|
|Fmaj7	A♭7	|G7	G♭7	||Fmaj7	|
|Fmaj7	A♭maj7	|D♭maj7	G♭maj7	||Fmaj7	|

Numerous turnaround reharmonization formulas exist, depending on how the target chord is prepared. The I chord substitutions used in the above example will be explained in greater depth in Chapter 9.

Tunes beginning on chords other than I

Here, the turnaround cadence must be adapted to prepare a return to the opening chord rather than to a I chord.

EXAMPLE 1 "All the Things You Are" (Jerome Kern)

End	Turnaround		Beginning	
|A♭maj7	|Gm7 (♭5)	C7 (♭9)	||Fm7	|

This standard in the key of A♭ major ends on the tonic, but begins on the relative minor (Fm7). Here, the turnaround resolves to the opening Fm7 chord, rather than A♭maj7, which is prepared by its II–V cadence (Gm7(♭5)–C7).

EXAMPLE 2 "Beautiful Love" (Victor Young)

End	Turnaround	Beginning	
|Dm	|Fm7	||Em7 (♭5)	|

This standard in D minor ends on the I chord (Dm) and begins on II (Em7(♭5)). The Fm7 in the turnaround, which serves to prepare the return to the first chord of the tune, is a parallel chord.

④ Answers

1

G major	E minor
C major	A minor
D major	B minor

B♭ major	G minor
F major	D minor
E♭ major	C minor

2

2.1 G major   A♭ major   **2.2** E♭ major   **2.3** D minor

3

– A♭ major = A♭ minor
– B minor = B major

4

The tonic function is typically applied to chords based on the **Ist** degree and is used to express a **sensation of rest** in a musical phrase.

The dominant function is typically applied to chords based on the **Vth** degree and is used to express a **sensation of tension** in a musical phrase.

The two chords that exercise a subdominant function: **II** and **IV**.

1

The perfect cadences in the following major keys

|D7 |Gmaj7 || |B♭7 |E♭maj7 || |A7 |Dmaj7 || |C7 |Fmaj7 ||

The perfect cadences in the following harmonic minor keys

|A7 |Dm^(maj7) || |C♯7 |F♯m^(maj7) || |E7 |Am^(maj7) || |G7 |Cm^(maj7) ||

The perfect cadences in the following major keys (there are several possibilities because at least one of the two chords must be inverted)

|E7 |Amaj7/C♯ || |F7/A |B♭maj7 || |B7 |Emaj7/B || |E♭7/B♭ |A♭maj7 ||

The imperfect cadences in the following harmonic minor keys

|B7/D♯ |Em^(maj7) || |D7 |Gm^(maj7)/B♭ || |F♯7/E |Bm^(maj7)/D || |G♯7 |C♯m^(maj7)/G♯ ||

2

Imperfect cadence	Perfect cadence	Imperfect cadence
Half cadence / Semicadence	Deceptive cadence	Plagal cadence

3

In major	|Gmaj7 |Dmaj7 ||	|G♭maj7 |D♭maj7 ||	|Dmaj7 |Amaj7 ||
In harmonic minor	|Am7 |Em^(maj7) ||	|B♭m7 |Fm^(maj7) ||	|Gm7 |Dm^(maj7) ||
In melodic minor	|F7 |Cm^(maj7) ||	|E7 |Bm^(maj7) ||	|A7 |Em^(maj7) ||

4

B♭m7: borrowed from F natural minor or F harmonic minor.
B7: borrowed from F♯ melodic minor.
E♭7: borrowed from B♭ melodic minor.

1

F: Gm7 – C7 – Fmaj7 　　Bb: Cm7 – F7 – Bbmaj7 　　Ab: Bbm7 – Eb7 – Abmaj7 　　D: Em7 – A7 – Dmaj7

G: Am7 (b5) – D7 – Gm(maj7) 　　B: C#m7 (b5) – F#7 – Bm(maj7) 　　A: Bm7 (b5) – E7 – Am(maj7) 　　Eb: Fm7 (b5) – Bb7 – Ebm(maj7)

C: Dm7 – G7 – Cm(maj7) 　　F: Gm7 – C7 – Fm(maj7) 　　D: Em7 – A7 – Dm(maj7) 　　G: Am7 – D7 – Gm(maj7)

2

"Tune Up" (Miles Davis)

| Em7 | **A7** | Dmaj7 | ✕ | **Dm7** | G7 |

| Cmaj7 | ✕ | Cm7 | F7 | **Bbmaj7** | Ebmaj7 |

"Alone Together" (Arthur Schwartz)

| Dm | Em7 (b5) A7 | **Dm** | Em7 (b5) A7 | Dm | **Am7 (b5) D7 (b9)** | Gm |

| ✕ | Bm7 E7 | **Gm7** C7 | F F7 | Em7 (b5) **A7** | Dmaj7 | Em7 (b5) A7 :||

"Honeysuckle Rose" (Thomas "Fats" Waller)

| **Gm7** | **C7** | Fmaj7 | ✕ | Am7 | D7 | **Gmaj7** | ✕ ||

"Lament" (J. J. Johnson)

| Fm | Eb7 Ab7 | **Dbmaj7** | Gm7 C7 | F |

| Am7 (b5) D7 | Gm7 | **Em7** A7 | Dm | |

"Have You Met Miss Jones" (bridge) **(Richard Rodgers)**

| Cm7 | F7 | **Bbmaj7** | **Abm7** Db7 | Gbmaj7 | Em7 A7 |

| **Dmaj7** | Abm7 Db7 | **Gbmaj7** | Gm7 **C7** | Fmaj7 | |

"Cherokee" (bridge) **(Ray Noble)**

| Cm7 | F7 | **Bbmaj7** | ✕ | C#m7 | F#7 | Bmaj7 | ✕ |

| Bm7 | **E7** | **Amaj7** | ✕ | **Am7** | D7 | Gmaj7 | ✕ |

| Gm7 | C7 | Cm7 | F7 | ||

"Invitation" (bridge) **(Bronislau Kaper & Ned Washington)**

| C#m7 | **F#7** | Bm | ✕ | Bm7 | **E7** | Am | ✕ |

| **Am7** | D7 | Gm | ✕ | Em7 (b5) | Eb7 | D7 | G7 :||

3

3.1

| Cmaj7 | Cm7 F7 | Bbmaj7 | Bbm7 Eb7 |
| Abmaj7 | Dm7 G7 (b9) | Cmaj7 | Dm7 G7 |

I — C major — II — V — Bb major — I — II — V — Ab major —

I — Ab major — II — V — C major — C minor — I — II — V — C major —

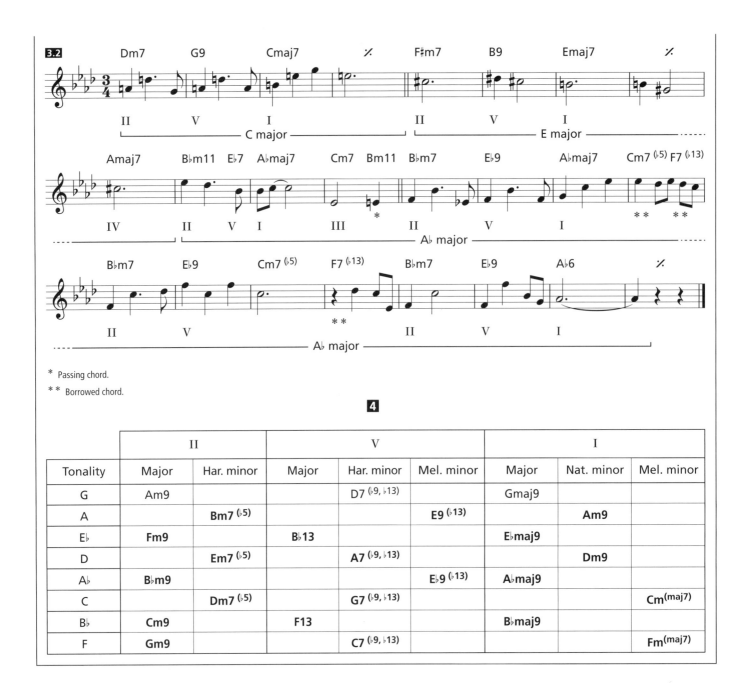

* Passing chord.
** Borrowed chord.

4

Tonality	II Major	II Har. minor	V Major	V Har. minor	V Mel. minor	I Major	I Nat. minor	I Mel. minor
G	Am9			D7 (♭9, ♭13)		Gmaj9		
A		Bm7 (♭5)			E9 (♭13)		Am9	
E♭	Fm9		B♭13			E♭maj9		
D		Em7 (♭5)		A7 (♭9, ♭13)			Dm9	
A♭	B♭m9				E♭9 (♭13)	A♭maj9		
C		Dm7 (♭5)		G7 (♭9, ♭13)				Cm(maj7)
B♭	Cm9		F13			B♭maj9		
F	Gm9			C7 (♭9, ♭13)				Fm(maj7)

EXERCISE 4

1

Tonality	IV Major	IV Har. minor	IV Mel. minor	V Major	V Har. minor	V Mel. minor	I Major	I Nat. minor	I Mel. minor
G	Cmaj9				D7 (♭9, ♭13)		Gmaj9		
F		B♭m9				C9 (♭13)			Fm(maj9)
A♭	D♭maj9			E♭13			A♭maj9		
C			F13		G9 (♭13)			Cm7	
A		Dm9			E7 (♭9, ♭13)		Amaj9		
E			A13		B7 (♭9, ♭13)				Em(maj9)
B♭		E♭m9		F13				B♭m7	
E♭	A♭maj9			B♭13					E♭m(maj9)

Tonality	VI Major	VI Har. minor	VI Mel. minor	V Major	V Har. minor	V Mel. minor	I Major	I Nat. minor	I Mel. minor
G	Em9				D7 (♭9, ♭13)		Gmaj9		
B		**Gmaj7**				F#9 (♭13)			**Bm(maj9)**
D		**B♭maj7**			A7 (♭9, ♭13)			**Dm7**	
C	**Am9**			G13					**Cm(maj9)**
A♭		**Fm9 (♭5)**				E♭9 (♭13)	A♭maj9		
E		**C#m9 (♭5)**				B9 (♭13)	Emaj9		
B♭	**Gm9**				F7 (♭9, ♭13)				**B♭m(maj9)**
E♭		**C♭maj7**			B♭7 (♭9, ♭13)			**E♭m7**	

1

In E♭ major |E♭maj7 |Cm7 |Fm7 |B♭7 |

In G harmonic minor |Gm(maj7) |E♭maj7 |Am7 (♭5) |D7 |

In C melodic minor |Cm(maj7) |Am7 (♭5) |Dm7 |G7 |

In E harmonic minor & melodic |Em(maj7) |Cmaj7 |F#m7 |B7 |
E harmonic minor   *E melodic minor*

In D melodic minor & harmonic |Dm(maj7) |Bm7 (♭5) |Em7 (♭5) |A7 |
D melodic minor   *D harmonic minor*

In B major & harmonic minor |Bmaj7 |G#m7 |C#m7 (♭5) |F#7 |
B major   *B harmonic minor*

2

"In a Sentimental Mood" (bridge in D♭ major) **(Duke Ellington)**

|D♭maj7   **B♭m7** |**E♭m7**   **Ab7** |**D♭maj7**   B♭7 |E♭7   A♭7 |
  I   VI   II   V   I

"Sophisticated Lady" (bridge in G major) **(Duke Ellington)**

|**Gmaj7**   **Em7** |**Am7**   **D7** |G7   G#dim7 |**Am7**   **D7** |
  I   VI   II   V   II   V

"Don't Blame Me" (in C major) **(Jimmy McHugh)**

|**Cmaj7**   Fm7   B♭7 |Em7   A7 |**Dm7**   **G7** |**Cmaj7**   **Am7** |
  I   III   II   V   I   VI

|**Dm7**   **G7** |Em7 (♭5)   A7 |**Dm7**   **G7** |**C6**   **G7**   :||
  II   V   II   V   II   V   I   V

3

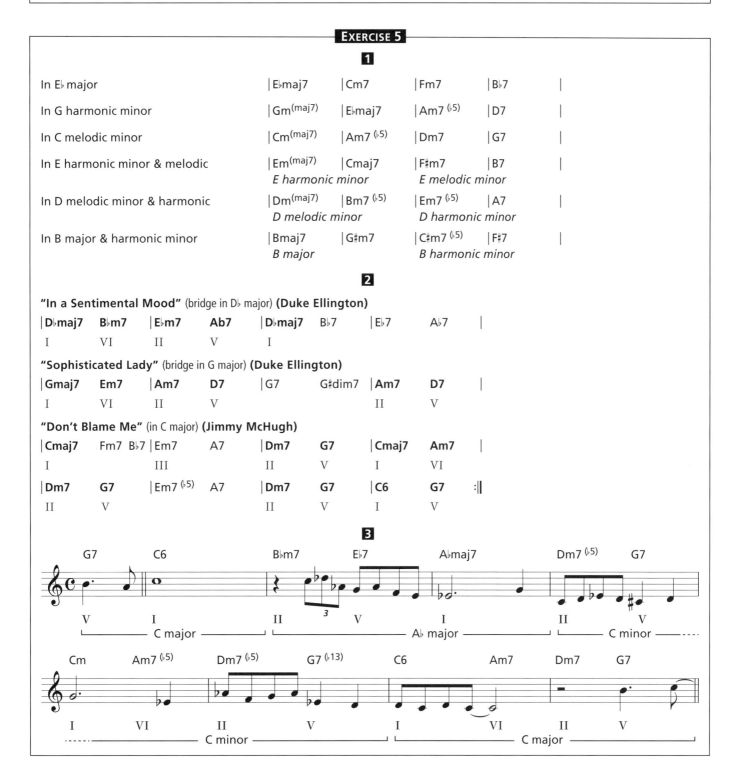

1

In G major	F7	Gmaj7	
In D major	C7	Dmaj7	
In B♭ major	A♭7	B♭maj7	

2

In A♭ major	D♭maj7	G♭7	A♭maj7	
In E♭ major	A♭maj7	D♭7	E♭maj7	
In B major	Emaj7	A7	Bmaj7	

3

In E major	Am7	D7	Emaj7	
In G major	Cm7	F7	Gmaj7	
In E♭ major	A♭m7	D♭7	E♭maj7	

1

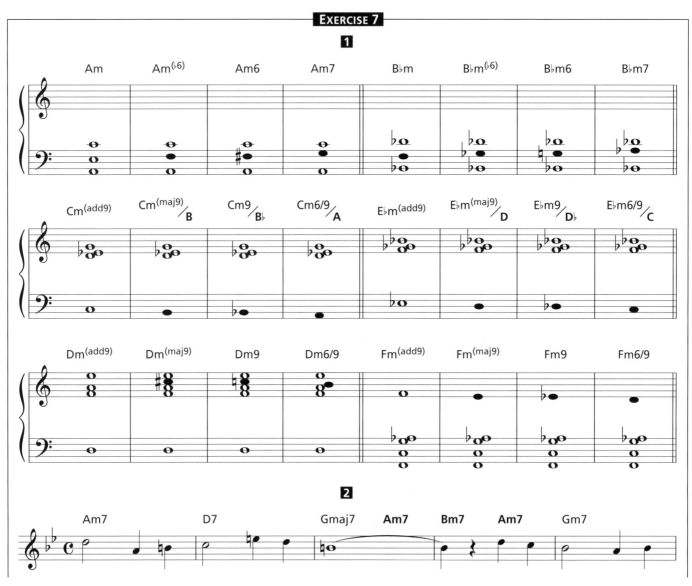

2

3

	I	$\text{I7}/7$	$\text{IV}/3$	$\text{IVm}/3$	$\text{I}/5$	
In G major	G	G7/F	C/E	Cm/E♭	G/D	‖
In B♭ major	B♭	B♭7/A♭	E♭/G	E♭m/G♭	B♭/F	‖
In E♭ major	E♭	E♭7/D♭	A♭/C	A♭m/C♭	E♭/B♭	‖
In A major	A	A7/G	D/F♯	Dm/F	A/E	‖

4

	I	$\text{I7}/3$	IV	♯IVdim7	$\text{I}/5$	
In D major	D	D7/F♯	G	G♯dim7	D/A	‖
In F major	F	F7/A	B♭	Bdim7	F/C	‖
In A♭ major	A♭	A♭7/C	D♭	Ddim7	A♭/E♭	‖
In E major	E	E7/G♯	A	A♯dim7	E/B	‖

CHAPTER 9
MODIFYING CHORD PROGRESSIONS

Because jazz standards[1] are part of the repertoire of many musicians, they provide an ideal source to assess and compare different interpretations of the same song, particularly since musicians tend to interpret a piece of music according to their own melodic, harmonic, and rhythmic personality. This chapter presents the main techniques used to enrich harmonies and modify chord progressions.

Harmonic modifications can be used to prepare the arrival of a target chord, introduce chords that are outside the tonality, reharmonize a melody, create a new bass line, or suggest a new harmonic approach when improvising.

To set up a target chord, we can add or modify one or several chords that precede it. Chord choices vary, depending on whether the changes are to be played over written melodies or during improvisations. This chapter focuses on target-chord preparation techniques and is divided into two parts. In the first part, we will look at one-chord preparations; in the second, at two-chord preparations.

Target-chord preparation using one chord

There are five ways to lead into a target chord using a single preparation chord:

- **X7sus4 chords:** which, in their tonal function, delay the arrival of the X7;
- **secondary dominants:** which enhance the arrival of the target chord by giving it the role of a temporary tonic;
- **chromatic dominants:** which are used as X7 substitutions;
- **diminished passing chords:** which give chords a tonic quality[2] by creating a chromatic movement in the bass;
- **parallel chords:** which have no harmonic function, but exercise a melodic harmonization role.

Target-chord preparation using two chords

Two types of chords may be used to set up the preparation chords mentioned above:

- secondary subdominants;
- chromatic subdominants.

Mastering these different chord-preparation principles requires a thorough understanding of the various cadences presented on functional harmony in Chapter 8 (p. 92).

---

1 Popular songs (and jazz tunes) that have stood the test of time and given rise to a great number of interpretations, which have themselves become permanent features of the musician's repertoire.
2 Referred to as "tonicization," the harmonic process whereby a given chord is assigned a secondary tonic function.

Part 1: Target-chord preparation using one chord

❶ X7sus4 chords

X7sus4 chords are closely related to dominant and subdominant chords. In sus4[3] chords, the 3rd of the X7 chord is replaced by the 4th. Sometimes, however, the 3rd can be added to the X7sus4 chord in certain positions to increase the functional ambiguity of the chord.

X7sus4 chords are most often used:

- to perform a subdominant function when preparing X7 chords;
- for their chord quality, rather than to exercise a specific function.

1.1 X7sus4 used in a subdominant function to prepare X7 chords

Tritone resolution (forced movement)

In tonal music, the tritone interval is the distance of six half-steps between any two given pitches, notably between the IVth and VIIth degrees of a scale with a leading tone.[4] These two notes, when sounded together in a harmonic cadence, require a half-step resolution in opposite directions. In other words, in a V–I chord progression, the leading tone must rise to the tonic, and the subdominant must descend to the mediant; this gravitational pull is natural in both the major and minor modes.

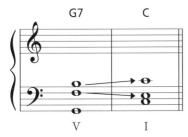

In the chapter on chord functions, we saw that the subdominant chords II and IV prepare the arrival of the dominant.

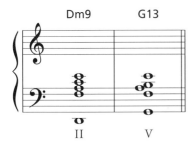

The X7sus4 chord[5] can also exercise a subdominant function to substitute, or prolong the minor seventh chord on the IInd degree.

EXAMPLES
Here, X7sus4 replaces IIm7:

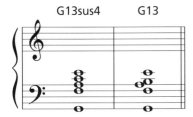

---

3 "Sus" = abbreviation for "suspended."
4 The VIIth degree of a scale is the note one half step below the tonic.
5 Depending on the extension notes used, the chord can be X9sus4 or X13sus4.

In the next cadence, the G7sus4 delays the arrival of the G13 dominant chord:

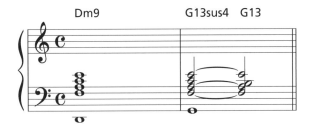

The only difference between these two examples is the bass of the two subdominant chords, Dm9 and G13sus4.

As mentioned above, an X7sus4 chord does not contain a 3rd. Since this chord lacks a tritone, it does not have a dominant function. When the X7sus4 tends naturally toward resolution in a cadence, it is used as a chord of preparation or transition, and can be aurally perceived as a continuation, or repetition, of the subdominant.

EXAMPLE

On beat 3 of measure 2 below, the E7sus4 prepares the arrival of the dominant E7 on beat 4; the perfect 4th in the melody resolves to the 3rd of the chord at the end of the measure.

1.2 Using X7sus4 chords

X7sus4 chords serve to delay the arrival of the X7. If the tempo permits, therefore, any X7 chord may be preceded by its X7sus4. Use X7sus4 chords according to your own musical taste, notably to enhance the melody and the harmony. In measure 2 below, G7sus4 is added to delay the arrival of G7.

EXAMPLE

X7sus4 chords with no specific function

Like all chords, the X7sus4 can be used for its color, rather than to serve a harmonic function. This is particularly common in modal music, as the following example shows:

Because of their duration, both these X7sus4 chords are used to express a "modal plateau."[6] In this context, they do not exercise a subdominant function and do not resolve.

❷ Secondary dominants: V7 of ...

V–I is the most important cadence in functional harmony, because of the sensation of tension and release created by the movement in the bass in the Circle of Fifths, and the presence of the tritone in the dominant chord.

This sensation is also created with **secondary dominants**, which are used to prepare any type of target chord, regardless of its function (Xmaj7, X7, Xm7, Xmin7(♭5), etc.). This is achieved by preceding the target chord with its V7, which assumes the role of a "temporary dominant."

Secondary dominants can be used in two ways; namely:

- to precede the target chord with its V7;
- to transform a chord into a V7 when it is part of a chord sequence in the Circle of Fifths.

2.1 Adding secondary dominants

Secondary dominants can be used to give a temporary tonic function to the target chord by preceding it with its dominant.

Take the following chord progression, for example:

|Cmaj7 |Dm7 |Em7 |Fmaj7 |G7 |Am7 |Bm7 (♭5)   :||

Adding secondary dominants before each chord produces the following progression:

|Cmaj7 **A7** |Dm7 **B7** |Em7 **C7** |Fmaj7 **D7** |G7 **E7** |Am7 **F♯7** |Bm7 (♭5) **G7** :||

---

6 The concept of modal plateau passages (term used in this book) is explained on p. 189.

Harmonization

This progression may be harmonized as follows:

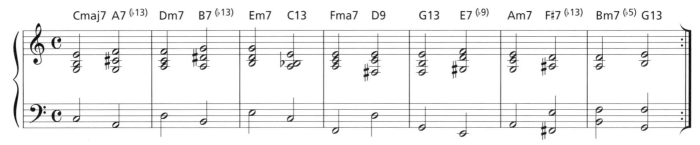

Chord symbols

Two types of chord symbols may be used to denote a secondary dominant chord in a harmonic analysis; namely:

- as V7/X (whereby X = the degree of the target chord), and
- as the 7th of the chord in question.

The secondary dominants in measures 1-3 of the harmonization above may be analyzed as follows:

- A7(♭13) = V7/II (i.e., V7 of D), or VI7 (A being the VIth degree);
- B7(♭13) = V7/III (i.e., V7 of E), or VII7 (B being the VIIth degree);
- C7 = V7/IV (i.e., V7 of F), or I7 (C being the Ist degree).

2.2 Modifying the quality of secondary dominant chords

We can also transform a chord into a secondary dominant by modifying the quality of its 3rd from minor to major.

I–VI–II–V cadence in C major:

Cmaj7	Am7	Dm7	G7
I	VI	II	V

Because the Am7, Dm7, and G7 chords in the above cadence follow the Circle of Cifths, the Am7 can be replaced by A7 to become the secondary dominant of Dm7:

Cmaj7	**A7**	Dm7	G7
I	VI7	II	V

Dm7 can also be replaced by D7 to become the secondary dominant of G7; A7 remains unchanged as the secondary dominant of D7:

Cmaj7	**A7**	**D7**	G7
I	VI7	II7	V

In the example below, we have retained the original chords and added the secondary dominants. This gives the following progression:

Cmaj7	Am7	**A7**	Dm7	**D7**	G7
I	VI	VI7	II	II7	V

Application

The following examples present two ways to use secondary dominants in themes (Ex. 1 and 2) and one when improvising (Ex. 3).

EXAMPLE 1
Changing chords into secondary dominants in a theme

Since this theme is in C minor, there should be a Dm7(♭5) in measure 2; the harmony and melody were written in such a way that the Dm7(♭5) could be changed to D7, which is the secondary dominant of G7.

EXAMPLE 2
Adding secondary dominants in a theme

The first eight measures of the following example illustrate two ways to use secondary dominants:

- the C7 and A7 chords on beat 3 of measures 4 and 8 are secondary dominants, added after their respective diatonic chords to prepare their target chords (Cmaj7–C7–leading to Fmaj7 in measure 4; and Am7–A7–leading to Dm7 in measure 8);
- the E7 chord in measure 7 replaces Em7, which belongs to the tonality.

In the same passage, the non-diatonic notes introduced by the E7 and A7 secondary dominants are also present in the melody; namely:

- G♯ on E7 (measure 7), and
- C♯ on A7 (measure 8).

EXAMPLE 3
Using secondary dominants in an improvisation

The next example illustrates how to transform diatonic chords into secondary dominants when improvising. Introducing different harmonic progressions in an improvisation offers a wider range of modal possibilities.

Adding secondary dominants

In the following excerpt, the A7 (beat 4 of measure 1) and D7 (beat 3 of measure 2) are added as secondary dominants.

Below, Dm is played throughout measure 4 and most of measure 5. The addition of D7 on beat 4 of measure 5 prepares the arrival of Gm7 and enriches the melody.

Changing chords into secondary dominants

This example features Am7(♭5) in measure 1:

By changing Am7(♭5) into A7 (the secondary dominant of D7), we obtain the following chord progression:

This works from a harmonic and a melodic point of view: the E♭, C, and F in the melody pose no problem for A7, since the first two notes are the enharmonic equivalents of #11 (D#) and B# (#9) of A7alt, and the third (F) is the ♭13. (See synthetic modes, Chapter 13.)

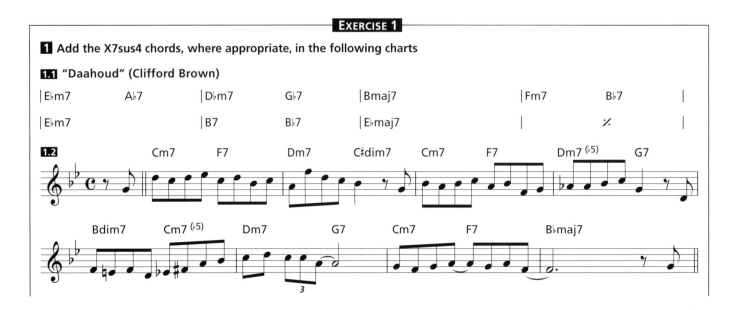

EXERCISE 1

1 Add the X7sus4 chords, where appropriate, in the following charts

1.1 "Daahoud" (Clifford Brown)

2 Give the secondary dominants of the following chords

Starting chord	Secondary dominant
Dm7	
Amaj7	
Bm7 (♭5)	
E♭m7	
E7	
D♭maj7	
Gm6	
F♯7	
B♭m(maj7)	

3 Write the names of the secondary dominants in the following chord charts

3.1 "Emily" (Johnny Mandel)

|Gmaj7 ... |Em7 ... |Am7 ... |D7 |

|Gmaj7 |G7 |Cmaj7 ... |F7 |

3.2 "Flamingo" (Ted Grouya)

|Fmaj7 Dm7 |Gm7 ... |Fm7 ... |B♭7 |

|D♭7 |Gm7 ... |Fmaj7 ... |Gm7 C7 |

3.3 Write the secondary dominants and analyze the color obtained

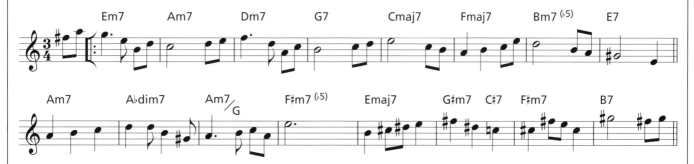

Answers, p. 149

❸ Chromatic dominants: ♭II7

3.1 X7 substitutes

X7 chords are characterized by the presence of the tritone between the 3rd and the 7th. This chord can be substituted by another X7 situated three whole steps above or below the root. This is a **tritone substitution**, which, in the new X7 chord, is analyzed as a **chromatic dominant**.

The tritone intervals of both X7 chords below sound identical because of the enharmonic relationship between B and C♭. The 3rd and the 7th of G7 become respectively the 7th and the 3rd of D♭7:

Having identified the tritone, we can now use it in a cadence. Take the II–V–I cadence in C major, for example:

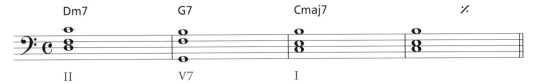

The following progression illustrates how D♭7, the **tritone substitute** of G7, can be used as the chromatic dominant of Cmaj7:

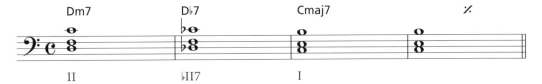

When there are no melodic constraints, it is possible to add the D♭7 and also retain the G7, as shown here. This implies that any chord may be prepared by the X7 chord, situated one half-step above.

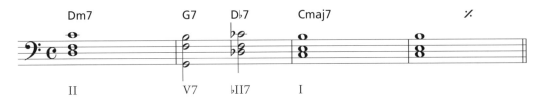

3.2 Augmented 6th chords

To understand the mechanism and relevance of the **chromatic dominant**, it is necessary to look at the augmented 6th chord, its closest equivalent in classical harmony. The **augmented 6th** is a dominant chord with a ♭5th. It is voiced in its second inversion and contains the enharmonic minor 7th interval, which is the characteristic interval of the augmented 6th chord.

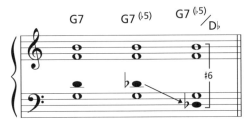

This chord almost always resolves to another dominant chord. It reinforces the melodic movement and need for resolution, notably in the bass, via a descending chromatic movement. A five-step breakdown of the progression from the dominant chord to its tritone substitute in the key of C major is given below:

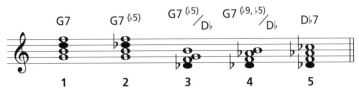

Step 1: The G7 dominant chord contains the B-F tritone interval. At this stage, the G7–C cadence (below) features only two notes requiring chromatic resolution: B (the leading tone) moving up one half-step to C (the tonic), and F (the subdominant) moving down one half-step to E (the mediant), as follows:

Step 2: Lower the 5th of the G7 (D), which becomes D♭.

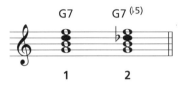

Step 3: Invert the chord; the diminished 5th is now voiced in the bass and the leading tone in the soprano. At this stage, the G7 chord contains three notes requiring chromatic resolution (F moving one half-step down to E, B up to C, and D♭ down to C).

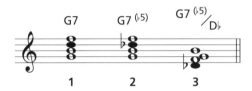

Step 4: To obtain a fourth note requiring chromatic resolution, we then raise the root of the dominant G chord by one half-step, to A♭.

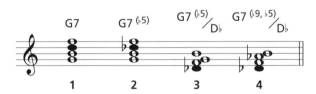

Here, every note of the chord is preceded by a chromatic movement leading up, or down, to the chord tones in the tonic chord: B rises to C, A♭ falls to G, F to E, and D♭ to C. This is the augmented 6th chord.

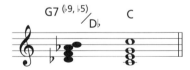

Step 5: Finally, by replacing B with its enharmonic equivalent (C♭), we obtain the chord of D♭7, the dominant substitute of G7.

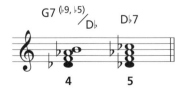

This five-step process illustrates the main interest of using dominant substitutes: to strengthen the **melodic movement and need for resolution.** In other words, the attraction toward the structural tones of the target chord is heightened by the chromatic relationships between each voice.

In this excerpt from Debussy's *La plus que lente*, the D♭7/G chord on beat 3 of the third measure may be thought of as a G7.

La plus que lente (Claude Debussy)

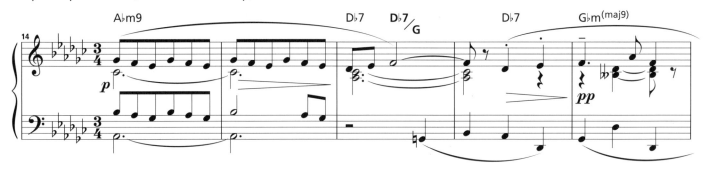

3.3 Tritone substitute table

All X7 chords can be substituted by another X7, regardless of their function (altered roots can take the name of their enharmonic equivalent; for example, D♭7 or C♯7. It is important to master these tritone substitutions so you can identify them at sight and play them in their proper context.

C7	G♭7
D♭7	G7
D7	A♭7
E♭7	A7
E7	B♭7
F7	B7

Measures 2 and 4 of the following theme illustrate two examples of chromatic dominants, as written by the composer.

3.4 Using chromatic dominant chords

Chromatic dominant chords can be used to add melodic and/or harmonic color to a theme, notably by:

- creating a specific bass line;
- attributing a specific function to a note in the melody.

Creating a specific movement in the bass line

In the following excerpt, the bass line descends by half step from B7 (on beat 3 of measure 1) to B♭, to A then to A♭ (in measures 2 and 3) before arriving on the root of Gm7 (measure 4). This chromatic descent is obtained by using inverted and chromatic dominant chords (B7 = substitute of F7; and A♭7 = substitute of D7).

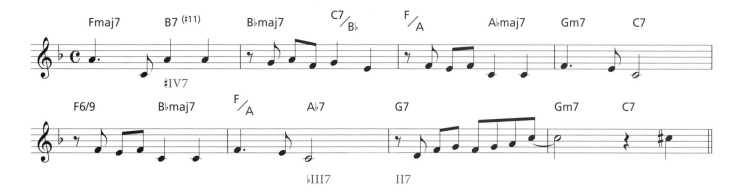

The next excerpt also shows how chromatic dominants can be used for voice-leading purposes to produce a smooth bass line: C7 (measure 2) = the substitute of F♯7; B♭7 (measure 3) = the substitute of E7, and A♭7 (measure 4) = the substitute of D7:

Note that these X7 chords are all one half step above their target chord, hence the name "chromatic dominant."

Original chord chart: |C♯m7 (♭5) C7 |Bm7   B♭7 |Am7   A♭7 |Gmaj7   ‖
          ⌞ half-step ⌟ ⌞ half-step ⌟ ⌞ half-step ⌟

Before their modification into chromatic dominants, these X7 chords form a series of II–V progressions through the Circle of Fifths.

X7 chords before chromatic-
dominant modification: |C♯m7 (♭5) **F♯7** |Bm7   **E7** |Am7   **D7** |Gmaj7   ‖
            II V   II V   II V

Attributing a specific color to a melody

Before using a tritone substitution in a theme, always analyze the relationship between the melody and the harmony, decide whether or not its use is justified, and ask yourself if it is indeed wise to second guess the composer's choice of chord.

Each of the three examples below proposes a tritone substitute (in parentheses) for their respective V7 chords. Note, however, that because the color of X7(♯11) is so important in all these themes, using tritone substitutes would not be a tasteful choice; in each case, the ♯11 would lose its melodic impact and become the root of a new chord.

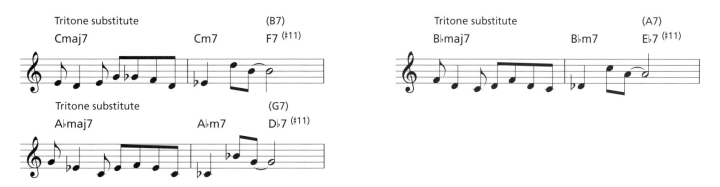

The following improvisation on Jimmy Van Heusen's "I Thought About You" illustrates several ways these secondary and chromatic dominants can be used for reharmonization purposes. Notice the predominance of X7 chords (secondary and chromatic dominants). This succession of X7 chords suggests that the original cadences have been modified.

To understand the role of each X7 chord, we must first determine what the original cadences are. The chart below features a series of subdominant-dominant cadences through the Circle of Fifths (B-E-A-D-G):

| Chords before modification | Bm7 (♭5) | E7 | Am7 | D7 (♭13) | Gm9 | D7 (♯9) | G7 | |
| Van Heusen chord chart | Bm7 (♭5) | B♭7 (♯11) | A7 | D7 (♭13) | G9 | A♭13 | G7 | |

Comparing these two charts shows that the following chords have been modified:

- Am7 to become A7 (secondary dominant of D), and:
- E7 to B♭7, and D7 to A♭7 (chromatic dominants).

Determining the original cadences can sometimes be a bit tricky. For example, Duke Ellington, one of the greatest jazz composers, often used different dominants in his compositions.

In the following excerpt, the succession of chromatic X7 chords in measure 2 indicates the presence of several different types of dominants. To begin the analysis, first separate the "real" chords (those that belong to the tonality) from those that have been modified or added.

While this eight-measure passage is in A♭ major, only three of the chords in the first three measures belong to the tonality: B♭m7, E♭7, and A♭maj7. Here again, the II–V–I cadence is the basic structure; the other chords (G♭7, F7, and E7) are dominant chromatic preparation chords.

The table below presents a target-chord preparation analysis working backward from right to left. Taking A♭maj7 as the target chord and preparing it with a succession of secondary dominants produces a series of descending X7 chords through the Circle of Fifths:

Target chord (TC): right to left chord analysis					
	5	4	3	2	1
Secondary dominants	V7 of F7	V7 of B♭7	V7 of E♭7	V7 of A♭maj7	A♭maj7 = TC
Chord name	C7	F7	B♭7	E♭7	A♭maj7

In the example below, the C7 and B♭7 chords above have been substituted (by G♭7 and E7) to produce a chromatic descent:

	5	4	3	2	1
Chord name	G♭7	F7	E7	E♭7	A♭maj7

Application: modifying chords

These four measures can be harmonized in several ways.

For example, applying chromatic dominants to the progression produces a descending chromatic bass line:

Application: adding chords

In the next example, the use of chromatic dominants is more complex, since the objective is to add a chord, not to substitute.

In the harmonized version of the first three bars, most of the original chords have been prepared by their chromatic dominant.

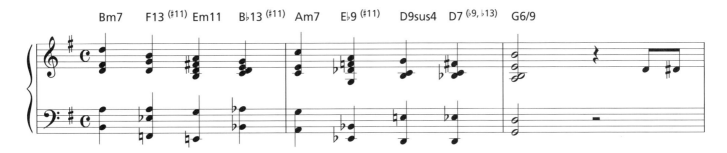

When analyzing themes, determine whether the dominant function is used as:
- the dominant of the tonality;
- the secondary dominant of the chord that follows;
- the chromatic dominant.

1 Insert chromatic dominants in the following chart only when they create a chromatic bass movement

|Gmaj7   Am7 |Bm7   E7 |Am7   D7 |Gmaj7 |

|B♭m7   E♭7 |Bm7   E7 |Am7 (♭5)   A♭7 |Gmaj7   D7 |

|Bm7   B♭m7 |Am7   D7 |Gmaj7 |C7   D7 |

|Gmaj7 |Em7   A7 |Am7 |C♯m7 (♭5)   F♯7 |

|Gmaj7 |Bm7 (♭5)   E7 |Am7   D7 |Gmaj7   D7 |

2 Insert chromatic dominants to obtain a chromatic movement resolving to the target chord. Write the chord symbol of the new chord.

④ Diminished seventh chords: V7(♭9)

4.1 Three diminished chords

As we saw in the chapters on chord construction, diminished 7th chords are built by stacking three minor 3rds to form a perfectly symmetrical chord. Taking enharmonic equivalents into consideration, we obtain four diminished chords containing the same notes.

Example

C♯dim7 and its related diminished chords

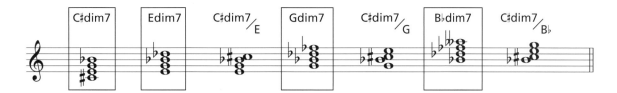

Every note in the C♯dim7 chord serves as the potential root of another diminished chord. The chords featured above in boxes indicate the four diminished chords thus obtained; the inversions of C♯dim7 give the actual pitches of the notes needed to make enharmonic equivalent comparisons.

Table of diminished chords

Every diminished chord generates another three diminished chords. As such, 12 diminished chords can be constructed out of three.

The table below lists the Xdim7 chords that contain the same notes. Note the enharmonic choice of roots in the table; for example, a G♭dim7 is usually referred to as an F♯dim7, which is more common.

Cdim7	E♭dim7	F♯dim7	Adim7
C♯dim7	Edim7	Gdim7	B♭dim7
Ddim7	Fdim7	A♭dim7	Bdim7

The diminished chord has two main functions; namely, when it is used as:

- a dominant chord without a root;
- a passing chord.

4.2 Secondary dominant chords without roots

Depending on the context, the diminished chord can be heard, and used, as an X7(♭9) without a root. To understand the principle, look at the C♯dim7 and A7(♭9) chords below.

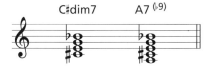

Note the close relationship between the two chords; the chord tones of C♯dim7 are in fact the 3rd, 5th, 7th, and ♭9 of A7(♭9). The diminished chord can therefore be used as a secondary dominant positioned one half-step below the target chord.

Example

|Cmaj7 |Am7 |Dm7 |G7   :‖|

All the chords in the previous example can be preceded by a diminished chord one half-step below, as follows:

|Cmaj7   **G♯dim7** |Am7   **C♯dim7** |Dm7   **F♯dim7** |G7   **Bdim7** :||

To determine the relationship between the function of the diminished chord and the X7(♭9), replace each Xdim7 chord with the target secondary dominant, taking into account the fact that the root of the Xdim7 is the 3rd of the dominant. For example:

- G♯dim7 may become E7(♭9);
- C♯dim7 may become A7(♭9);
- F♯dim7 may become D7(♭9);
- Bdim7 may become G7(♭9).

In both instances, the F♯dim7 chords in measures 1 and 2 below are heard as rootless, dominant D7(♭9) chords.

Application

The Xdim7 chords in measures 1 and 2 below do not figure in the original composition, but may be added by the performer as secondary dominants.

4.3 Passing chords

A **passing diminished chord** can be used as a chromatic transition between two diatonic chords. Both diatonic chords may be voiced in root position or in one of their two inversions to create a chromatic movement in the bass.

Ascending motion

The Xdim7 can be used as a passing chord in an ascending progression of chords in root position. This example features a diatonic I–II–III–IV progression in F major, which has been enriched by adding the ♯Idim7 and ♯IIdim7 passing chords to create a chromatic bass line.

In the following example, the diatonic I–II–I progression is enriched by adding ♯Idim7, ♯IIdim7 passing chords that take us to the first inversion of the Ist degree.

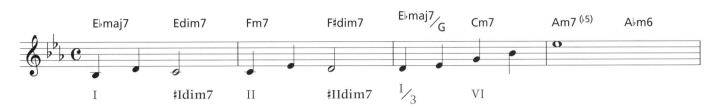

In the next example, the diminished passing chords on beat 4 of measures 2 and 4 prepare the first and second inversions of the tonic chord (measures 3 and 5).

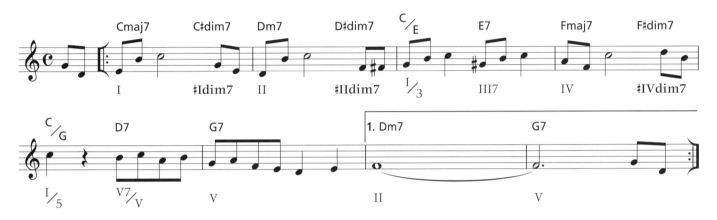

Descending motion

The same principle applies for a descending series of Xdim7 chords, where one of the two diatonic chords is inverted. Many chord charts, however, confuse the first inversion of the tonic (I) with a III chord (based on the mediant). For example, the B♭/D in the chart below is often incorrectly labeled Dm7.

Likewise, the A♭maj7/C in measure 4 below is often incorrectly labeled Cm7.

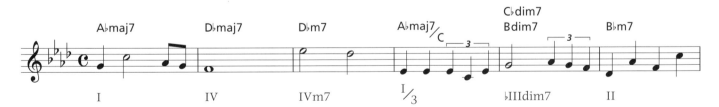

Adding passing Xdim7 chords

Passing Xdim7 chords may be added in chord progressions to create new bass lines and new chromatic resolutions in the melody, or to give chords a temporary tonic function.

Stride[7] piano players regularly use the Xdm7 as a passing chord to enhance the accompaniment, as demonstrated in the following example.

---

7 A jazz piano style developed from ragtime at the beginning of the 1920s, where the roots of the chords are played in the left hand on the strong beats, and the chords on the weak beats.

|F | ∕. |Gm7 |C7 |

Xdim7 chords may be used to enrich this cadence:

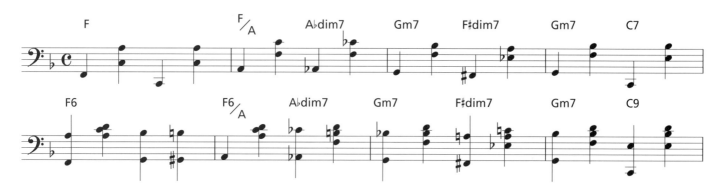

Reminder

The table below lists three of the target-chord preparation chords studied in this chapter (the secondary dominant, chromatic dominant, and diminished chord) and illustrates how these three preparation chords can be used to set up the Dm7 chord in a |Cmaj7 | Am7 | Dm7 | G7 | progression:

Secondary dominant or V7 | ...	|Cmaj7	|A7	|Dm7	|G7	|
	|Cmaj7	|Am7 **A7**	|Dm7	|G7	|
Chromatic dominant	|Cmaj7	|E♭7	|Dm7	|G7	|
Diminished chord	|Cmaj7	|C♯dim7	|Dm7	|G7	|

Some chord-progression variants

Several variations of the basic | Cmaj7 | Am7 | Dm7 | G7 | chord progression are given below:

Ex. 1 |Cmaj7 |A7 |D7 |G7   ‖   **Ex. 2** |Cmaj7 |A7 |D7 |D♭7   ‖
        I   VI7   II7   V   I   VI7   II7   ♭II7

Ex. 3 |Cmaj7 |E♭7 |D7 |D♭7   ‖   **Ex. 4** |Cmaj7 |C♯dim7 |Dm7 |G7   ‖
        I   ♭III7   II7   ♭II7   I   ♯Idim7   II   V

Ex. 5 |Cmaj7 |C♯dim7 |Dm7 |D♭7   ‖   **Ex. 6** |Cmaj7 |E♭7 |Dm7 |D♭7   ‖
        I   ♯Idim7   II   ♭II7   I   ♭III7   II   ♭II7

EXERCISE 3

1 Write the names of the V7 chords containing the chord tones of the following Xdim7 chords

F♯dim7 = D7 $^{(♭9)}$ G♯dim7 =   Cdim7 =   Gdim7 =   C♯dim7 =   Edim7 =

2 Add the X7dim7 chords in the following theme

3 Complete the following chart with diminished and secondary dominant chords

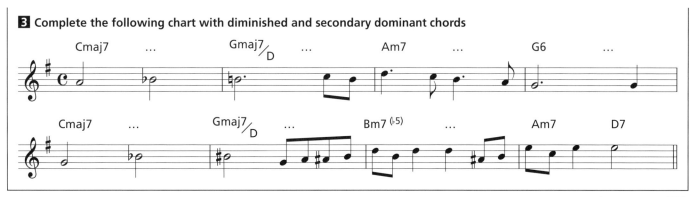

Answers, p. 150

⑤ Parallel chords

5.1 Parallel chords: the basics

While the process of using parallel chords to prepare target chords goes beyond the scope of functional harmony, it is an interesting harmonization technique nonetheless. This involves placing a chord with the same quality a second above or below the target chord. The movement of voices does not have to be parallel. This technique can be used to harmonize themes where the harmony must be perfectly attuned to the melody, or for improvisation purposes. Stripped of their harmonic function, these chords should be considered as passing chords used to harmonize specific notes in the melody.

The following example, written in the style of Bill Evans, features two types of parallel-chord preparation; X7–X7 and Xmaj7–Xmaj7. The B7 in measure 1 prepares B♭7sus4, and the Emaj7 and Amaj7 chords in measures 1 and 2 respectively prepare the E♭maj7 and A♭maj7 chords that follow.

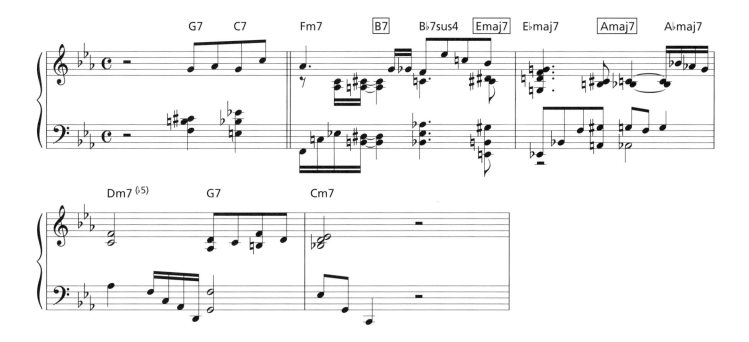

Application

Four examples of parallel-chord preparation are given below.

EXAMPLE 1

Parallel-chord preparation of B♭m7 with Cm7. This new chord creates a descending movement in the bass, harmonizes the melody, and prepares the quality of the B♭m7:

As illustrated in the Bill Evans style harmonization above, the quality of the preparation chord can differ slightly from that of the target chord. This is the case in Example 2, where the Fm7 pickup prepares the Em7(♭5) on beat 1 of measure 1:

EXAMPLE 2

EXAMPLE 3

Here, most of the chords are minor 7ths.

EXAMPLE 4

This passage contains three types of parallel chords: Xmin7, Xmaj7(♯5), and X7.

⑥ Answers

1

1.1 "Daahoud" (Clifford Brown)

|E♭m7   /   **A♭7sus4** A♭7 |D♭m7   **G♭7sus4** G♭7 |Bmaj7 |Fm7   /   **B♭7sus4** B♭7 |

|E♭m7   **B7sus4** B7 **B♭7sus4** B♭7 |E♭maj7 | ⁄. |

1.2 "Everything Happens to Me" (Matt Denis)

|Cm7   /   **F7sus4** F7 |Dm7   C♯dim7 |Cm7   F7 |Dm7 (♭5) /   **G7sus4** G7 |

|Bdim7   Cm7 (♭5) |Dm7   /   **G7sus4** G7 |Cm7   F7 |B♭maj7 |

2

Starting chord	Secondary dominant
Dm7	**A7**
Amaj7	**E7**
Bm7 (♭5)	**F♯7**
E♭m7	**B♭7**
E7	**B7**
D♭maj7	**A♭7**
Gm6	**D7**
F♯7	**C♯7**
B♭m(maj7)	**F7**

3

3.1 "Emily" (Johnny Mandel)

|Gmaj7 **B7** |Em7 **E7** |Am7 **A7** |D7 |

|Gmaj7 |G7 |Cmaj7 **C7** |F7 |

3.2 "Flamingo" (Ted Grouya)

|Fmaj7   Dm7 |Gm7 **C7** |Fm7 **F7** |B♭7 |

|D♭7 |Gm7 **C7** |Fmaj7 **D7** |Gm7   C7 |

3.3

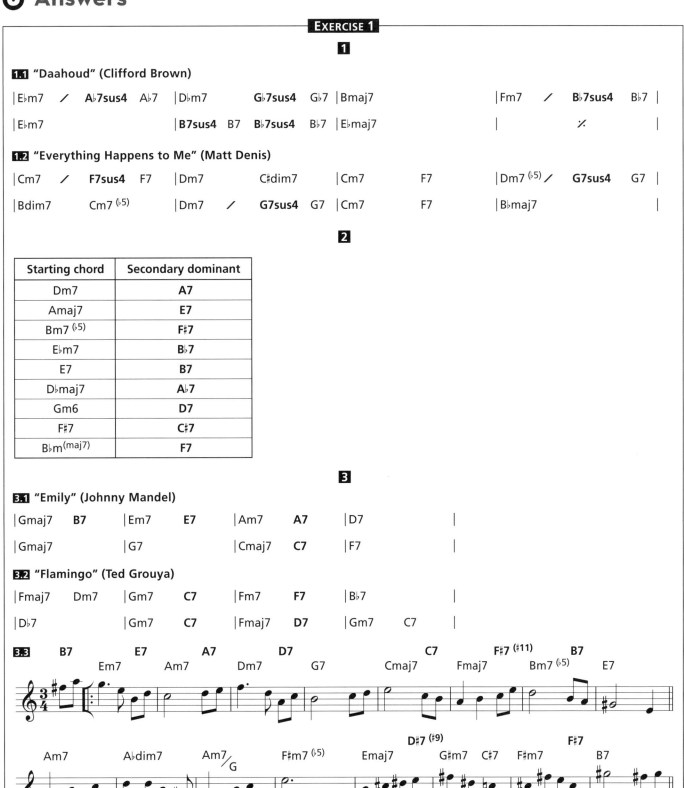

1

Gmaj7	Am7	Bm7	**B♭7**	Am7	**A♭7**	Gmaj7		
B♭m7	**A7**	Bm7	**B♭7**	Am7 (♭5)	**A♭7**	Gmaj7	D7	
Bm7	B♭m7	Am7	**A♭7**	Gmaj7		**F♯7**		
Gmaj7		Em7	A7	Am7		C♯m7 (♭5)	F♯7	
Gmaj7		Bm7 (♭5)	**B♭7**	Am7	**A♭7**	Gmaj7	D7	

2

2.1

F	E7	E♭7	D7 / D♭7	C7		Cm7	**B7**	
B♭7	Fdim7	Cm7	**A♭7**	Gm7	**G♭7**	F	**G♭7** :‖ F	‖
Dm7	**D♭7**	Cm7	**B7**	B♭m7	E♭7	Am7	**A♭7**	
Gm7	**A♭7**	Gm7	C7	Am7	**A♭7**	Gm7	C7	‖

2.2

Dm7	**D♭7**	Cm7	**B7**	B♭6		‖ Fm7	**E7**	E♭maj7	
Fm7	**E7**	E♭maj7		Em7	**E♭7**	Dmaj7		Gm7	C7

2.3

D7	**A♭9**	G7	**D♭7**	C7		Fmaj7		B7	**F9**	E7	**B♭7**	A7	**E♭9**	Dm7 /	
Dm7		G7		Am7		D7		Dm7 **A♭7**	G7	**D♭7**	Cmaj7	A7		:‖

2.4

F6	/	D7	**A♭9** (♯11)	G7	**D♭7** (♯11)	C7	**G♭7** (♯11)	F6		F♯dim7		G7	**D♭7** (♭9)	C7	**G♭7** (♯11)	
F6	/	D7	**A♭7** (♯11)	Gm7	/	A7	**E♭9**	Dm7		G7		Gm7	/	C7	**G♭7** (♯11) :‖	

1

F♯dim7 = D7 (♭9)   G♯dim7 = E7 (♭9)   Cdim7 = A♭7 (♭9)   Gdim7 = E♭7 (♭9)   C♯dim7 = A7 (♭9)   Edim7 = C7 (♭9)

2

Fmaj7	**F♯dim7**	Gm7	**G♯dim7**	Am7	**Bdim7** Cm7 F7	B♭maj7	E♭9	
Fmaj7	**F♯dim7**	Gm7		F6	Dm7	G7	**Bdim7** C7	:‖

3

Cmaj7	**C♯dim7**	Gmaj7/D	**E7**	Am7	**D7**	G6	**D♭7** (♯11)	
Cmaj7	**C♯dim7**	Gmaj7/D	**F♯7**	Bm7 (♭5)	**G♯dim7**	Am7	**D7**	:‖

Part 2: Target-chord preparation using two chords

❶ Secondary subdominants

In the first part of this chapter, we studied the five ways to prepare a target chord using one preparation chord, five options that already offer many possibilities. We will now go one step further and prepare a target chord with two chords by preceding preparatory secondary dominant and chromatic secondary chords with their subdominant chords.

1.1 II–V of ...

The **secondary subdominant** performs the same function as a subdominant, but differs in that it does not belong to the key center. Instead, it is borrowed from another major or minor tonality.

Just as the secondary dominant can be used to precede the target chord with its V7, the addition of the secondary subdominant makes it possible to create a | IIm7–V7 | or | IIm7(♭5)–V7 | cadence for any target chord. This secondary cadence serves to enhance the target chord by giving it a **temporary tonic function.**

In the following example, the Fmaj7 in measure 3 is the passing tonic that serves to prepare G7 in measure 4:

| Cmaj7 | | ✗ | Fmaj7 | G7 | |

We can attribute a passing tonic function to this Fmaj7 chord by preparing it with its II–V. These Gm7–C7 chords in measure 2 are not part of a modulation to F major, but are borrowed from the tonality of F major.

| Cmaj7 | | Gm7   C7 | Fmaj7 | G7 | |
| | | IIm7   V7 | IV | | |

In the following theme, the A♭maj7 in measure 3 becomes a temporary Ist degree prepared by its II–V (B♭m7–E♭7).

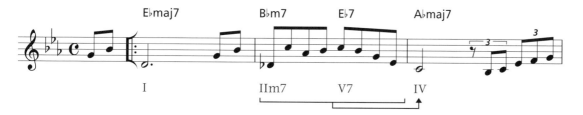

Depending on the musical context or one's personal choice, it is possible to borrow this secondary cadence from a minor tonality.

Example

Going back to the original Cmaj7–Fmaj7–G7 progression above, we can prepare the Fmaj7 with a Gm7(♭5)–C7(♭9) cadence borrowed from F harmonic minor:

| Cmaj7 | | Gm7 (♭5)   C7 (♭9) | Fmaj7 | G7 | |
| | | IIm7 (♭5)   V7 | IV | | |

In the next excerpt, Dm7 in measure 3 becomes a temporary 1st degree prepared by its II–V, Em7(♭5)–A7.

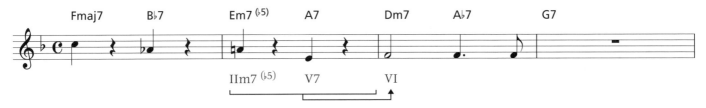

The following example in E♭ major presents a secondary cadence in measure 2 (Gm7(♭5)–C7(♭9)), which serves to prepare the Fm7 in measure 3.

1.2 IVm7–♭VII7 of ...

The same principle may be applied when using secondary subdominants to prepare ♭VII7 chords in ♭VII7–I cadences.

EXAMPLE
Take the following chord progression in C major:

|Cmaj7 | % |B♭7 | % |
I   ♭VII7

Then, prepare the B♭7 in measure 4 by preceding it with its subdominant to create a II–V chord progression, which is the IVm7–♭VII7 cadence in C:

|Cmaj7 | % |Fm7 |B♭7 |
I   IVm7   ♭VII7

The next two examples illustrate how this IVm7–♭VII7 cadence can be used in themes: Fm7–B♭7 in measures 3 and 4 of example 1, and A♭m7–D♭7 in measure 4 of example 2.

Example 1

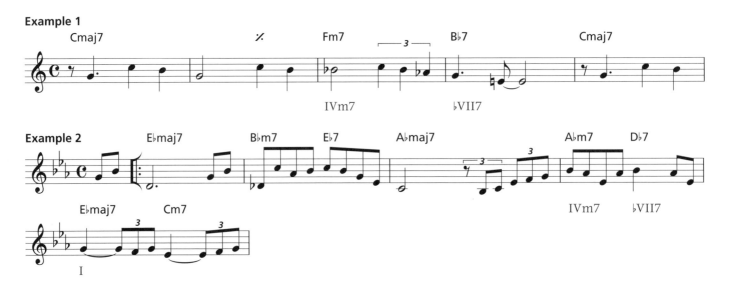

Example 2

❷ Chromatic subdominants

The **chromatic subdominant** can be used to prepare the chromatic dominant and produce the sensation of a II–V cadence. This is symbolized by the chords ♭VIm7 or ♭VIm7(♭5), which generally resolve to ♭II7.

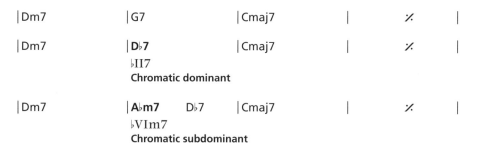

The chromatic subdominant sometimes resolves to the X7 chord one half-step below. In the following chart, the A♭m7 chromatic subdominant resolves down one half step to G7:

|Dm7 |A♭m7   G7 |Cmaj7 | ╱. |

In the next example, the A♭m7(♭5) chromatic subdominant on beat 1 of measure 4 resolves to the D♭9 chromatic dominant on beat 3, which in turn resolves down one half step to Cmaj7 in measure 5.

Look at the melody below:

In the following harmonization of this melody, the subdominant chromatic chord (♭VIm7) in measure 4 was added by the performer.

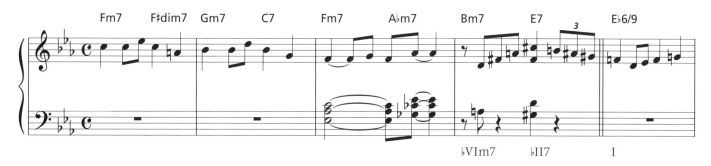

Summary list of subdominant and dominant chords covered in this chapter

All the chord preparations presented in this chapter are listed in the table below.

|Cmaj7	|Am7	**|Dm7** Subdominant	**|G7** Dominant	|
|Cmaj7	**|A7sus4 A7** X7sus4 prepares and delays arrival of X7	|Dm7	|G7	|
|Cmaj7	**|C#dim7** Dim7 one half step before target chord	|Dm7	|G7	|
|Cmaj7	**|A7** Secondary dominant	|Dm7	|G7	|
|Cmaj7	**|Em7** A7 Secondary subdominant	|Dm7	|G7	|
|Cmaj7	**|E♭7** Chromatic dominant	|Dm7	|G7	|
|Cmaj7	**|B♭m7** E♭7 Chromatic subdominant	|Dm7	|G7	|
|Cmaj7	**|B♭m7** A7 Chromatic subdominant	|Dm7	|G7	|

The various subdominant, dominant, and tonic chord possibilities that serve to create the cadences studied in this chapter are listed below.

Subdominants
IIm7
IIm7 (♭5)
II7
♭II7
IVmaj7 or IV6
IVm7 or IVm6
IVm7 (♭5)
IV7
#IVdim7
♭VImaj7
VImin7 (♭5)
♭VI7
♭VII7

Dominants
V7
♭II7
VIIdim7

Tonics
Imaj
Imin

1 Write the IIm7—V7 of the following target chords

Fmaj7:   Am7:   Bmaj7:   A♭maj7:   E♭7:   Cm7:

2 Write the IVm7—♭VII7 of the following target chords

Dmaj7:   Gmaj7:   B♭maj7:   Fmaj7:

3 Analyze the following passage

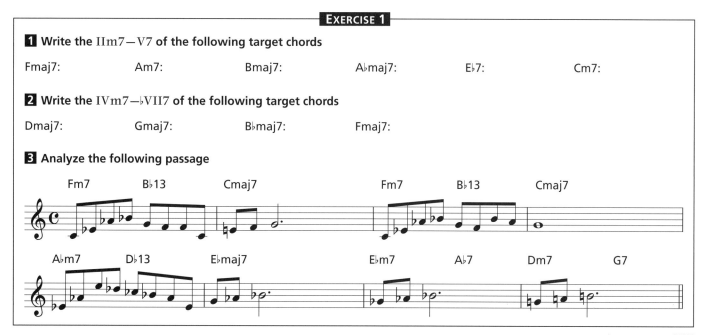

Answers, p. 155

❸ Answers

1

Fmaj7: **Gm7—C7**   Am7: **Bm7—E7**   Bmaj7: **C♯m7—F♯7**   A♭maj7: **B♭m7—E♭7**   E♭7: **Fm7—B♭7**   Cm7: **Dm7—G7**

2

Dmaj7: **Gm7—C7**   Gmaj7: **Cm7—F7**   B♭maj7: **E♭m7—A♭7**   Fmaj7: **B♭m7—E♭7**

3

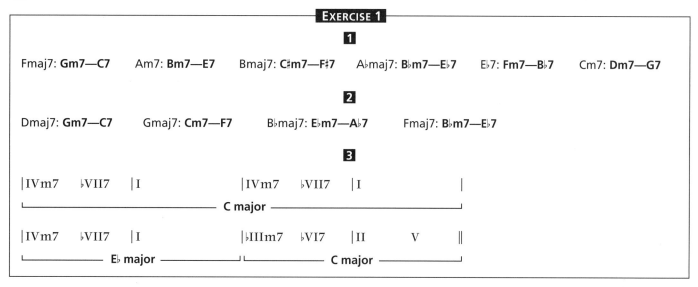

CHAPTER 10
HARMONIC ANALYSIS

Harmonic analysis can facilitate your understanding of, and approach to, a piece of music, by:

- ensuring a correct interpretation (i.e., using the right scales or modes for each chord);
- highlighting the chord-choice possibilities you can use to modify the original harmonies;
- helping you memorize chord progressions.

❶ Main terms

Using harmonic analysis to gain an understanding of how a theme develops can help you memorize chord progressions and apply new harmonic principles in your compositions, arrangements, and improvisations. The main terms involved in harmonic analysis are defined below.[1]

1.1 Structure

The structure of a piece of music is determined by identifying the melodic passages that are repeated. This indicates which jazz-standard form the tune is written in (ABA, AABA, ABAC, rhythm changes or blues, etc.).

1.2 Harmonic rhythm

Harmonic rhythm indicates the number of chords per measure and the presence of tonal and/or modal plateau[2] passages. Sometimes, both can be found in the same composition, as in "One Finger Snap" (Ex. 1.6 below).

1.3 Determining tonality

The key signature, together with the first and last cadence, determines the main tonality of a tune. Tonality (major or minor) does not specify whether there are any modulating passages in the composition. While a key signature with no sharps or flats generally indicates the tonalities of C major or A minor, it may also be used for themes with no defined tonality.

1.4 Chord names and symbols

Once the tonality has been defined, chords are attributed Roman-numeral names to identify the cadences, borrowed chords, substitutions and modulations, etc.

---

1 Rhythmic analysis is not covered in this book.
2 Modal plateau: term used in this book to define the use of one chord spanning several measures for the purposes of establishing a mode. See p. 189.

1.5 The tonal plateau

Here, all the chords in a progression have a tonal center and a defined function. This is functional harmony.

EXAMPLE

"I Can't Get Started" (Vernon Duke); measures 1-8

|Cmaj7   Am7 |Dm7   G7 |E7   Am7 $^{(\flat5)}$ |D7   G7sus4 |

|Cmaj7   Am7 |Dm7   G7 |E7   A7 |D7   G7sus4 ‖

1.6 The modal plateau

A modal plateau consists of one chord that spans several measures for the purposes of establishing a mode, not a tonal center.

EXAMPLE

"One Finger Snap" (Herbie Hancock); measures 1-20

This composition comprises three modal plateau passages in measures 1-12, followed by a series of tonal cadences in measures 13-20.

|Gm7 | | ∥ | ∥ | ∥ |

|B♭m7 | | ∥ | ∥ | ∥ |

|E♭m7 | | ∥ | ∥ | ∥ |

|Gm7 $^{(\flat5)}$ |C7 |Fm7 $^{(\flat5)}$ |B♭7 |

|E♭maj7 | ∥ |Dm7 $^{(\flat5)}$ |G7 :‖

1.7 The atonal plateau

Chord progressions in atonal plateau passages have no established key center.

EXAMPLE

"Pee Wee" (Tony Williams)

Here, no tonality is established and we move from one mode to another via a series of chord progressions.

|D♭maj7 |E♭/D♭ |F/D♭ |Dm7 |

|E♭7 $^{(\sharp9)}$ |E7 |G♭maj7 $^{(\sharp11)}$ | ∥ |

|G7sus4 |G7 |F7sus4 |D♭maj7 $^{(\sharp11)}$ |

|G♭maj7 |G7sus4 |G7 |Fm7   D♭maj7 |

|G♭maj7 $^{(\sharp11)}$ |D♭7sus4 |F/D♭ | ∥ | ∥ ‖

1.8 Modulation

To enable a modulation, the ear must have enough time to become acquainted with the original tonality so that it can hear the change in key. In general, cadences are used to prepare modulations, which can be confirmed if enough time is allowed for the new tonality to settle in.

The theme below begins in D minor and modulates to its relative major (F) by measure 8. It then shifts into D♭ major in measure 9, prepared by an E♭m7–A♭7 cadence. This modulation from F major to D♭ major represents a tonal descent of a major 3rd, a common interval used in modulations.

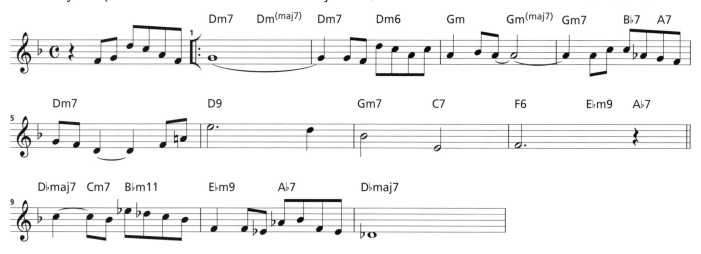

1.9 Borrowed chords (modal mixture)

This term applies to chords that do not belong to the tonality, but are "borrowed" from another key and do not result in a modulation.

EXAMPLE

The following II–V–I chord cadence in C major contains G7(♭13), a chord borrowed from C minor. This cadence does not modulate.

|Dm7 |G7 (♭13) |Cmaj7 | ⁒   :‖

❷ Analysis of themes

2.1 "Tune Up" (Miles Davis)

From a pedagogical standpoint, this piece is interesting because it comprises a succession of diatonic cadences.

|Em7 |A7 |Dmaj7 | ⁒ |
II   V   I

5
|Dm7 |G7 |Cmaj7 | ⁒ |
II   V   I

9
|Cm7 |F7 |B♭maj7 |Gm7 |
II   V   I   VI

13
|Em7 |A7 |Dmaj7 | ⁒   ‖
II   V   I

Structure: 16-measure AA form.
Harmonic rhythm: one chord per measure.
Tonality: D major.
Modulations: to C major (measures 5-8) and to B♭ (measures 9-12).

2.2 "Manhã de Carnaval/Black Orpheus" (Luiz Bonfá); measures 1-16

```
|Am              |Bm7 (♭5)   E7 (♭9)   |Am              |Bm7 (♭5)   E7 (♭9)   |
 I               II         V          I               II         V
5
|Am              |Dm7       G7         |Cmaj7           |A7 (♭9)              |
 I               II        V           I               VI7
9
|Dm7             |G7                   |Cmaj7           |Fmaj7               |
 II              V                     I               IV
13
|Bm7 (♭5)        |E7                   |Am              |Bm7 (♭5)   E7 (♭9)  ||
 II              V                     I               II         V
```

Structure: 32-measure AB form.
Harmonic rhythm: one or two chords per measure.
Tonality: A minor.
Modulations: to C major (measures 6-12) then to A minor.

2.3 "There Will Never Be Another You" (Harry Warren)

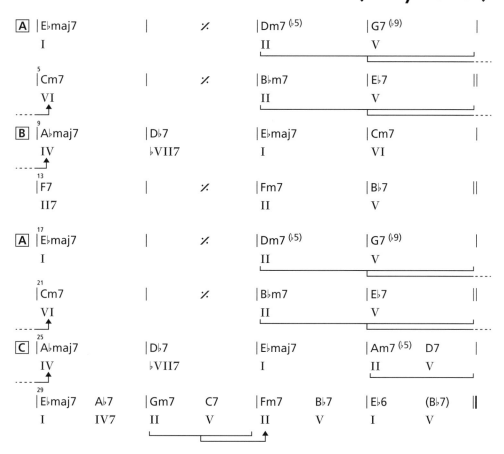

Structure: 32-measure ABAC form.
Harmonic rhythm: variable.
Tonality: E♭ major.
Secondary subdominants

- measures 3-4: | Dm7(♭5) G7(♭9) | Cm7|. Dm7(♭5) is both the 7th tonal (diatonic) degree of E♭ major and the secondary subdominant of the II–V progression of VI;
- measures 7-8: | B♭m7 E♭7 | A♭maj7|;
- measure 30: | Gm7 C7 | Fm7|.

♭VII7–I cadence: measures 10 and 26 | D♭7–E♭maj7 |.
Borrowed from: A♭7 to E♭ melodic minor: measure 29 | E♭maj7–A♭7 |.

2.4 "Tenderly" (Walter Gross); measures 1-16

|Ebmaj7	|Ab7	|Ebm7	|Ab7	
I	IV7	I	IV

5 |Fm7	|Db7	|Ebmaj7	|Gm7 (b5) C7 (b9)	
II	bVII7	I	II V

9 |Fm7 (b5)	|Bb7 (b9)	|Fm7 (b5)	|Bb7 Bdim7	
II	V	II	V #Vdim7

13 |Cm7	|F7	|Fm7	|Bb7	‖
VI	II7	II	V

Structure: 32-measure ABAC form.

Harmonic rhythm: one chord per measure.

Tonality at beginning and end: essentially Eb major (despite the presence of numerous passages in Eb minor).

Although the piece does not modulate, on several occasions it borrows chords from other tonalities:

- measure 2: Ab7, borrowed from Eb melodic minor;
- measure 3: Ebm7, borrowed from Eb Aeolian;
- measure 4: Ab7, borrowed from Eb melodic minor;
- measure 6: Db7, borrowed from Ab melodic minor;
- measure 8: the | Gm7(b5) C7(b9) | cadence, borrowed from F harmonic minor;
- measure 9-12: the | Fm7(b5) Bb7(b9) | cadence, borrowed from Eb harmonic minor;
- measure 12: Bdim7, a passing chord borrowed from C harmonic minor;
- measure 14: F7, the IInd altered degree, which relates to several different modes.

Measures 1-4: various types of plagal cadences.

Measures 6-7: bVII7–Imaj7 cadence.

Measure 12: use of dim7 passing chord; this Bdim7 chord may be analyzed as a rootless G7(b9) dominant chord.

Measure 14: the IInd degree is altered to become II7 in a IIm7–V7 harmonic progression.

EXERCISE 1

1 Analyze the three musical excerpts below

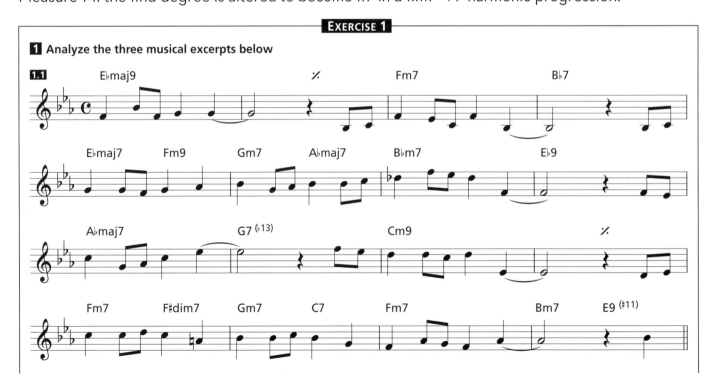

1.1

Ebmaj9   ⁒   Fm7   Bb7

Ebmaj7   Fm9   Gm7   Abmaj7   Bbm7   Eb9

Abmaj7   G7 (b13)   Cm9   ⁒

Fm7   F#dim7   Gm7   C7   Fm7   Bm7   E9 (#11)

Answers, p. 161-162

❸ Answers

1.1

Structure: 32-measure AA form.
Key: E♭ major.

Measures 1-4
This passage expresses the Ist degree (E♭), which is followed by its II—V.

Measures 5-6
A progression of diatonic chords, going from the Ist to the IVth degrees (A♭maj7).

Measures 7-8
A II—V cadence built on the IVth degree (the E♭7, being the secondary dominant prepared by its subdominant B♭m7, resolves to A♭maj7, in measure 9, which assumes a temporary tonic function).

Measures 9-10
After resolving to the IVth degree (temporary tonic), the melody then moves on to another secondary dominant: G7 (♭13): V of VI. The VIth degree (Cm7) is tonal and heard in measures 11 and 12.

Measures 13-14

The Fm7, a diatonic chord (IInd degree), is followed by an F♯dim7 which may be considered a D7 $^{(♭9)}$/F♯. This is a secondary dominant which serves to prepare the IIIrd degree (Gm7) in measure 14.

The Gm7 chord assumes a temporary tonic function and is also the subdominant of a II—V cadence which enables a return to the harmonic progression. In other words, the F♯dim7 acts as the V of III (Gm7) which is heard as the subdominant of a new cadence.

Mesures 15-16

The Fm7 is prepared by a II—V cadence. In measure 16, the chromatic dominant of the Ist degree, E9 $^{(♯11)}$, is prepared by its subdominant (Bm9). Note that the augmented 11th of the chromatic dominant (A♯) is indispensable in that it is the enharmonic equivalent of B♭, which is in the melody.

1.2

Structure: 16 measures.
Key: essentially F minor.

Measures 1-2

Ist degree of F minor (F melodic minor given the presence of D natural and E natural in the melody).

Measures 3-4

II—V borrowed from F harmonic major (A♮ in the melody).

Measures 5-6

Return to degree I of F minor.

Measures 7-14

Series of II—V chord progressions throughout the circle of fifths: Cm7—F7 in B♭ major; B♭m7—E♭7 in A♭ major; A♭m7—D♭7 in G♭ major; G♭m7—C♭7 in F♭ major (enharmonic of E major).

Measures 15-16

II—V cadence in F enabling the return to F minor at the beginning of the theme. The Gm7 is in the key of F major while the V is in F harmonic minor.

1.3

Key: E♭ major.

Measure 3

A♭13 is borrowed from E♭ melodic minor. This chord is both the IVth degree of a plagal cadence and the sub V of the Gm7 chord that follows.

Measure 4

G♭dim7; a passing chord between Gm7 and Fm7.

Measures 7-8

E♭7sus4 and E♭7 are pivot chords that exercise a tonic function to conclude the II—V—I cadence in E♭ major, and act as secondary dominants of A♭maj7.

Measure 10

Preparation of E♭maj7 with the modal cadence IVm7—♭VII7—Imaj7.

Measure 11

D♭13 functions as the chromatic dominant of C7.

Measure 14

Cm7—F7 which is the II—V cadence used to prepare the arrival of the Vth degree (B♭7) in the final measure, which is preceded by its subdominant.

CHAPTER 11
THE THREE MUSICAL SYSTEMS

Modes

For the aspiring jazz musician, modes can be either a source of wonder or one of sheer terror. How many times have you heard fellow musicians say, "Modes are great!" or "Modes are too complicated; I can't understand a thing!" Although having a solid understanding of modes and how to use them is not a prerequisite for playing beautiful music, it is useful if you want to enrich your melodic and harmonic vocabulary.

Being able to use modes correctly requires mastering all their specific characteristics. For example, knowing that in an Xm7 chord, the major 6th is the Natural Characteristic Degree (see page 171) of the Dorian mode is all well and good, but never takes precedence over the ability to recognize these specific pitches by ear, an aural skill which, for every mode, requires a certain amount of time and practice. All too often, the eagerness to learn and understand can push students to go too far, too fast, cut corners and, consequently, fail to achieve their objectives. Trying to learn and master everything as quickly as possible and gorging oneself with a maximum amount of information is pointless; it is a bit like a thirsty traveler trying to fill an empty glass with water from Victoria Falls. If he actually survives the ordeal, and the glass doesn't break in the process, the best he can hope for is a somewhat damp, but still very empty, glass! Knowing how to take your time is essential, so you can digest one piece of information before moving on to the next.

Modes may be approached from intellectual, aural, and technical points of view. Taken together, all these approaches will help you understand the enigma, and master the art, of modal harmony. In the previous chapters, we studied the functions of chords. In this chapter, we will learn other ways to color chords and musical phrases; in particular, how to use the characteristic degrees of the different modes to add color to chords, without modifying their function.

❶ The natural diatonic system

Scales in the **diatonic system** comprise a series of seven conjunct notes, each with a different name and pitch. This diatonic system can be natural (with the necessary alterations written in the key signature), or altered (in which case, not all the alterations can be written in the key signature).

Let's take the C major scale to illustrate the natural diatonic system.

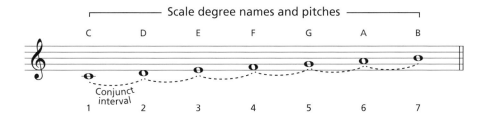

By respecting the diatonic relationship between all the notes of the scale, we obtain seven different names for the conjunct degrees.

The natural diatonic system may be organized into three circles, forming six different series of notes:

- the circle of fifths or fourths:

  5ths →   ← 4ths
  F – C – G – D – A – E – B

- the circle of thirds or sixths:

  3rds →   ← 6ths
  C – E – G – B – D – F – A

- the circle of seconds or sevenths:

  2nds →   ← 7ths
  C – D – E – F – G – A – B

1.1 Accidentals and key signatures

In major keys

Whatever the major scale or natural diatonic mode[1], the compulsory sharps or flats are placed in the key signature immediately after the treble and/or bass clef(s) to indicate the tonality. This is not possible for **synthetic modes**,[2] where at least one alteration is an accidental.

EXAMPLE
D major scale

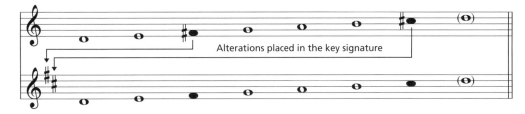

Note that:

- both the altered notes, F♯ and C♯, are compulsory; these cannot be written as G♭ and D♭, since all seven notes in the scale must have different names and respect the diatonic system;
- both sharps must be placed in the key signature, according to the order of sharps.

In minor keys

In the following example in D harmonic minor, both the B♭ and C♯ are compulsory. B♭ must be placed in the key signature, indicating, in this case, the tonality of D minor (the relative minor of F major). On the other hand, because C♯ is an accidental, it cannot be included in the key signature. Consequently, every time a C is encountered, it must be sharped. This is an example of a **synthetic mode**, which belongs to an altered diatonic system. (See Chapter 13, p. 203.)

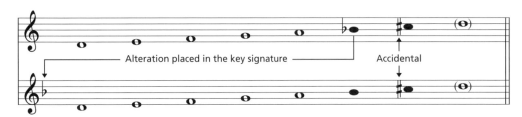

---

1   Natural diatonic modes: modes derived from the major scale. See Chapter 12, p. 169.
2   Synthetic modes: name given to modes derived from the melodic minor, harmonic minor, harmonic major, and double harmonic major scales. See Chapter 13, p. 203.

❷ The chromatic system

The **chromatic system** is defined by the 12-degree, equal-temperament tuning system upon which Western music is based. These degrees (five of which have the same name, but a different sound when sharped or flatted, such as G-G♯ or E-E♭, etc.), move by half-step to form the **chromatic scale**:

The chromatic scale has been a feature of the tonal system since the Renaissance. Several 19th century composers made great use of this scale, but it was not until the beginning of the 20th century that composers such as Alban Berg, Arnold Schoenberg, and Anton Webern began to take it beyond the tonal system and use it as the structural basis for their 12-tone compositions (dodecaphony).[3]

2.1 Different roles of chromaticism[4]

In the tonal system, chromaticism is often used to add color to the melody and the harmony. This causes a dissonance and a resolution to a specific note. These chromatic (or non-diatonic) notes can be encountered in different forms, depending on their characteristics (appoggiaturas, trills, etc.). Diatonic degrees can therefore be mixed with altered chromatic degrees.

Four types of chromatic passages are illustrated below. These examples throw light on the difference in how dissonant/consonant relationships are perceived. This distinction varies, depending on the duration and rhythmic position of the dissonance and the tonal context.

Short chromatic passage

Longer chromatic passages (tonal chromaticism)

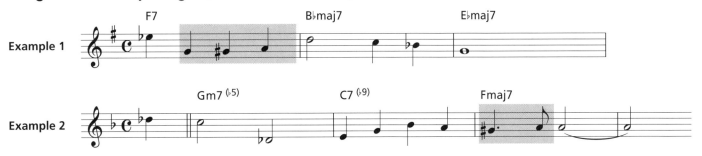

Longer chromatic passages (atonal chromaticism)

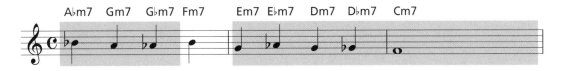

---

3 A composition technique that gives equal weight to all 12 degrees of the chromatic scale.
4 From the ancient Greek chrôma = color.

Chromaticism in relation to the tonal center

Unlike the example above, the chromaticism below is used in a tonal context. The harmonic chromatic movements in this theme distance us from, then bring us back, to the tonality.

> Melodic and harmonic chromaticism play an important role in establishing the consonance or dissonance of a musical phrase; in other words, the relationship between stability and instability, or tension and resolution.
>
> Dissonance is not a variable that can be measured scientifically, but rather an aesthetic choice of the composer perceived by the listener according to his or her musical culture and experience.

❸ Enharmonic equivalents

Using **enharmonic equivalents** makes it possible to attribute two different names to the same note.

EXAMPLES

While enharmonic equivalents can simplify the writing and reading of music, they should be used properly and with a certain degree of caution to avoid confusion.

3.1 Usable enharmonic intervals

In addition to simplifying writing, enharmonic equivalents can also be useful from an acoustics and musical point of view. Take, for example, the chord progression, C7(♭9, ♭13)–Fm11. Over the C7 chord, we could play C Locrian ♭4[5] (below), which is the mode based on the VIIth degree of D♭ melodic minor.

---

5 Also known as the Altered Scale; see Synthetic Modes, Chapter 13, p. 205.

In the C Locrian ♭4 mode, several notes may be heard as enharmonic intervals, depending on their association to C7. For example:

- E♭ may be aurally perceived as an augmented 9th, or a minor 10th;
- F♭, as a major 3rd;
- G♭, as an augmented 4th or a diminished 5th.

The characteristic pitches of the chord (root, 3rd, and 7th) and the extensions (the 9ths, 11th, and 13th) are possible when we use enharmonic equivalents. In this case, it is the ear that decides. In certain jazz lead sheets, enharmonic equivalents are sometimes used to avoid double flats and double sharps when writing chord symbols and melodies.

3.2 Enharmonic equivalents to be avoided

However, simplifying musical notation has its limits. Why is it important to use a note's precise name? When we refer to a D♭7 chord, is it correct to say that the 7th of the chord is B rather than C♭? The two examples below should shed some light on the subject.

EXAMPLE 1

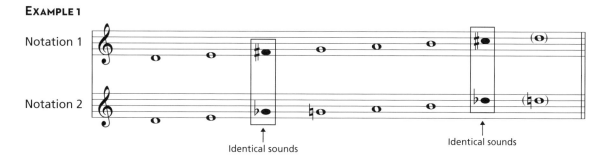

If you played the two scales above (on a tempered instrument), the ear would not detect any difference. In both cases, the whole steps and half steps are in the same place. The difference becomes apparent only during the analysis.

Writing the five-note chords corresponding to the 1st degree of these two modes, gives:

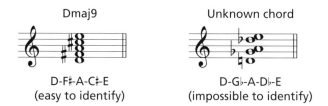

Writing errors arising from the use of enharmonic equivalents, as in the second chord example above, can cause total confusion when analyzing chord names, the colors of notes, and the corresponding modes. This can make it considerably more difficult to organize one's thoughts and convey what one wants to other musicians.

EXAMPLE 2

In many lead sheets, such as those in the *Real Book*, X7 chord-symbol errors are far too frequent. This is notably the case with the X7(♭13, 9) chord which is often incorrectly labeled as X7(♯5). While the confusion between the ♯5 and the ♭13 enharmonic equivalents may seem a mere detail, it is in fact very important.

To better understand this enharmonic inaccuracy, let's take the II–V–I cadence in C minor:

|Dm7 (♭5) |G7 (♯5) |Cm | ⁄. |

To get to the source of the confusion, find the notes and the mode corresponding to G7(♯5).

In the diatonic system, a D♯ is followed by an E, which is not the note we are looking for in this G7 in C minor. In addition, it is impossible to classify this mode in the diatonic system, since no parent scale contains these seven notes.

Now let's write the notes for the same chord labeled as G7(9, ♭13) and compare the results.

Chord tones	G	B	D	F	A	E♭		
Mode	G	A	B	C	D	E♭	F	(G)

This clearly shows that the notion of ♯5 is incorrect because ♭6 is a chord tone and a degree of the mode. This mode (G Mixolydian ♭6)[6] is derived from the C melodic minor parent scale.

_____
6 See the Mixolydian ♭6 in Chapter 13, Synthetic Modes, p. 204.

Chapter 12
NATURAL DIATONIC MODES

❶ Origin of modes

Taking each degree of a major scale as the root or, to be more exact, the potential modal tonic of a new sequence of notes, and retaining all the notes in the original major scale, we obtain seven different modes. The major scale is called the **parent scale** and the seven modes derived from the parent scale are called the natural **diatonic modes**. Collectively known as the **church (or ecclesiastic) modes**, each is assigned a specific name, the exact origin of which is still uncertain.

The nomenclature characterizing the natural diatonic modes proposed in 1547 by Heinrich Glarean (1488-1563) in his treatise on ecclesiastic modes, entitled *Dodecachordon* (one of the most acclaimed and influential books on music theory written during the Renaissance), is still used today. This nomenclature has a logic that is both semantic and scientific. While the names of these modes are the same as those used in jazz nomenclature, this is not the case for synthetic modes,[1] where the choice in name attributed to any given mode is important in that it must define the mode's specific characteristics.[2]

Through time, the church modes, upon which the music of the Middle Ages was based, gradually gave way to the emergence of the major and minor systems, introduced to give new momentum to music and offer greater melodic and harmonic possibilities. Later, however, composers and improvisers began to renew their interest in the modes, and to use them in their music.

During the 1950-60s, the compositions of some jazz musicians — such as Bill Evans, George Russell, and Gil Evans — began to reflect the influence of the early 20th century "French School" composers (Debussy, Ravel, Fauré, et al.).

1.1 The seven modes derived from the major scale

All seven degrees of the major scale serve as the modal tonic of a mode. Because the tonic is displaced for each of these modes, the whole-step/half-step interval sequences are also modified. This produces the **seven natural modes** belonging to the natural diatonic system.

The seven natural modes derived from the diatonic scale of C major can be transposed to any of the 12 degrees of the octave.

---

1 See Synthetic Modes, Chapter 13, p. 203.
2 For example, the mode built on the 2nd degree of the melodic minor (Phrygian ♮6) is often incorrectly referred to as the Dorian ♭2.
   See Chapter 13, nomenclature, p. 205.

Names of the natural diatonic modes

The names of the natural modes always correspond to the respective degree of the major scale upon which they are built.

Mode	Degree of major scale
Ionian	I
Dorian	II
Phrygian	III
Lydian	IV
Mixolydian	V
Aeolian	VI
Locrian	VII

EXAMPLE

Taking the scale of C major, let's build the seven modes derived from the seven degrees of the scale.

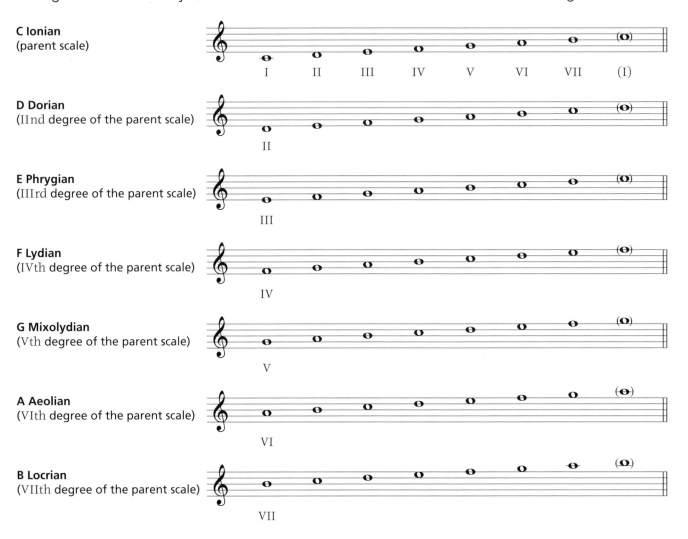

The seven modes above are all derived from the notes of the C major scale, in which every degree becomes a modal tonic. No alteration is added; the only modification is the order of whole-step (2) and half-step (1) intervals, which is adjusted to produce a new sequence of notes, specific to each mode.

1.2 Analysis of the natural diatonic modes

Modal analysis is based on the order of half-step and whole-step intervals. It is easier to calculate intervals by half-step units. This avoids writing and thinking in terms of 0.5 tones and 1.5 tones.

As for the major and minor scales, the writing system used in modal analyses is based on the smallest possible interval, that is to say the half-step, which equals "1." As such, we use:

- 1 to represent one half step;
- 2 to represent one whole step (= 2 half steps);
- 3 to represent one-and-a-half steps (= three half steps);
- 4 to represent two whole steps (= four half steps).

In this book, we use the term **Natural Characteristic Degree (NCD)** to indicate the natural degree that defines the color of a mode. This NCD is harmonically and melodically essential to define the mode.

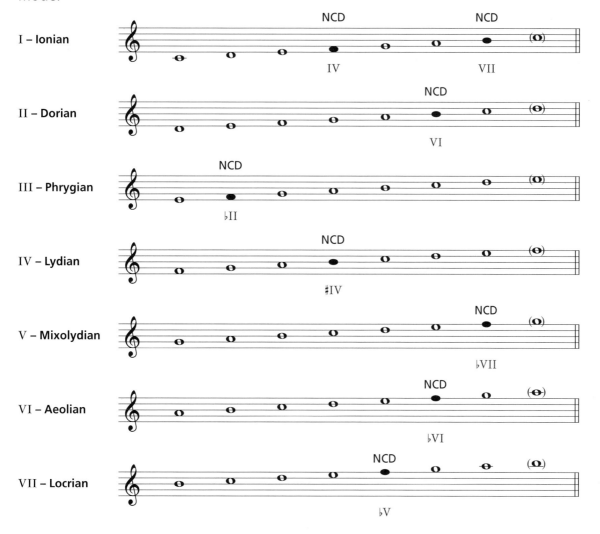

1.3 Transposition of the seven natural modes onto the modal tonic of C

To simplify and clarify the analysis of these natural modes, let's transpose them onto the same modal tonic (C). This produces the following set of seven **parallel modes**; that is to say, a series of seven modes with the same modal tonic (C Ionian, C Dorian, C Phrygian, etc.):

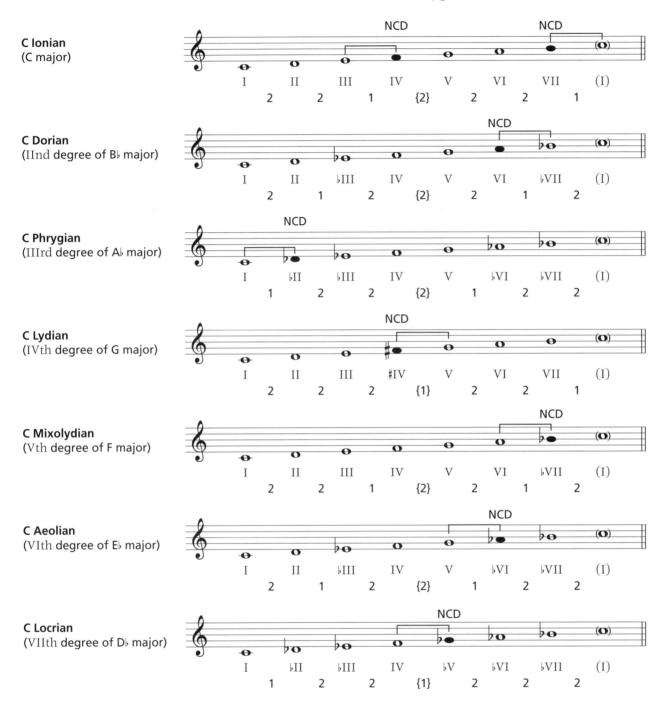

1.4 The modal fragment

Every NCD is preceded, or followed, by a note a half step below or above it; collectively, these two notes are called the **modal fragment**. To express the characteristic color of a mode, play the root, the 3rd, and the modal fragment, melodically and harmonically. Note that, in the modes listed above, the modal fragment of every mode is indicated by a horizontal bracket placed above the two notes in question.

Two examples of chord voicings expressing the colors of the C Dorian and C Lydian modes are given below:

Chord expressing the color of C Dorian:
modal fragment = A-B♭.

Chord expressing the color of C Lydian:
modal fragment = F♯-G.

1.5 Tetrachord analysis

As we saw in Chapter 5, a **tetrachord** comprises four conjunct degrees. All heptatonic (seven-note) scales and modes, therefore, contain a lower and an upper tetrachord. The C major scale, for example, contains these two tetrachords:

Example in the scale of C major:

- C D E F = lower tetrachord;
- G A B C = upper tetrachord.

These two tetrachords are separated by a variable "connector" interval represented by the symbol {i}.

Degree	I	II	III	IV	V	VI	VII	(I)
Tetrachord	└─ lower ─┘				{i}	└─ upper ─┘		

As for the major and minor systems, our analysis of the lower and upper tetrachords in the natural diatonic modes, as presented in the table below, is also built on half-step interval units.

Mode	Lower tetrachord	Connector interval {i}	Upper tetrachord
Ionian	2 2 1	2	2 2 1
Dorian	2 1 2	2	2 1 2
Phrygian	1 2 2	2	1 2 2
Lydian	2 2 2	1	2 2 1
Mixolydian	2 2 1	2	2 1 2
Aeolian	2 1 2	2	1 2 2
Locrian	1 2 2	1	2 2 2

The natural system comprises four types of tetrachords.

Tetrachord	Order of intervals	*Ambitus**
Major	2 2 1	Perfect 4th
Minor	2 1 2	Perfect 4th
Phrygian	1 2 2	Perfect 4th
Lydian	2 2 2	Augmented 4th

* Melodic or instrumental range from the lowest to the highest note.

The seven modes may be divided into two categories ; namely, those whose tetrachords are:

- identical (Ionian, Dorian, and Phrygian);
- different (Lydian, Mixolydian, Aeolian, and Locrian).

1.6 Distinguishing the natural modes

Every mode comprises the same number of notes (7) and the same number of whole-steps (5) and half-steps (2).

For example, the C Dorian mode:

- expresses a Cm13 chord;
- comprises two minor tetrachords (2-1-2) separated by a connector interval {i} = 2;
- contains the modal fragment, A-B♭.

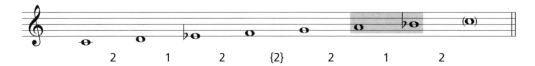

Melodic example

This improvised four-measure melodic phrase is characteristic of the D Dorian mode, with the presence of the root, the minor 3rd, and the B-C modal fragment.

Harmonic example

This famous riff from Miles Davis's "So What" has become a reference Dorian-mode harmonic progression.

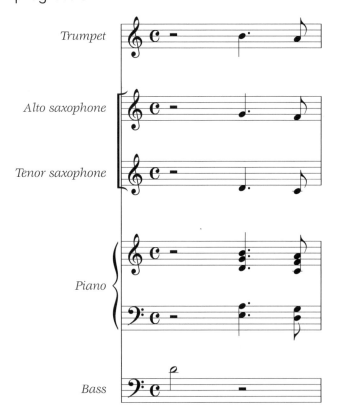

There are many different ways to express a mode harmonically. Two possible voicings for C Dorian are given below:

1.7 Altered degrees

To identify the **altered degrees** present in any given mode, compare the mode in question with its parallel major scale. The ability to identify these altered degrees makes it possible to rapidly construct a mode, determine the differences between it and the parallel major scale, and draw comparisons between it and the other modes.

For example, compare the scale of D major with the modes of D Mixolydian, D Lydian, and D Locrian below. The altered degree of each of these modes is indicated by an Arabic numeral:

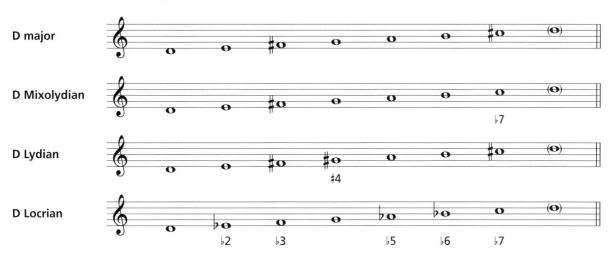

EXERCISE 1

1 Name and write the seven natural modes derived from the G major scale

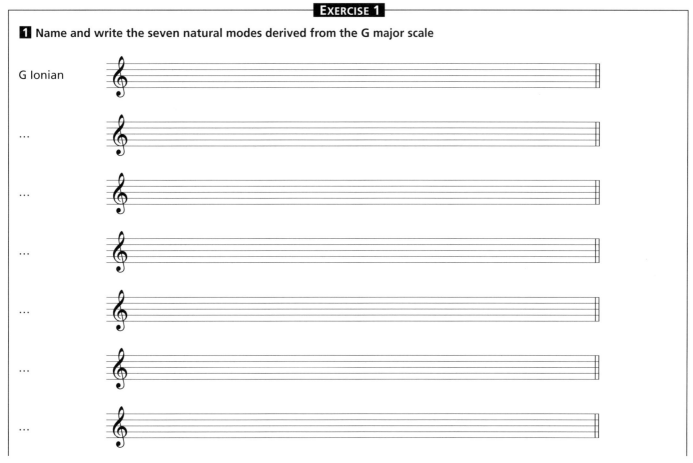

2 Name and write the seven natural modes with F as the modal tonic

F Ionian

...

...

...

...

...

...

3 Write the name(s) of the Natural Characteristic Degree(s) of the following modes

D Ionian: E♭ Dorian: A Phrygian:

B♭ Lydian: D♭ Mixolydian: G Aeolian: C♯ Locrian:

4 Write the names of the notes comprising the modal fragments of the following modes

E♭ Ionian: A♭ Dorian: G Phrygian: E Lydian:

B♭ Mixolydian: D Aeolian: A Locrian:

5 On the staff, write the notes of the following tetrachords

Major (2 2 1) of:

D   A   G♭

Minor (2 1 2) of:

B   E   F♯

Phrygian (1 2 2) of:

A♭   D♭   G

Lydian (2 2 2) of:

E♭   A   E

6 Write the name of the parent scales of the following modes

A Ionian: E♭ Dorian: D Phrygian: B♭ Lydian:

F Mixolydian: G Aeolian: F Locrian:

7 Write the names of the altered notes of the following modes (using the major scale as your reference)

G Dorian: E Phrygian: A♭ Lydian: B Mixolydian:

D Aeolian: F Locrian:

Answers, p. 200-201

❷ Reorganization of the natural diatonic scale

Modes can also be arranged in a way that does not follow their diatonic order, but according to the type of sensation they evoke. Classifying modes from darkest to brightest, or rather from the most minor-sounding to the most major-sounding, provides the full sound-color spectrum modes have to offer.

Classification of modes from the most minor to the most major

Modes derived from C major	Mode
	B Locrian: Xm7 ($^{♭5}$) ($^{♭9, 11, ♭13}$)
	E Phrygian: Xm7 ($^{♭9, 11, ♭13}$)
	A Aeolian: Xm7 ($^{9, 11, ♭13}$)
	D Dorian: Xm7 ($^{9, 11, 13}$)
	G Mixolydian: X7 ($^{9, 11, 13}$)
	C Ionian: Xmaj7 ($^{9, 11, 13}$)
	F Lydian: Xmaj7 ($^{9, ♯11, 13}$)

Transposition onto the same modal tonic

Modes derived from C major	Transposition onto same modal tonic

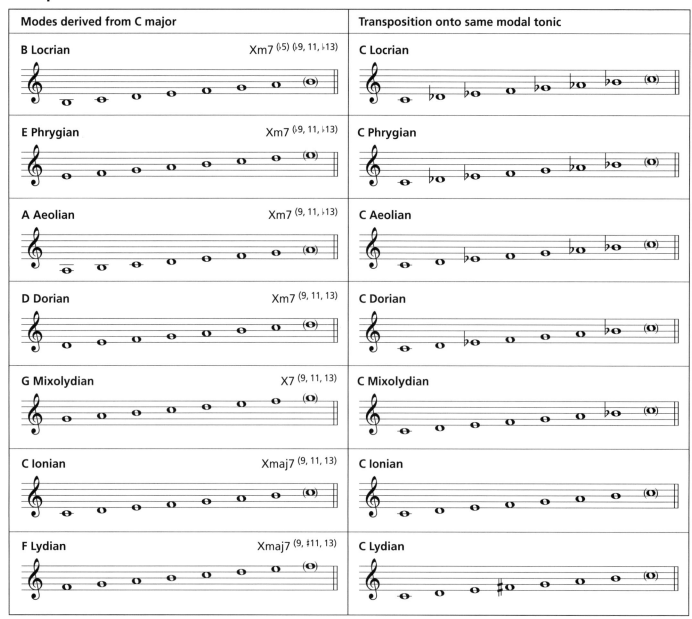

It is interesting to note that, when classifying modes from minor-to-major (or dark-to-light), the movement from the Locrian (the darkest mode) to the Lydian (the brightest) takes us through the descending Circle of Fifths.

VII	III	VI	II	V	I	IV
B	E	A	D	G	C	F

This symmetrical division of the octave by perfect 5ths makes it possible to distinguish the neighboring modes and employ the technique of mirror writing, presented on p. 181.

We will endeavor, with varying degrees of ease and difficulty, to determine a symmetrical division of the octave, and thus establish the same system of analysis for the four other parent scales in the next chapter.

2.1 Summary table

The summary table below lists all the natural modes derived from C major, going left to right from darkest to brightest. This list:

- is arranged according to the Circle of Fifths;
- shows the neighboring modes (with one alteration);
- specifies the Natural Characteristic Degree(s) of every mode.

Circle of fifths (neighboring modes from one column to the next)

"Dark" / "Light"

Degree	VII	III	VI	II	V	I	IV
Mode	B Locrian	E Phrygian	A Aeolian	D Dorian	G Mixolydian	C Ionian	F Lydian
NCD	Diminished 5th	Minor 2nd	Minor 6th	Major 6th	Minor 7th	Perfect 4th & Major 7th	Augmented 4th

This classification makes it possible to distinguish the modal degrees (VII, III, VI, II) on the left, and the tonal degrees (V, I, IV) on the right.

The **modal zone** comprises four modal (or weak) degrees. These degrees do not indicate the tonality, or have a direct gravitational pull toward the Ist degree. This zone includes the minor modes (Locrian, Phrygian, Aeolian, and Dorian).

The **tonal zone** comprises three tonal (or strong) degrees that can define a tonality. Degrees V and IV have a strong gravitational pull toward the Ist degree, as in perfect (V–I) and plagal (IV–I) cadences. This zone contains three major modes (Mixolydian, Ionian, and Lydian).

2.2 Parallel neighboring modes

Modifying the Natural Characteristic Degree of a mode automatically takes us to its neighboring mode.

EXAMPLES

Raising the diminished 5th in C Locrian gives C Phrygian.

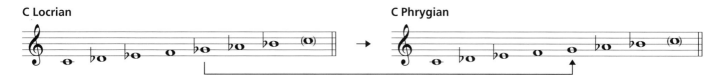

Lowering the major 6th in C Dorian gives C Aeolian.

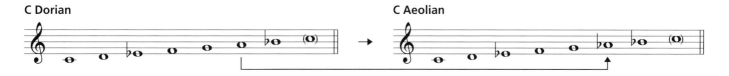

❸ Difference between tonality, scales, and modes

Confusion between the concepts of tonality, scale, and mode can sometimes compromise analytical accuracy. Let's take a closer look at the differences between these three concepts.

3.1 Tonality

The tonality of a piece of music is determined by the succession and frequency of the tonal chords built on degrees I, IV, and V. Major and minor tonalities determine the range of the composition. A piece of music written in F major may be transposed into G major, for example, to accommodate the tessitura[3] of a vocalist or instrumentalist. This changes the range, but not the melodic and harmonic structure of the music. The major or minor tonality imposes the use of tonal degrees I and V, but does not restrict the use of non-diatonic notes or chords. As we saw on pp. 131 and 135, the use of secondary and chromatic dominants for example does not imply modulation.

EXAMPLE
"Satin Doll" (Duke Ellington)

```
|Dm7    G7    |     ⁒     |Em7    A7    |     ⁒      |

|Am7    D7    |A♭m7   D♭7 |Cmaj7  G7    |Em7 ⁽♭5⁾ A7  :‖
```

The key center throughout these first eight measures is C major, despite the presence of non-diatonic notes with chords A7, D7, A♭m7, D♭7, and Em7(♭5). C remains the tonal center throughout the passage.

3.2 Scales

While the C major scale comprises seven notes (C, D, E, F, G, A, B), their presence in a musical passage does not necessarily imply that the tonality is C. As we have seen, all these notes may also serve as the modal tonics upon which the seven natural modes are constructed. According to this principle, F Lydian contains the same notes as C major but does not imply the tonality of C major. In this case, these notes are expressed in a modal context.

EXAMPLE
"Wave" (Antônio Carlos Jobim)

```
|Dmaj7       |B♭dim7     |Am7        |D7         |

|Gmaj7       |Gm6        |F♯7        |B7         |

|Bm7    E7   |B♭7    A7  |Dm7    G7  |     ⁒     :‖
```

Here, we can use the notes of the C major scale in the last two measures, without actually being in the tonality of C.

3.3 Modes

Every mode has a characteristic color, determined by its specific interval structure. If a musical phrase in C Phrygian moves into C Lydian, the color changes, but the range does not. **Modality** characterizes the use of modes during a musical phrase. Modal passages can be of varying lengths or span an entire theme.

---

3 Instrumental or vocal range.

"On Green Dolphin Street" (Bronislau Kaper & Ned Washington)

Here, we move from one modal color to the next without changing the range. C remains the modal tonic throughout the entire eight-measure passage.

Transposition is the technique used to move the tonality, and thus the range, of an entire theme (or a section) into another key without altering the intervals. This is a common practice in vocal music and is used to adapt the melodic range (*ambitus*) of a piece of music to accommodate the tessitura of the vocalist or instrumentalist in question.

EXAMPLE
Theme written in the key of G minor:

Same theme transposed into D minor:

❹ Mirror harmony

Mirror harmony,[4] a writing technique used essentially for its symmetrical interest rather than for voice-leading purposes, can be used to establish other inter-modal relationships. From the original melodic line, it is possible to create several different types of mirror images, depending on whether the symmetrical axis (i.e., the mirror) is horizontal or vertical. This technique provides three possible writing techniques.

4.1 Retrograde

In a retrograde (vertical mirror), only the order of notes is inverted; the mode remains unchanged. The retrograde of the ascending C Ionian mode is the descending C Ionian:

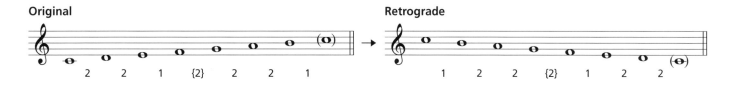

---

4 Writing technique where each voice retains its melodic independence within the chords.

4.2 Melodic inversion

In a melodic inversion (horizontal mirror), the melody is turned upside down. The order of intervals remains the same as the original, resulting in a modulation. When inverted, the ascending C Ionian mode becomes the descending C Phrygian:

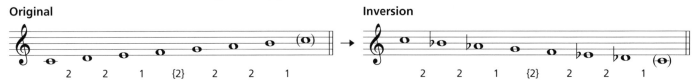

4.3 Retrograde inversion

In a retrograde inversion (literally, backward and upside down), the original melody retains the same progression of notes, but the order of intervals is inverted, resulting in a modulation. The retrograde inversion of an ascending C Ionian mode is the ascending C Phrygian:

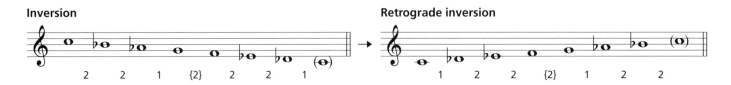

EXAMPLES

Taking the 12-tone row from Bill Evans's "Twelve Tone Tune Two," let's apply a retrograde, a melodic inversion, and a retrograde inversion. Many such examples can be found in the works of Johann Sebastian Bach, one of the masters of musical symmetry.

Original 12-tone row

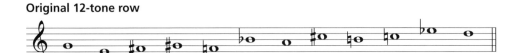

Retrograde (musical line in reverse order)

Inversion (ascending interval when inverted descends, and vice versa)

Retrograde inversion (melody reversed and intervals inverted)

Another notable example of mirror writing is found in the rondeau "Ma fin est mon commencement et mon commencement ma fin" by French composer Guillaume de Machaut (1300-1377). Note the examples of mirror writing in the ten-measure excerpt below. Here, the melodic line in the *triplum*[5] from measures 1-10 is a horizontal inversion of the line voiced in the *cantus*[6] from measures 10 back to 1. Likewise, in the tenor voice, the musical line in measures 6-10 is a mirror of measures 5-1. This is called a musical palindrome.

4.4 Mirror relationships in modes

Every natural mode has its own mirror mode, with the exception of the Dorian mode, which is a palindrome (i.e., containing the same sequence of intervals in both directions).

Mode	Lower tetrachord	{i}	Upper tetrachord	Retrograde inversion	Lower tetrachord	{i}	Upper tetrachord
Ionian	2 2 1	2	2 2 1	Phrygian	1 2 2	2	1 2 2
Dorian	2 1 2	2	2 1 2	Dorian	2 1 2	2	2 1 2
Lydian	2 2 2	1	2 2 1	Locrian	1 2 2	1	2 2 2
Mixolydian	2 2 1	2	2 1 2	Aeolian	2 1 2	2	1 2 2

4.5 Summary table

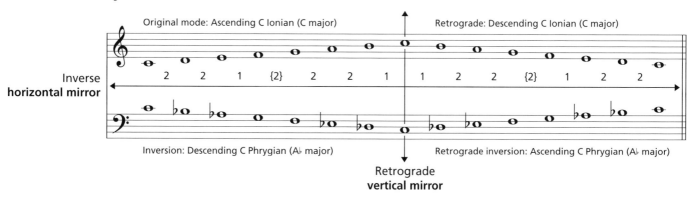

---

5 Latin name designating the third voice in Ars Antiqua polyphony of the 12th and 13th centuries.
6 Latin name designating the top contrapuntal voice in medieval polyphony.

❺ Presence of natural modes in themes

In **functional harmony**, a tonal function is attributed to each chord built on the degrees of the scale. These functions may be divided into three categories:

- **subdominant:** tension-preparation chords;
- **dominant:** tension-function chords;
- **tonic:** resolution-function chords.

Chord progressions follow a logic that may correspond to a cultural trend or an aesthetic preference. When we studied chord functions in Chapter 8, we saw that many compositions contain dominant–tonic (V–I) and subdominant–dominant–tonic (IV–V–I) progressions.

In the Middle Ages, **modal harmony** was used principally in plainsong (a monophonic vocal piece) and in secular music (consisting mainly of ornate monodies sometimes accompanied by a drone).[7] Toward the end of the 19th century, composers started to renew their interest in modal harmony; the predominance of major and minor tonalities began to wane, leaving greater room for modality. Since modal harmony is not functional, chords do not have a tonic, dominant, or pre-dominant function, but rather serve to express a specific color.

While modal aspects were already present in the blues, it wasn't until the 1959 release of Miles Davis's album *Kind of Blue* that modal harmony became an integral feature of jazz. This was later developed in the works of musicians such as John Coltrane, Bill Evans, George Russell, Herbie Hancock, Wayne Shorter, et al.

5.1 Presentation of diatonic natural modes

Let's look at some ways to use these natural diatonic modes. The aim here is not to review all the harmonic and melodic possibilities, but rather to provide some examples of how to use them.

5.1.1 Ionian

The Ionian mode is associated with major chords. In general, although the perfect 4th is one of the two NCDs of the mode, it is rarely featured in a tonal context, let alone in cadences. The IVth is reserved for modal purposes or in melodies using appoggiatura notes.

In the example below, the IVth degree of the Ionian mode is in the melody. The non-tonal Fmaj9 chord expresses a B♭. The diatonic-triad harmonization reinforces the modal color.

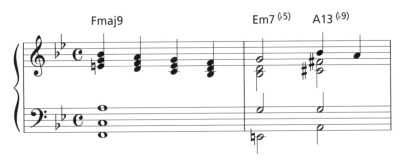

---

7 Bass note played throughout a vocal or instrumental piece.

5.1.2 Dorian

The Dorian mode is associated with minor 7th chords with a major 6th. The first two beats in measure 2 below illustrate how to harmonize a melody in triads. These triads are diatonic, derived from the Dorian mode; they feature the major 6th (C♯), which is the NCD of E Dorian.

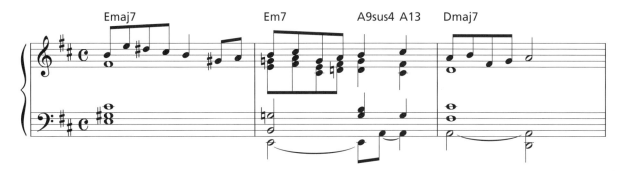

The following example illustrates another diatonic triad harmonization (second inversion). Note that the first two beats of measure 1 utilize all the notes of the D Dorian mode; D is featured in the bass clef and, in the treble clef, C, F, and A are voiced on the first eighth note, followed by D, G, and B on the second, and B, E, and G on the fourth. This is an example of a pandiatonic chord.[8]

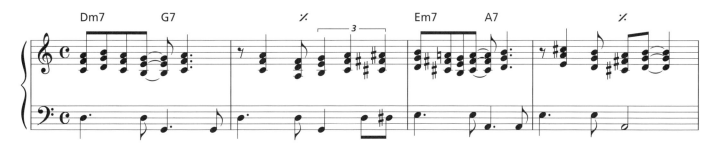

5.1.3 Phrygian

The Phrygian mode is associated with a minor chord. In addition, this mode is often chosen because of its Spanish sound (although it would be a pity to limit its use to this context).

In many progressions, the Phrygian mode is used with the Phrygian ♭3[9] mode to create a certain degree of ambiguity around the 3rd. This is the case in the following example, where the 3rd (G) alternates between the major (G♯) and the minor (G♮). The overall color here is clearly Phrygian.

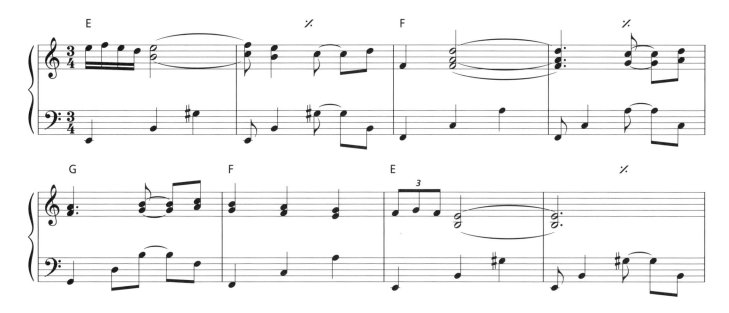

---

8 Pandiatonic composition uses all seven notes of the diatonic scale, melodically or harmonically.
9 See Chapter 13, Synthetic Modes, p. 203.

The Phrygian mode may also exercise a "dominant" function and, as such, be used to substitute the dominant.

Subdominant function	"Dominant" function	Tonic function
V7sus4	V Phrygian	I

In the following II–V–I cadence in D major, the Phrygian takes the place of the dominant chord. This unusual harmonization is made possible because the 3rd (C♯) — the leading tone — is not expressed in the melody. Notice how the voice leading of the inner parts prepares the 3rd of D major (F♯) in measure 3, with E on beat 1 of measure 2 rising to F (♭13 of Am) on beat 3, and up to F♯ on beat 1 of measure 3.

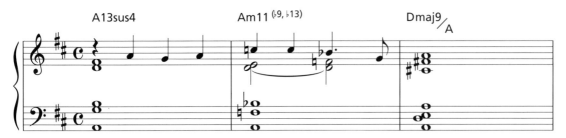

5.1.4 Lydian

The Lydian mode can be used on the Ist degree. This is the case in the following example (in the style of Bill Evans) where the A(add 9) chord in measure 1 expresses a D♯ in the alto voice. Note how the NCD of A Lydian marks the beginning of the voice-leading passage, which moves in ascending chromatic motion from one measure to the next (D♯ to E to E♯ to F♯).

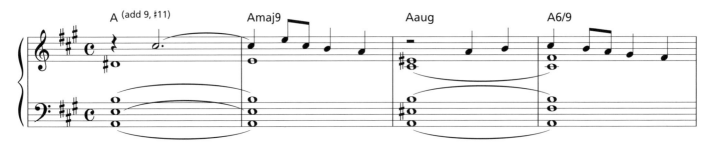

5.1.5 Mixolydian

The Mixolydian mode is associated with dominant and sus4 chords.

In the following musical excerpt, the A13 in measure 2 is prepared by a sus4 (A9sus4) in measure 1. Here, the G in the alto voice descends to F♯ in measure 2, as does the D to C♯. The harmonization of these two measures uses notes from the Mixolydian mode. The first chord in measure 3 (D13sus4) presents another voicing (1, 4-3, 7, 9, 13) for the Mixolydian mode.

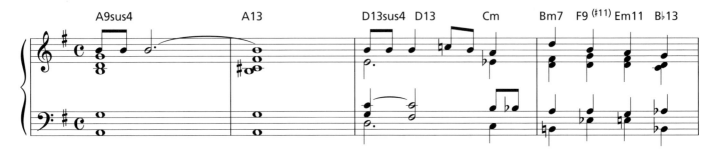

The example below gives another voicing (1, 9, 4, 7) for the G9sus4 in measure 2 and a 1, 7, 3, 13, 9 voicing for the G13 dominant in measure 4.

5.1.6 Aeolian

The Aeolian mode is associated with any minor chord that clearly expresses its NCD, the minor 6th.

This is the case with regard to the Cm7(♭6) chord in measure 5 of the following excerpt. Note that the 9th of the chord is expressed in measure 6. Measures 5-6 feature all the notes of the mode.

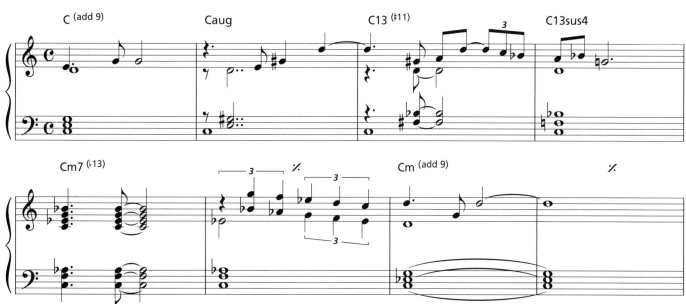

In the following example, F is voiced in the melody (measure 2). The context is Aeolian and the theme can be harmonized as such.

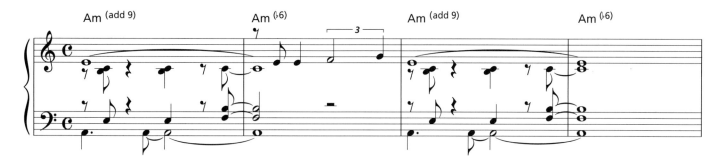

5.1.7 Locrian

The Locrian mode is associated with Xm7(♭5) chords. While the perfect 11th may be added as an extension note (being the IVth degree of the mode), the IInd degree (minor 9th on a minor chord) is to be avoided.

In the following theme, the chord progression presents two voicings for the Xm7(♭5): the second inversion of the chord in measure 2 and a 1, 5, 3, 11, 7 voicing in measure 4. The Gm7(♭5) in measure 2, which is not featured in the original chord chart, moves to F in measure 3 and may be perceived as a minor plagal cadence; that is to say, a B♭m6 (IVm) resolving to its 1st degree (Fmaj).

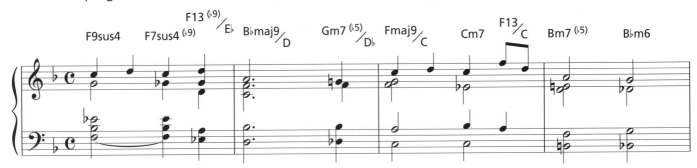

Note that the descending chromatic movement in the bass throughout these four measures is achieved by using chord inversions. The combination of functional and modal harmony in the same composition is often found in jazz, and offers a wide range of melodic and harmonic possibilities.

The following examples present several contexts where we can apply natural modes.

5.2 Modal cadences

While a modal cadence serves to provide the color of a mode, the tonal cadence installs and confirms a key center. These two types of cadences may be combined to form a modal mixture.[10] The modal cadence must feature the Natural Characteristic Degree(s) (and the Altered Characteristic Degree,[11] in the case of synthetic modes) that express the specific color of the mode in question. There are many different types of modal cadences and many ways to interpret them. Some examples are given below:

Ionian
No modal cadence here, since the Ionian mode installs a tonality.

Dorian
IIm7–Im7   ♭VIImaj7–Im7
Dm7–Cm7   B♭maj7–Cm7

Phrygian
♭IImaj7–Im7   ♭VIIm7–Im7
D♭maj7–Cm7   B♭m7–Cm7

Lydian
II7–Imaj7   VIIm7–Imaj7
D7–Cmaj7   Bm7–Cmaj7

Mixolydian
Vm7–I7   ♭VIImaj7–I7
Gm7–C7   B♭maj7–C7

Aeolian
IVm7–Im7   ♭VII7–Im7
Fm7–Cm7   B♭7–Cm7

---

10 Also known as a borrowed chord (term used in this book) and a modal interchange.
11 Altered Characteristic Degree (ACD). See Chapter 13, Synthetic Modes, p. 207 .

Locrian

There is no typical cadence for this mode because of the instability of the Xm7(♭5) target chord. It is possible, however, to alter the Ist degree to obtain a cadence, for example:

♭IIIm7–Imaj

E♭m7–Cmaj7

Using this type of cadence in a tonal context makes it possible to replace one or more tonal chords and enrich a chord progression, by creating new movements in the bass and colors that are outside the tonality. These changes should always take into account the melody to avoid any unwanted clashes.

Take a II–V–I chord progression in C major, with no melodic restrictions:

|Dm7 |G7 |Cmaj7 |
II   V   I

Now, let's modify the tonic preparation by using different modal cadences:

1. Modal cadence in C Aeolian

|A♭maj7 |B♭7 |Cmaj7 |
VI   VII   I
└——— C Aeolian ———┘└— C Ionian —┘

2. Modal cadence in C Phrygian

|D♭maj7 |B♭m7 |Cmaj7 |
II   VII   I
└——— C Phrygian ———┘└— C Ionian —┘

5.3 Using modal plateau passages

A **modal plateau**[12] is a modal passage that contains no harmonic movement. This type of writing is often encountered in jazz, in many different forms. A modal plateau can span the entire length of a composition or be limited to part of the theme, in which case it may be combined with passages that use functional harmony.

5.3.1 Modal plateau passages used throughout an entire theme

All the musical examples below are modal and are based on a succession of modes.

"So What" (Miles Davis)

This theme (in AABA form) is built on the Dorian mode, which modulates between the two modal tonics, D and E♭.

A |├——————— Dm7 • D Dorian (8 measures) ———————┤‖
B |├——————— E♭m7 • E♭ Dorian (8 measures) ———————┤‖

---

12 Term used in this book. See Chapter 10, p. 157.

"Saga of Harrison Crabfeathers" (Steve Kuhn)

This theme alternates between the Aeolian and the Lydian modes, based on different modal tonics.

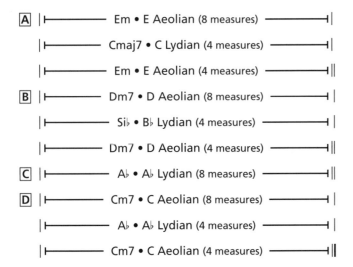

"Flamenco Sketches" (Miles Davis)

This theme is structured around a succession of five modes, with an open-ended number of measures per mode. The structure of the piece is determined by the order of the modes, not the number of measures.

| C Ionian |

| A♭ Mixolydian |

| B♭ Ionian |

| D Phrygian ♮3* |

| G Dorian |

* Phrygian ♮3: Vth degree of the harmonic minor scale (see Chapter 13, p. 231).

5.3.2 The modal plateau used in a part of a theme

The following examples contain a mixture of modal and functional harmony. This type of writing offers a wider choice of colors and atmospheres. The modal plateau can create a sensation of suspended time that breaks with the temporal structure of the piece. This is achieved by providing a unique color over several measures, which is then contrasted by a series of functional cadences. Modal plateau passages can vary in length.

Part A of the following theme is modal and part B is tonal. In the introduction and interlude passages, you can play the G Dorian or Aeolian over the Gm7, and in Part A, the B♭ Dorian or Aeolian on the B♭m7 and E♭ Dorian or Aeolian on the E♭m7.

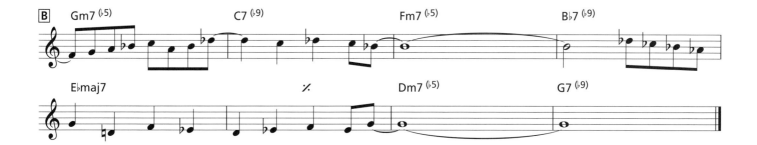

5.3.3 Introductions, interludes, and codas

The absence of functional cadences in modal music can create a floating sensation, as if time has stopped. Cycles based on the number of measures (defined or not, as in "Flamenco Sketches") structure the form while creating a sensation of suspense.

Used in free-form jazz, this effect can also be employed in introductions, interludes, and codas. The three examples below illustrate how this effect can be used over:

- an eight-measure pedal;[13] this offers a wide range of harmonic and melodic choices (Ex. 1);
- a melody written with imposed harmonies (Ex. 2);
- an ostinato over a pedal with imposed harmonies (Ex. 3).

EXAMPLE 1

The chord chart below consists of an eight-measure modal passage in A♭. Although the A♭ Mixolydian mode is frequently played over such a passage, another approach is to use an A♭ pedal as a bass over which you apply the harmonies of your choice. Eight-measure sections such as this can be found in interludes and in the middle of themes.

EXAMPLE 2

The eight measures in the following example alternate between the G Lydian and F♯ Aeolian modes.

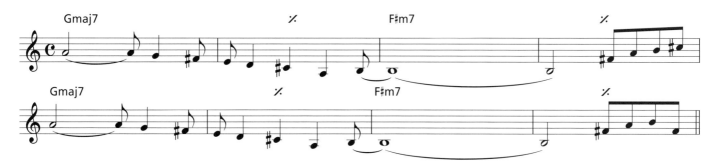

EXAMPLE 3

The following introduction is built on an ostinato in the mode of C Dorian.

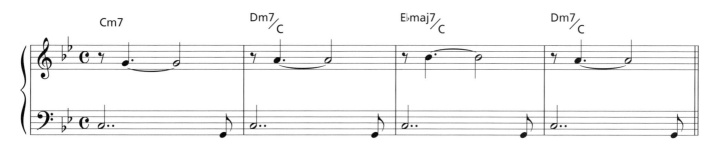

---

13   A note maintained throughout a passage of several measures.

5.3.4 Parallel modulation

Parallel modulation involves changing the mode, but not the tonic. This produces a series of **parallel modes.** Although the modal tonic does not change, we can modulate from one mode to another.

EXAMPLE 1

"On Green Dolphin Street" (Bronislau Kaper & Ned Washington)

This theme starts with eight measures moving through a series of four parallel mode modulations.

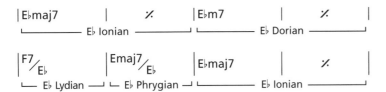

EXAMPLE 2

In the following example, the first eight measures comprise two parallel modes. These modes are suggested by the harmony, but can be modified at any time by the performer.

- D Mixolydian, played over D7sus4;
- D Ionian, over Dmaj7.

In measures 9 to 12, there is a shift in style from modal to functional harmony, with a II–V–I cadence in G major and a V–I in B♭ major.

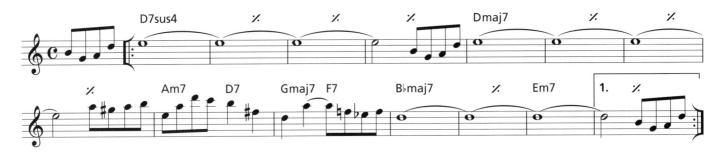

5.3.5 Modal mixtures (borrowed chords)

Modal mixtures are chords that are "borrowed" from one or several chords in the parallel major or minor scales or the parallel modes for the purposes of modifying — for varying lengths of time — the diatonic colors of a scale or a mode.

EXAMPLE

Plagal cadence in C major

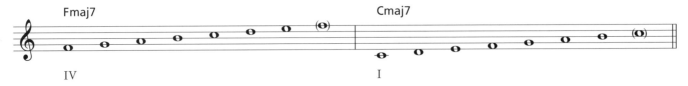

The Fmaj7 in the cadence above can be modified by borrowing the IVth degree of C melodic minor to produce F7(♯11). The impact of the borrowed chord (which introduces an E♭) transforms the scale of C major into C melodic minor and, as such, temporarily modifies the color of C major, as illustrated in the modified chart below:

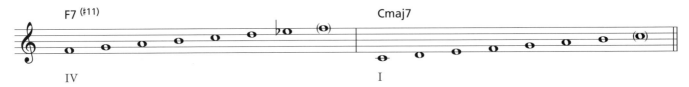

Comment

A modal-mixture or borrowed chord (terms used in this book) is also known as a modal interchange, although this nomenclature is not really appropriate, because the movement of the borrowed chord is in one direction only. In the preceeding example, while the F7 is borrowed from C melodic minor, the Fmaj7 cannot, under any circumstances, replace the borrowed F7 chord. It is therefore more precise to use the terms modal-mixture, borrowed mode, or modal cadence than modal interchange.

In the next example, the theme begins with a II–V–I cadence and plays on the ambiguity between the tonalities of C minor and C major. The first two measures are in C minor, with the II and V using the borrowed chord from C harmonic minor, resolving to I (C major) in measures 3 and 4.

5.3.6 Modulation

In the following examples, the modes change on every chord. In this context, it would be appropriate to use the term modulation to define the different changes in mode, although in conventional musical terminology this would be considered a change in tonality.

Two measures per mode
The theme below begins with an eight-measure passage built on a series of Xmaj7(#11) chords and their corresponding Lydian modes. The next eight measures comprise a series of functional harmonic cadences.

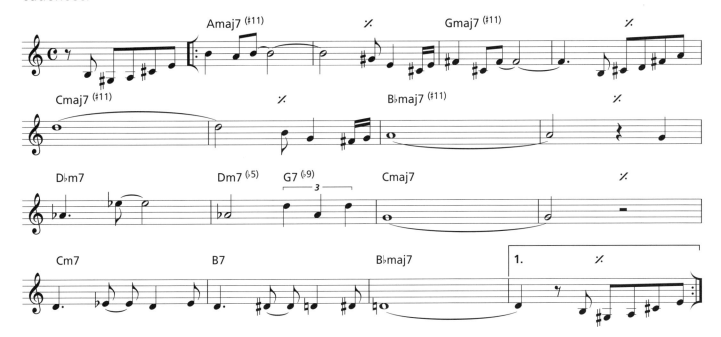

In the next two examples, the modes change from measure to measure or during the same measure.

One measure per mode

"Speak No Evil" (Wayne Shorter)

The first eight measures of the theme alternate between Cm7 and D♭maj7. Two types of modal approach can be used to tackle this type of cadence, namely:

- using one mode per chord: this gives C Dorian on the Cm7 chords and D♭ Lydian on the D♭maj7 chords;
- using a common mode for both chords; C Phrygian for Cm7 and D♭maj7.

Two modes per measure

In this example, there are two chords per measure, i.e., one mode per chord.

5.4 Two approaches to modal harmony

The study of modes offers the possibility of approaching a piece of music from two harmonic points of view, either by:

- respecting the original chord changes; or
- modifying the harmony.

Both approaches require a thorough understanding of all of the notions addressed in this book.

5.4.1 Respecting the original chord changes

The tonal dominance of the natural major, as well as the harmonic and melodic minors, can be bypassed through the use of modes. The combination of functional and modal harmony opens up a wide range of new musical possibilities in jazz.

Modal analysis is sometimes used incorrectly in tonal contexts. For example, analyzing the following progression from a modal point of view would be inappropriate, because all the chords in the cadence stem from the same tonality, C major.

It would be incorrect to refer to D Dorian for the Dm7 chord, G Mixolydian for the G7 or C Ionian for the Cmaj7, since this is a perfect II–V–I cadence in C major with no non-diatonic notes. The particular characteristic of modes is that each one has a specific color, which can be enhanced melodically or harmonically.

The next example uses the same perfect cadence. Here, however, notes borrowed from other scales have been added to the chords built on the Vth degree – G7(♭13) – and on the Ist degree – Cmaj7(♯11). Although the ♭13 of G and the ♯11 of C do not belong to the key of C major, this is still a perfect II–V–I cadence in C major.

The G Mixolydian ♭6[14] and C Lydian modes must be used to portray the colors of the harmonic alterations.

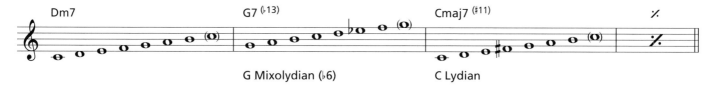

Both examples illustrate the importance of modal analysis.

In the next three examples, our analyses are based on the original compositions, with no modifications.

EXAMPLE 1

The first six measures of the following theme (based on the E♭maj7 and D♭maj7 chords) alternate between the E♭ Ionian and D♭ Lydian modes. The augmented 4th, which is present in the melody in measure 2 (G), suggests the D♭ Lydian mode. The II–V–I cadence beginning in measure 7 ends on a short passage in G major in measure 9. We then move on to a F7–Gmaj7 modal cadence that calls for the modes of G Ionian and F Lydian ♭7.[15]

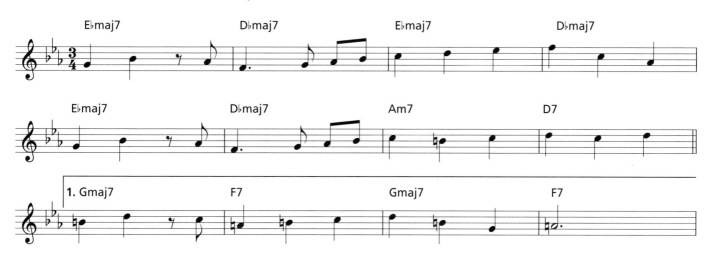

EXAMPLE 2

In this example, the two-measure ostinato based on the A Aeolian mode dictates the modal color to the piece.

---

14   See Synthetic Modes, Chapter 13, p. 204.
15   See Synthetic Modes, Chapter 13, p. 204.

Example 3

Here, the first eight measures, like the entire theme, are built on two modes: the Dorian and the Lydian. The Natural Characteristic Degrees of these modes (in boxes) are particularly present in the melody.

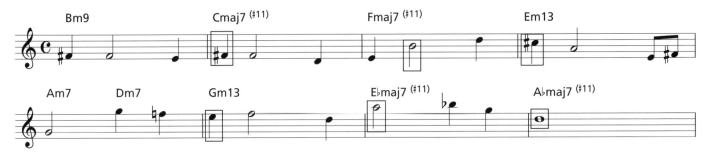

5.4.2 Modifying the written harmony

Up to this point, we have applied the functional harmonic principles imposed by theory to respect the original chord progressions. However, having a thorough understanding of modes also makes it possible to modify the harmony according to one's own aesthetic choices to obtain new colors when harmonizing a melody or improvising. Some examples are given below.

Example 1

Over the E♭m7 in measure 3, the E♭ Phrygian mode can be used instead of E♭ Dorian to give the musical phrase a different color.

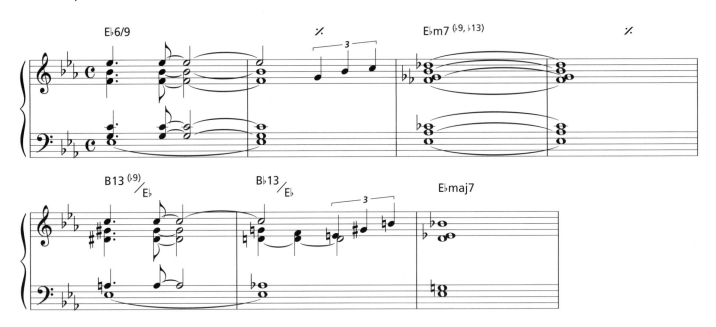

EXAMPLE 2

The Lydian mode is frequently used at the end of a piece, as in the following example ending on Cmaj9(#11). Note the close proximity between the 5th and the NCD of Cmaj9(#11) (G and F#, respectively) and the second inversion of the D major triad in the inner voices of the chord:

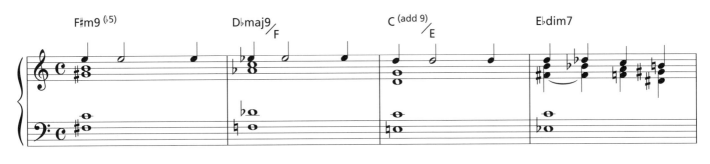

5.5 Combined modal and tonal cadences

We have just seen how modes can be used to change the color of chords. It is also possible to modify a tonal cadence by using a modal cadence.

In jazz, this type of cadence is often used in a tonal context to replace one or several tonal chords in order to enrich the chord progressions by introducing a new bass movement and adding colors that are outside the tonality. These changes should always take the melody into account to avoid unwanted clashes.

Let's use a II–V–I in C major with no melodic restrictions, and modify the tonic preparation by employing different modal cadences:

Dm7	G7	Cmaj7	
II	V	I	

Modal cadence of ...	**C Aeolian**				**C Phrygian**			
	Abmaj7	Bb7	Cmaj7		Dbmaj7	Bbm7	Cmaj7	
	└── C Aeolian ──┘ └─ C Ionian ─┘				└── C Phrygian ──┘ └─ C Ionian ─┘			

The modal II–I and VII–I progressions in C below will enable you to hear the modes and become acquainted with their respective colors:

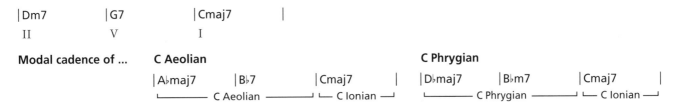

II–I			
Ionian	Xm7—Xmaj7	Dm7—Cmaj7
Dorian	Xm7—Xm7	Dm7—Cm7
Phrygian	Xmaj7—Xm7	Dbmaj7—Cm7
Lydian	X7—Xmaj7	D7—Cmaj7
Mixolydian	Xm7 – X7	Dm7—C7
Aeolian	Xm7 (b5)—Xm7	Dm7 (b5)—Cm7
Locrian	Xmaj7—Xm7 (b5)	Dbmaj7—Cm7 (b5)

VII–I			
Ionian	Xm7 (b5)—Xmaj7	Bm7 (b5)—Cmaj7
Dorian	Xmaj7—Xm7	Bbmaj7—Cm7
Phrygian	Xm7—Xm7	Bbm7—Cm7
Lydian	Xm7—Xmaj7	Bm7—Cmaj7
Mixolydian	Xmaj7—X7	Bbmaj7—C7
Aeolian	X7—Xm7	Bb7—Cm7
Locrian	Xm7—Xm7 (b5)	Bbm7—Cm7 (b5)

1 Define the following terms

Major scale	Tonality	NCD	Borrowed chord
Parent scale	Modal fragment	Parallel modes	Modulation
Mode	Tetrachord	Parallel modulation	Transposition

2 Mirror writing

2.1 Write the retrogrades of the following

Twelve tone row derived from
Twelve Tone Tune (Bill Evans)

2.2 Write the inversion

2.3 Write the retrograde inversion

3 Transpose the following musical passage in E♭ into F and B♭

4 Write the names of the chords in the following modal cadences

II-I of...	A Dorian:	B♭ Lydian:	F Phrygian:
VII-I of...	E♭ Aeolian:	A♭ Mixolydian:	D Lydian:

5 Write the names of the natural modes to be used with the following chords

B♭maj13 (♯11):	Gm13:	Amaj13:	E♭7sus4:
Bm9 (♭13):	Dm7 (♭5):	A♭13:	F6/9:

6 Write the names of the chords corresponding to the following modes

A Dorian:	G Phrygian:	D Lydian:	F♯ Mixolydian:
E♭ Aeolian:	C♯ Locrian:		

7 Name the two modes used in measures 1-5 of the following 3 musical excerpts

7.1

⓺ Answers

1

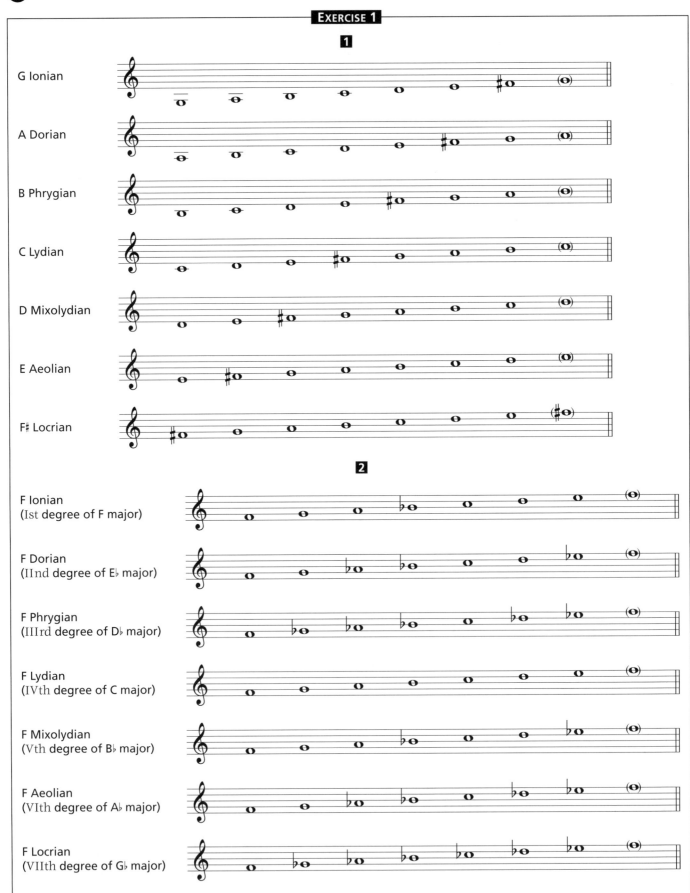

G Ionian

A Dorian

B Phrygian

C Lydian

D Mixolydian

E Aeolian

F# Locrian

2

F Ionian
(Ist degree of F major)

F Dorian
(IInd degree of E♭ major)

F Phrygian
(IIIrd degree of D♭ major)

F Lydian
(IVth degree of C major)

F Mixolydian
(Vth degree of B♭ major)

F Aeolian
(VIth degree of A♭ major)

F Locrian
(VIIth degree of G♭ major)

D Ionian: G & C♯ (two NCDs for the Ionian mode)   E♭ Dorian: C   A Phrygian: B♭

B♭ Lydian: E   D♭ Mixolydian: C♭   G Aeolian: E♭   C♯ Locrian: G

4

E♭ Ionian: G - A♭ and D - E♭   A♭ Dorian: F - G♭   G Phrygian: G - A♭   E Lydian: A♯ - B

B♭ Mixolydian: G - A♭   D Aeolian: A - B♭   A Locrian: D - E♭

5

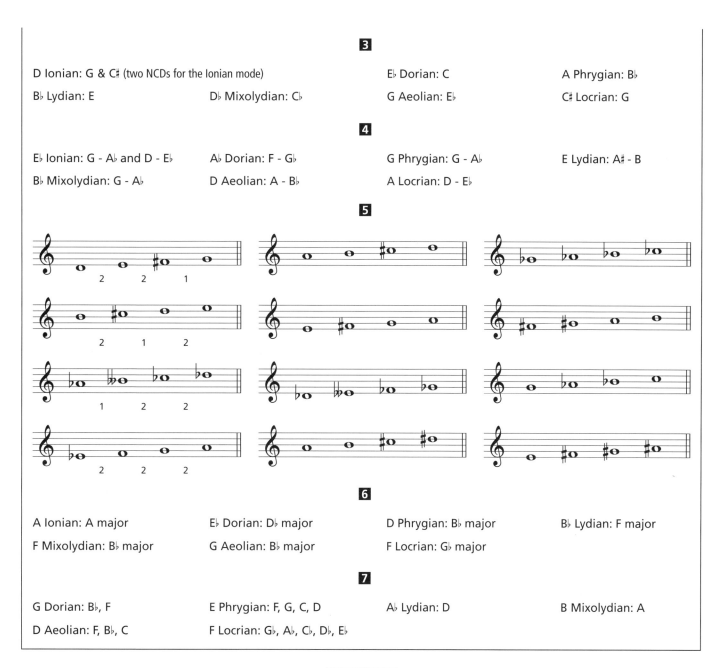

6

A Ionian: A major   E♭ Dorian: D♭ major   D Phrygian: B♭ major   B♭ Lydian: F major

F Mixolydian: B♭ major   G Aeolian: B♭ major   F Locrian: G♭ major

7

G Dorian: B♭, F   E Phrygian: F, G, C, D   A♭ Lydian: D   B Mixolydian: A

D Aeolian: F, B♭, C   F Locrian: G♭, A♭, C♭, D♭, E♭

EXERCISE 2

1

Major scale: a sequence of seven notes with different names and pitches and which are organized in an ordered series of intervals: 2 2 1 2 2 2 1 (see p. 83).

Parent scale: a sequence of seven notes where each degree can become the modal tonic of a mode. In this book, we focus on five heptatonic parent scales, namely; the major, harmonic minor, melodic minor, harmonic major and double harmonic major scales (see p. 181).

Mode: a sequence of notes whose characteristic color is defined by an ordered series of intervals specific to the mode in question (see p. 40).

Tonality : indicated by the succession and frequency of the tonal chords built on degrees I, IV and V. Whether major or minor, the tonality determines the range of a piece of music (see p. 191).

Modal fragment: the combination of the NCD and the neighboring note, one half-step above or below that precedes it (see p. 184).

Tetrachord: succession of four conjunct degrees (see p. 185)

NCD: abbreviation for Natural Characteristic Degree which indicates the note(s) that characterizes the color of the mode (see p. 183).

Parallel modes: modes based on the same modal tonic; ex. C Ionian and C Mixolydian (see p. 204).

Parallel modulation: movement from one mode to another mode, both with the same modal tonic, ex. passage from C Dorian to C Lydian (see p. 204).

Borrowed chord: chord borrowed from a tonality or mode other than that of the cadence (see p. 205).

Modulation: technique which enables the transition from one tonality to another (see p. 205).

Transposition: technique used to alter the range of a musical passage or piece without modifying the intervals (see p. 192).

2.1 Retrograde
(musical line in reverse order)

Row derived from *Twelve Tone Tune* (Bill Evans)

2.2 Melodic inversion
(ascending interval, when inverted, descends, and vice versa)

2.3 Retrograde inversion
(melody reversed and intervals inverted)

3

4

II-I of…	A Dorian: **Bm7 – Am7**	B♭ Lydian: **C7 – B♭maj7**	F Phrygian: **G♭maj7 – Fm7**
VII-I of…	E♭ Aeolian: **D♭7 – E♭m7**	A♭ Mixolydian: **G♭maj7 – A♭7**	D Lydian: **C♯m7 – Dmaj7**

5

B♭maj13 (♯11): **B♭ Lydian**	Gm13: **G Dorian**	Amaj13: **A Ionian**	E♭7sus4: **E♭ Mixolydian**
Bm9 (♭13): **B Aeolian**	Dm7 (♭5): **D Locrian**	A♭13: **A♭ Mixolydian**	F6/9: **F Ionian**

6

A Dorian: **Am13**	G Phrygian: **Gm7** (♭9, ♭13)	D Lydian: **Dmaj13** (♯11)	F♯ Mixolydian: **F♯13**
E♭ Aeolian: **E♭m9** (♭13)	C♯ Locrian: **C♯m7** (♭5, ♭9)		

7

7.1 C Locrian (measures 1-2) then C Phrygian (measures 3-5).

7.2 G Mixolydian.

7.3 Dorian mode in C, F, E and B.

CHAPTER 13
SYNTHETIC MODES

In this chapter, we will focus on the four parent scales related to the melodic minor, harmonic minor, harmonic major, and double harmonic major systems.

These four parent scales provide 28 **synthetic modes**, for which we have applied the same principles used in our study of the natural modes. While the names of the natural modes are the same in all books on music theory, the names of the synthetic modes vary from one text to another. In this book, we use the nomenclature employed by Bernard Maury,[1] which, we believe, is the most precise.

When analyzing modes, two important points should be taken into account:

- every natural mode has its own specific Natural Characteristic Degree(s) (NCD). These never change, which justifies using the mode's precise name;
- while natural diatonic modes are analyzed by drawing comparisons with their parallel major scales (for example, F Dorian vis-à-vis its reference scale of F major), synthetic diatonic modes draw comparisons with their parallel natural modes (for example, F Dorian ♭5 analyzed in relation to F Dorian). Note that, in addition to their respective NCDs, every synthetic mode also contains an Altered Characteristic Degree (ACD). [2]

Part 1: The melodic minor system

❶ Modes derived from the melodic minor scale

The melodic minor system is the next area of study after the major diatonic system, since there is only one degree that differentiates the two systems: their respective IIIrd degrees. The melodic minor is the most common system after the major.

Taking the scale of C melodic minor as the parent scale, we obtain seven synthetic modes derived from the melodic minor system.

1.1 Sequence of descending 5ths

The seven degrees of the melodic minor scale can be organized as a sequence of descending 5ths, as follows:

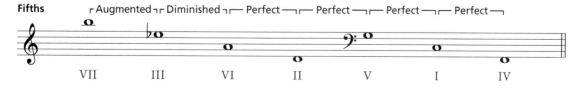

---

1 See Foreword, p. iv.
2 Analysis of modes (Section 1.4 , p. 205) and Altered Characteristic Degrees (Section 1.7, p. 207.)

When organized by descending 5ths, the melodic minor system contains an augmented 5th and a diminished 5th. Unlike the major diatonic system, therefore, the melodic minor cannot be organized as a sequence of perfect 5ths, but rather produces a **synthetic diatonic sequence**. In an asymmetrical sequence of this kind, there are no neighboring modes or mirror relationships in the same system. To obtain symmetry in the sequence, we must try to reorganize the order of 5ths.

1.2 Symmetrical sequence

As for the natural modes, we have reorganized the series of notes in the melodic minor by descending major 2nds and perfect 5ths. This produces a sequence that is both symmetrical and which serves as the basis for analyzing and drawing comparisons between the modes.

1.3 Origin of modes

As mentioned above, the melodic minor is a parent scale in which every degree serves as a modal tonic to produce seven **synthetic modes**.

Taking the seven notes of the C melodic minor parent scale as a basis to determine the seven synthetic modes related to this system, we note that, in addition to having a Natural Characteristic Degree (found in the natural diatonic modes), all the synthetic modes listed below also contain an Altered Characteristic Degree (ACD).[3]

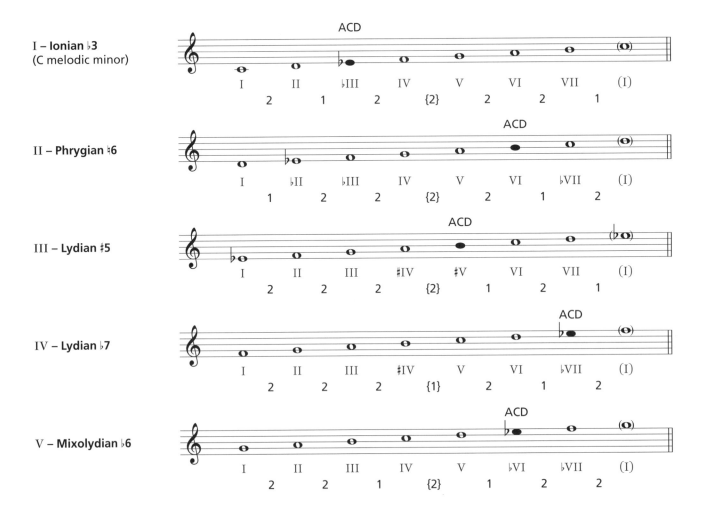

---

3 Analysis of modes (Section 1.4 , p. 205) and Altered Characteristic Degree, (Section 1.7, p. 207).

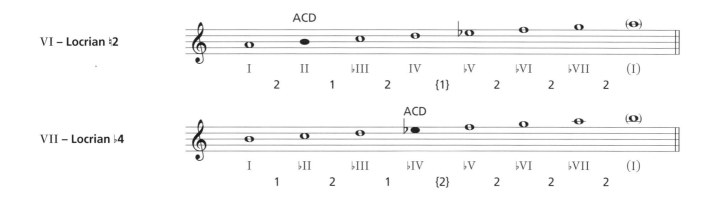

This system does not contain a Dorian or an Aeolian mode, but rather two Lydian and two Locrian modes, which are retrograde inversions. Lydian, played backward and upside down, becomes Locrian, and vice versa.

Nomenclature

A certain ambiguity surrounds the Phrygian ♮6,[4] which is frequently referred to as the Dorian ♭2. Aside from the distinct Phrygian sound of the mode itself, Bernard Maury's teachings on the subject revealed a strong preference for using Phrygian ♮6 over Dorian ♭2. In his classes and master classes,[5] Maury based his argument on a set of three theoretical criteria:

- the function of the Dorian mode is limited exclusively to minor chords, while that of the Phrygian mode (which can also be employed with minor chords) is more frequently used with X7sus4(♭9) chords;
- the ♭2 of the Dorian mode creates a ♭9 with an Xm7, an interval to be avoided in a minor 7th chord. Conversely, the ♭9 is the Natural Characteristic Degree of the Phrygian mode. Referring to this mode as a Phrygian ♮6, we obtain an enriched X13sus4(♭9);
- the retrograde inversion (RI) of the Dorian ♭2 mode produces a Dorian ♮7, whereas the RI of Phrygian ♮6 is Ionian ♭3, which is more representative of the Ist degree.

The Ionian ♭3 mode is also known as the Ionian minor.

The Lydian ♯5 mode is also known as the Lydian augmented.

The Lydian ♭7 mode is also known as the Mixolydian ♯4, the Lydian Dominant, the Acoustic Mode (as used by Debussy), and the Bartók Scale.

The Locrian ♭4 is also known as the Altered Scale and the Superlocrian.

1.4 Analysis of modes

As in our analysis of the natural diatonic modes, we will transpose the seven synthetic modes onto the same modal tonic to facilitate the analysis of, and draw comparisons between, the modes. The major scale is still the reference scale used to indicate the altered degrees present in the synthetic modes of the melodic minor.

Because every mode has its own specific Natural Characteristic Degree that never changes, it is important to employ a nomenclature that is precise (or relevant). As already mentioned, in addition to their specific NCDs, synthetic modes have an Altered Characteristic Degree (ACD) that differentiates them from the natural modes. For example, the difference between the Ionian and the Ionian ♭3 modes is the quality of their respective IIIrd degrees.

---

4 Also known as Phrygian natural 6.
5 Notably at Berklee in 1989.

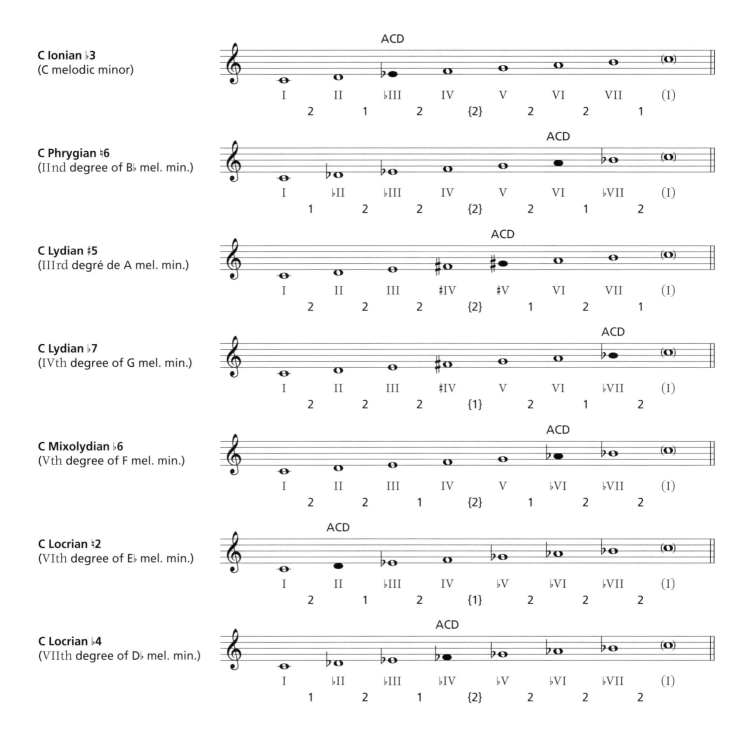

1.5 Tetrachord analysis: melodic minor modes

An analysis of the lower and upper tetrachords present in the seven synthetic modes derived from the melodic minor is presented in the table below.

Mode	Lower tetrachord	Connector interval {i}	Upper tetrachord
Ionian ♭3	2 1 2	2	2 2 1
Phrygian ♮6	1 2 2	2	2 1 2
Lydian ♯5	2 2 2	2	1 2 1
Lydian ♭7	2 2 2	1	2 1 2
Mixolydian ♭6	2 2 1	2	1 2 2
Locrian ♮2	2 1 2	1	2 2 2
Locrian ♭4	1 2 1	2	2 2 2

In addition to the four tetrachords already encountered in the major system, the melodic minor system introduces the diminished 1-2-1 tetrachord, with an *ambitus* spanning a diminished 4th.

Unlike the natural modes, none of the lower and upper tetrachords contained in the synthetic modes derived from the melodic minor system are the same. Conversely, there is still one palindromic[6] mode: the Mixolydian ♭6.

1.6 Differentiating the synthetic modes

Synthetic modes can be compared with their parallel natural-mode equivalents. In addition to sharing the same NCDs as their natural diatonic modes, synthetic modes contain an Altered Characteristic Degree (ACD), indicated in their names.

1.7 Altered Characteristic Degrees

In the same way Natural Characteristic Degrees enable us to recognize the natural diatonic modes, the presence of Altered Degrees in a mode makes it possible to rapidly identify the synthetic modes and facilitates their comparison. It is therefore essential to memorize the ACDs of the synthetic modes.

EXAMPLE

In the example below, the presence of ♯5 (the ACD of G Lydian ♯5) indicates the difference between this mode and the natural G Lydian. It is important to remember that ♯4 is the Natural Characteristic Degree of all Lydian modes.

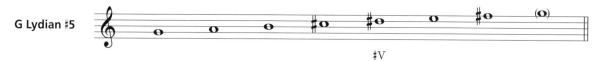

EXERCISE 1

1 Write the seven modes derived from the F melodic minor scale

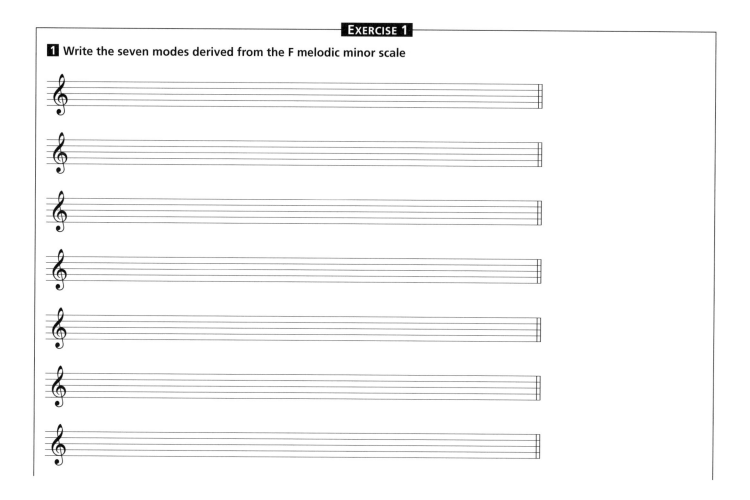

---

6 A palindrome is a word, group of words or set of figures that is identical when read from left to right and vice versa.

2 Write the seven modes derived from the melodic minor scale with G as the modal tonic

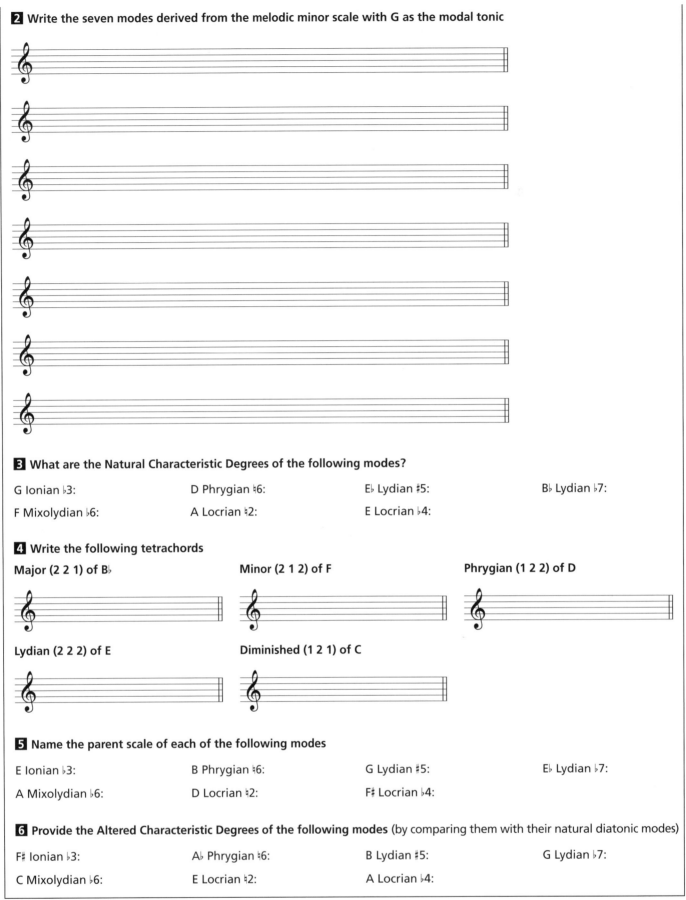

3 What are the Natural Characteristic Degrees of the following modes?

G Ionian ♭3:   D Phrygian ♮6:   E♭ Lydian #5:   B♭ Lydian ♭7:

F Mixolydian ♭6:   A Locrian ♮2:   E Locrian ♭4:

4 Write the following tetrachords

Major (2 2 1) of B♭   Minor (2 1 2) of F   Phrygian (1 2 2) of D

Lydian (2 2 2) of E   Diminished (1 2 1) of C

5 Name the parent scale of each of the following modes

E Ionian ♭3:   B Phrygian ♮6:   G Lydian #5:   E♭ Lydian ♭7:

A Mixolydian ♭6:   D Locrian ♮2:   F# Locrian ♭4:

6 Provide the Altered Characteristic Degrees of the following modes (by comparing them with their natural diatonic modes)

F# Ionian ♭3:   A♭ Phrygian ♮6:   B Lydian #5:   G Lydian ♭7:

C Mixolydian ♭6:   E Locrian ♮2:   A Locrian ♭4:

Answers, p. 215-216

1.8 Reorganization of the melodic minor scale

By reorganizing the symmetrical scale, we can obtain the neighboring modes and thus classify the modes from "darkest" to "brightest."

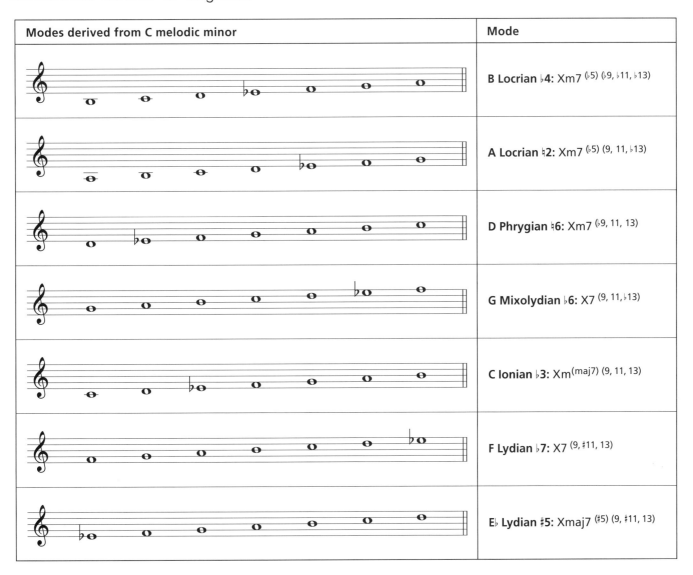

Modes derived from C melodic minor	Mode
	B Locrian ♭4: Xm7 (♭5) (♭9, ♭11, ♭13)
	A Locrian ♮2: Xm7 (♭5) (9, 11, ♭13)
	D Phrygian ♮6: Xm7 (♭9, 11, 13)
	G Mixolydian ♭6: X7 (9, 11, ♭13)
	C Ionian ♭3: Xm(maj7) (9, 11, 13)
	F Lydian ♭7: X7 (9, ♯11, 13)
	E♭ Lydian ♯5: Xmaj7 (♯5) (9, ♯11, 13)

1.9 Mirror harmony

The mirror-writing techniques used in the natural modes also apply to the synthetic modes derived from the melodic minor system. The relationships between the following modes remain the same:

- Lydian and Locrian;
- Ionian and Phrygian.

Note that the Mixolydian ♭6 mode remains unchanged because it is a palindrome.

To obtain the name of the ACD in the "mirror" synthetic mode, inverse the altered note of the first mode as you would for an interval. In this way:

- Ionian ♭3 becomes Phrygian ♮6;
- Lydian ♯5 becomes Locrian ♭4;
- Lydian ♭7 becomes Locrian ♮2;
- Mixolydian ♭6 remains Mixolydian ♭6.

1.10 Tetrachord summary table

The chart below show the melodic minor modes and their retograde inversions:

Mode	Lower tetrachord	{i}	Upper tetrachord	Retrograde inversion	Lower tetrachord	{i}	Upper tetrachord
Ionian ♭3	2 1 2	2	2 2 1	Phrygian ♮6	1 2 2	2	2 1 2
Lydian ♯5	2 2 2	2	1 2 1	Locrian ♭4	1 2 1	2	2 2 2
Lydian ♭7	2 2 2	1	2 1 2	Locrian ♮2	2 1 2	1	2 2 2
Mixolydian ♭6	2 2 1	2	1 2 2	Mixolydian ♭6	2 2 1	2	1 2 2

❷ Using melodic minor modes in themes

Modes derived from the melodic minor are frequently used in jazz. In this section, we will see how these synthetic modes can be applied in themes. First, let's look at how they can be used in a II–V–I cadence.

EXAMPLE 1
Original cadence in C major:

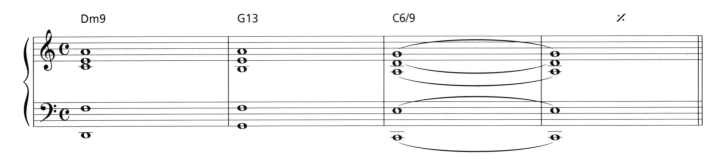

EXAMPLE 2
G13 becomes G13(♯11), which is associated with G Lydian ♭7:

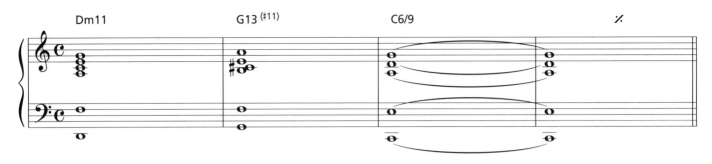

EXAMPLE 3
G13 becomes G9(♭13), which is associated with G Mixolydian ♭6:

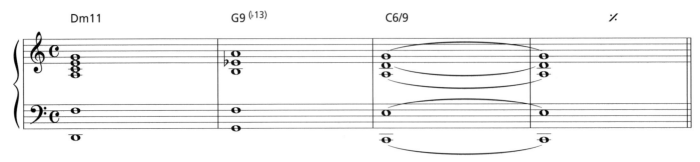

Example 4

G13 becomes G7sus4(♭9), which is associated with G Phrygian ♮6, then G7 alt, with G Locrian ♭4:

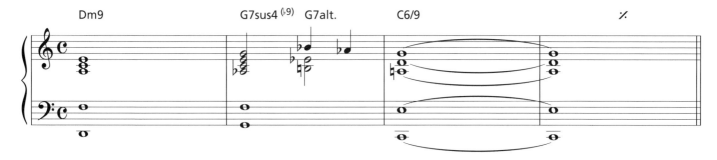

Example 5

Dm9 becomes Dm9(♭5), which is associated with D Locrian ♮2.[7] G7(♭9, ♭13) is associated with G Locrian ♭4, and Cmaj13(♯5, ♯11) with C Lydian ♯5:

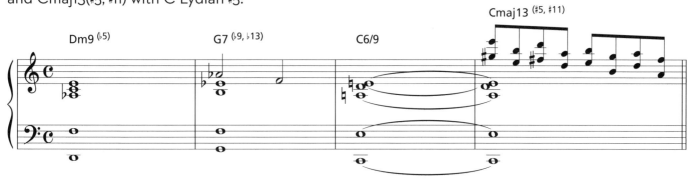

Example 6

In the following minor cadence, Dm9(♭5) is associated with D Locrian ♮2, G7(♭10, ♭13) with G Locrian ♭4 and Cm(maj13) with C Ionian ♭3:

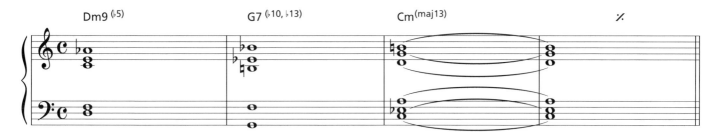

2.1 Ionian ♭3

Ionian ♭3 is used with minor chords such as Xm(maj7), Xm6, and Xm6/9. Note, however, that Xm (maj7) chords offer the most interesting contrast because the juxtaposition of a minor 3rd and a major 7th creates a certain ambiguity with regard to the sound, but not to the function.

Example 1

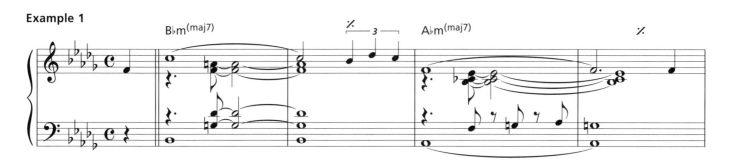

---

7 Also known as Locrian natural 2.

Example 2

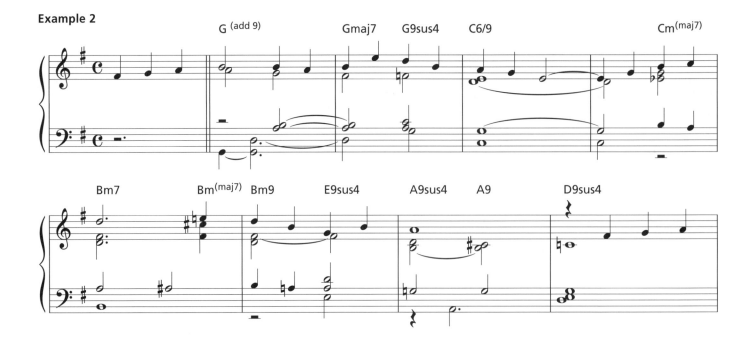

2.2 Phrygian ♮6

The NCD of this mode is the minor 2nd, an interval not usually associated with a minor chord. It is more interesting to use this mode over an X7sus4(♭9). The ACD also voices the major 13th, which enriches the chord. The Phrygian ♮6 is therefore most often used with X13sus4(♭9) chords.

Example 1

Example 2

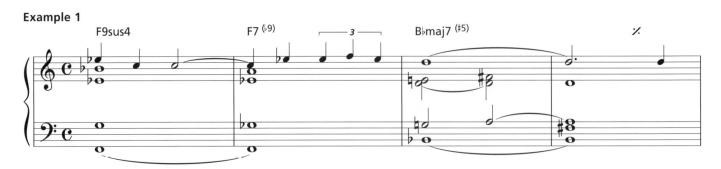

2.3 Lydian ♯5

The Lydian ♯5 mode is used with major chords such as the Xmaj7(♯11) and Xmaj7(♯5). When the melody permits, this mode may be used to create additional dissonance when harmonizing major chords.

Example 1

Example 2

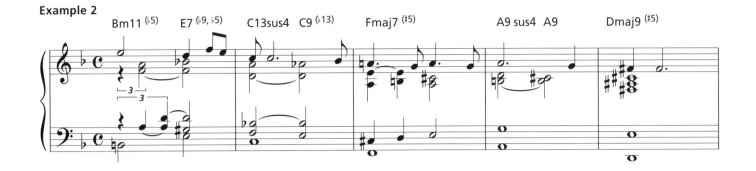

2.4 Lydian ♭7 [8]

The color of X13(#11) chords is most often found in passing harmonic passages. The chord can be the Vth degree or any other dominant chord.

2.5 Mixolydian ♭6 [9]

This mode combines the major 9th and minor 13th of an X7 chord, as illustrated in C7(♭13) in Example 1, and in E♭9(♭13) in Example 2 below.

Example 1

Example 2

---

8 Also known as the Lydian dominant, the Bartók Scale, and the Acoustic Scale.
9 Mixed major.

2.6 Locrian ♮2

In certain musical phrases, the major 2nd of this mode may sound too dissonant, depending on the context. Used mainly with IIm7(♭5) chords, the major 2nd voices the major 3rd of the tonality, which is in fact in the minor. Note the presence of F♯ in the II–V (Em11(♭5)–A7) cadence in D minor in Example 1, below, and that of C♯ in the II–V–I cadence (Bm9(♭5)–E7–Am) in Example 2.

Example 1

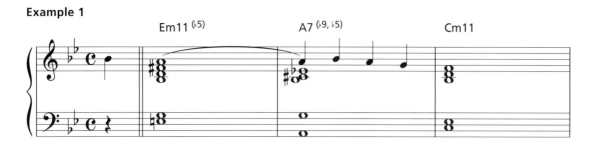

Example 2

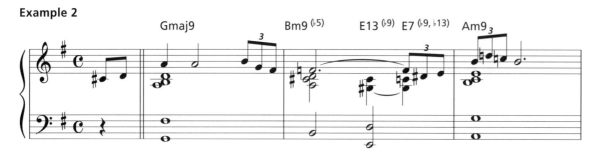

2.7 Locrian ♭4 [10]

This mode is frequently used over X7 chords, where every extension note (color) is altered. Because all the X7 extensions (♭9, ♯9, ♯11, and ♭13) can be altered in this mode, it is typically referred to as X7alt.

Example 1

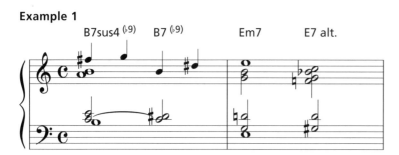

Example 2

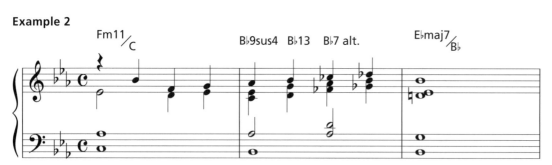

EXERCISE 2

1

F13 sus4 (♭9): F Phrygian ♮6	E7 (♯11): E Lydian ♭7	Bm(maj7): B Ionian ♭3
A♭maj9 (♯5): A♭ Lydian ♯5	B♭9 (♭13): B♭ Mixolydian ♭6	D7 (♭9, ♯11): D Locrian ♭4
Fm9 (♭5): F Locrian ♮2		

---

10 Also known as the Altered Scale (or Superlocrian).

Locrian ♭4	|B♭m7	E♭7	A♭maj7	D♭maj7	
		E♭7 (♭9, ♯9, ♯11, ♭13)			
Lydian ♯5	|Fm7	B♭m7	E♭7	A♭maj7 (♯5)	
					A♭maj7 (♯5, ♯11)
Phrygian ♮6	|F7	∕.	B♭maj7	E♭maj7	
	F13sus4 (♭9)				
Ionian ♭3	|Cm	∕.	A♭m6	G7	
	Cm(maj7)				
Locrian ♮2	|Fm7 (♭5)	B♭7	E♭m7	A♭7	
	Fm11 (♭5)				
Lydian ♭7	|Bm7	Am7	D7	Gmaj7	
			D13 (♯11)		
Mixolydian ♭6	|Cm7	F7	B♭maj7	Gm7	
		F9 (♭13)			

❷ Answers

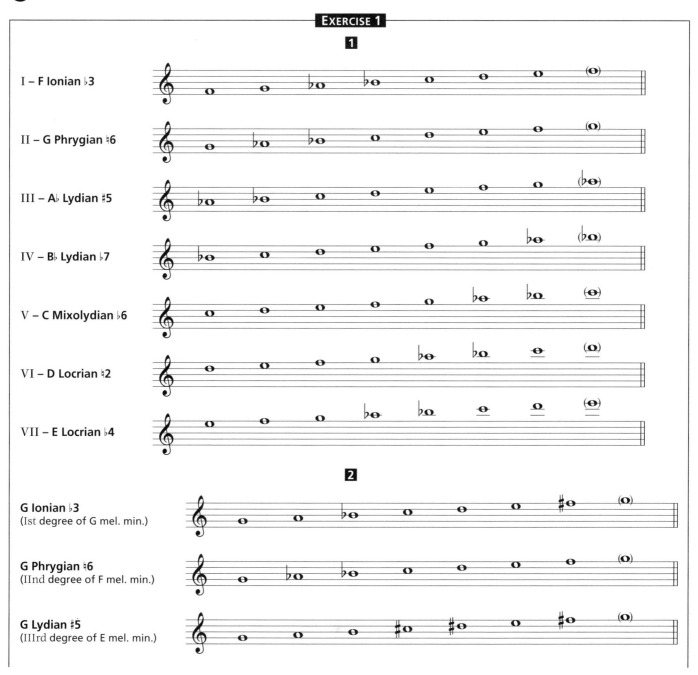

EXERCISE 1

1

I – F Ionian ♭3

II – G Phrygian ♮6

III – A♭ Lydian ♯5

IV – B♭ Lydian ♭7

V – C Mixolydian ♭6

VI – D Locrian ♮2

VII – E Locrian ♭4

2

G Ionian ♭3
(Ist degree of G mel. min.)

G Phrygian ♮6
(IInd degree of F mel. min.)

G Lydian ♯5
(IIIrd degree of E mel. min.)

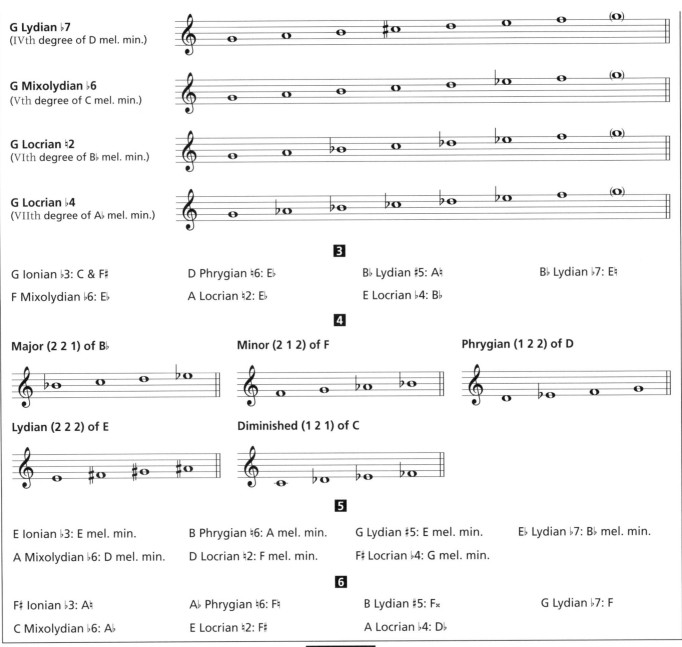

G Lydian ♭7
(IVth degree of D mel. min.)

G Mixolydian ♭6
(Vth degree of C mel. min.)

G Locrian ♮2
(VIth degree of B♭ mel. min.)

G Locrian ♭4
(VIIth degree of A♭ mel. min.)

3

G Ionian ♭3: C & F♯   D Phrygian ♮6: E♭   B♭ Lydian ♯5: A♮   B♭ Lydian ♭7: E♮

F Mixolydian ♭6: E♭   A Locrian ♮2: E♭   E Locrian ♭4: B♭

4

Major (2 2 1) of B♭   **Minor (2 1 2) of F**   **Phrygian (1 2 2) of D**

Lydian (2 2 2) of E   **Diminished (1 2 1) of C**

5

E Ionian ♭3: E mel. min.   B Phrygian ♮6: A mel. min.   G Lydian ♯5: E mel. min.   E♭ Lydian ♭7: B♭ mel. min.

A Mixolydian ♭6: D mel. min.   D Locrian ♮2: F mel. min.   F♯ Locrian ♭4: G mel. min.

6

F♯ Ionian ♭3: A♮   A♭ Phrygian ♮6: F♮   B Lydian ♯5: F×   G Lydian ♭7: F

C Mixolydian ♭6: A♭   E Locrian ♮2: F♯   A Locrian ♭4: D♭

EXERCISE 2

1

F13 sus4 (♭9): F Phrygian ♮6   E7 (♯11): E Lydian ♭7   Bm(maj7): B Ionian ♭3

A♭maj9 (♯5): A♭ Lydian ♯5   B♭9 (♭13): B♭ Mixolydian ♭6   D7 (♭9, ♯11): D Locrian ♭4

Fm9 (♭5): F Locrian ♮2

2

Locrian ♭4	|B♭m7	|E♭7 **E♭7 (♭9, ♯9, ♯11, ♭13)**	|A♭maj7	|D♭maj7	
Lydian ♯5	|Fm7	|B♭m7	|E♭7	|A♭maj7 (♯5) **A♭maj7 (♯5, ♯11)**	
Phrygian ♮6	|F7 **F13sus4 (♭9)**	| ✕	|B♭maj7	|E♭maj7	
Ionian ♭3	|Cm **Cm(maj7)**	| ✕	|A♭m6	|G7	
Locrian ♮2	|Fm7 (♭5) **Fm11 (♭5)**	|B♭7	|E♭m7	|A♭7	
Lydian ♭7	|Bm7	|Am7	|D7 **D13 (♯11)**	|Gmaj7	
Mixolydian ♭6	|Cm7	|F7 **F9 (♭13)**	|B♭maj7	|Gm7	

Part 2: The harmonic minor system

❶ Modes derived from the harmonic minor scale

The harmonic minor system differs from the major system in that the IIIrd and VIth degrees are lowered.

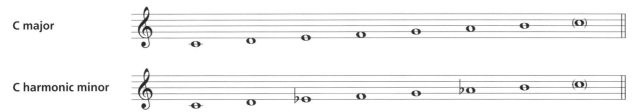

1.1 Sequence of descending 5ths

The harmonic minor system cannot be organized as a series of perfect 5ths and, as such, produces a **synthetic diatonic sequence.**

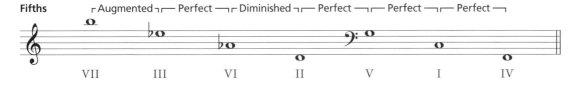

1.2 Symmetrical sequence

Although the seven degrees of the harmonic minor system cannot be organized symmetrically, mirror writing is still possible and provides the same retrograde inversion possibilities as the major harmonic system (see p. 182), as well as neighboring modes.

1.3 Origin of modes

The harmonic minor scale is another parent scale that produces seven new synthetic modes built on the seven degrees of the scale.

While we used the C major scale to illustrate the origin of the major and melodic minor systems, from a pedagogical standpoint, it is more interesting to base our analysis of the harmonic minor system on the relative minor of the major system. Note that this approach causes a slight change in the order, and a modification in the names, of the modes. Only the ACD (present in the names of the synthetic modes) indicates the difference between the synthetic modes and their parallel natural diatonic mode.

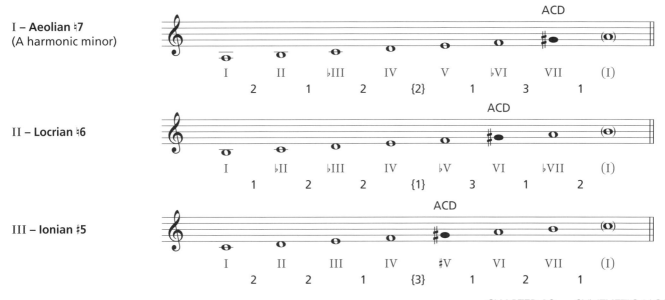

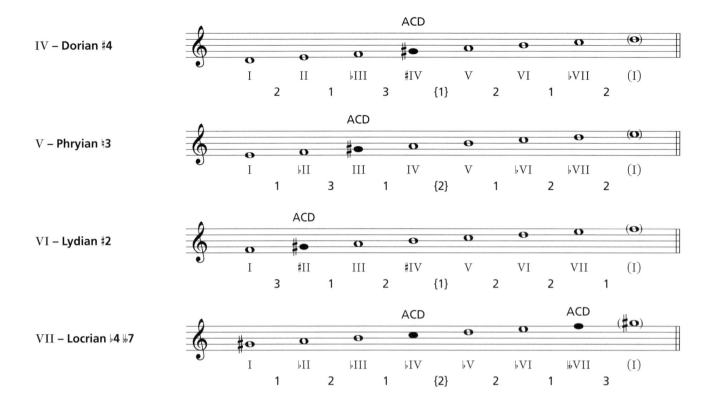

1.4 Analysis of modes

Transposing these seven synthetic modes onto the same modal tonic facilitates their analysis and makes it possible to draw comparisons between them. Here, we use the natural diatonic mode as the reference to analyze the altered degrees of the synthetic modes.

The NCDs of these synthetic modes are the same as in the parallel natural modes; only the ACDs change, depending on the synthetic mode in question.

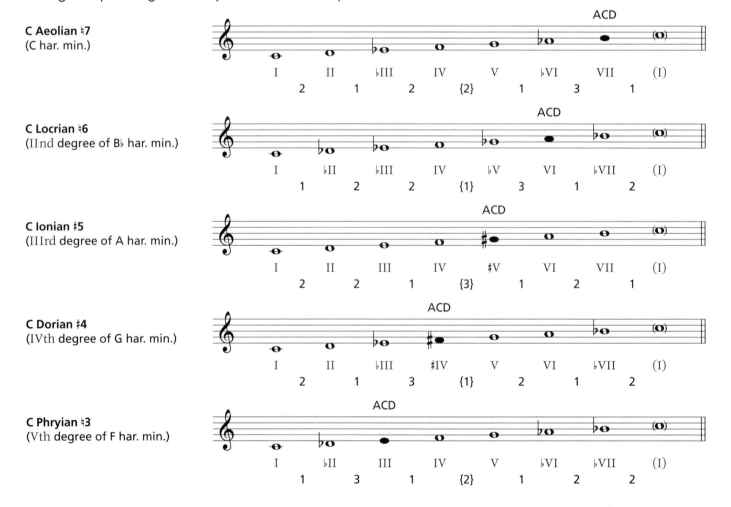

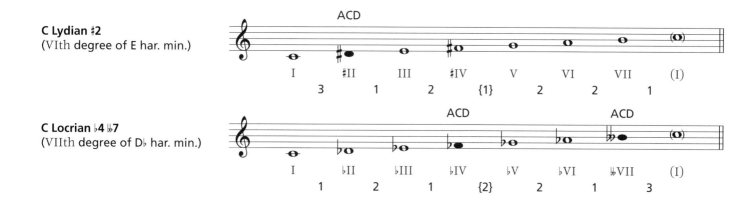

C Lydian ♯2
(VIth degree of E har. min.)

C Locrian ♭4 ♭♭7
(VIIth degree of D♭ har. min.)

1.5 Tetrachord analysis: harmonic minor modes

An analysis of the lower and upper tetrachords present in the seven synthetic modes derived from the harmonic minor is presented in the table below.

Mode	Lower tetrachord	Connector interval {i}	Upper tetrachord
Aeolian ♮7	2 1 2	2	1 3 1
Locrian ♮6	1 2 2	1	3 1 2
Ionian ♯5	2 2 1	3	1 2 1
Dorian ♯4	2 1 3	1	2 1 2
Phrygian ♮3	1 3 1	2	1 2 2
Lydian ♯2	3 1 2	1	2 2 1
Locrian ♭4 ♭♭7	1 2 1	2	2 1 3

For the first time, we encounter the augmented 2nd interval, which creates three new tetrachords:

- the harmonic tetrachord (1 3 1): *ambitus* of a perfect 4th;
- the Lydian ♯2 tetrachord (3 1 2): *ambitus* of an augmented 4th;
- the minor ♯4 tetrachord (2 1 3): *ambitus* of an augmented 4th.

As in the case of the modes derived from the melodic minor scale, none of the lower and upper tetrachords contained in these modes are the same. This system produces no palindromic modes.

1.6 Mirror harmony

Here, mirror harmony is based on the harmonic minor and harmonic major systems. This nomenclature is interesting given the logical correspondence between the names of the modes and their Altered Characteristic Degrees.

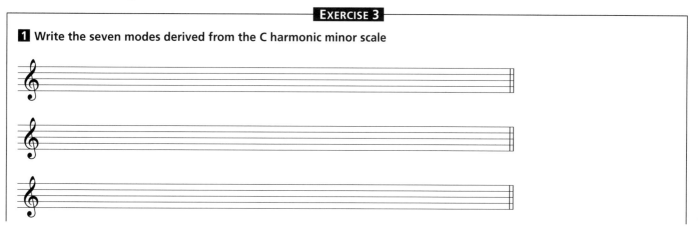

EXERCISE 3

1 Write the seven modes derived from the C harmonic minor scale

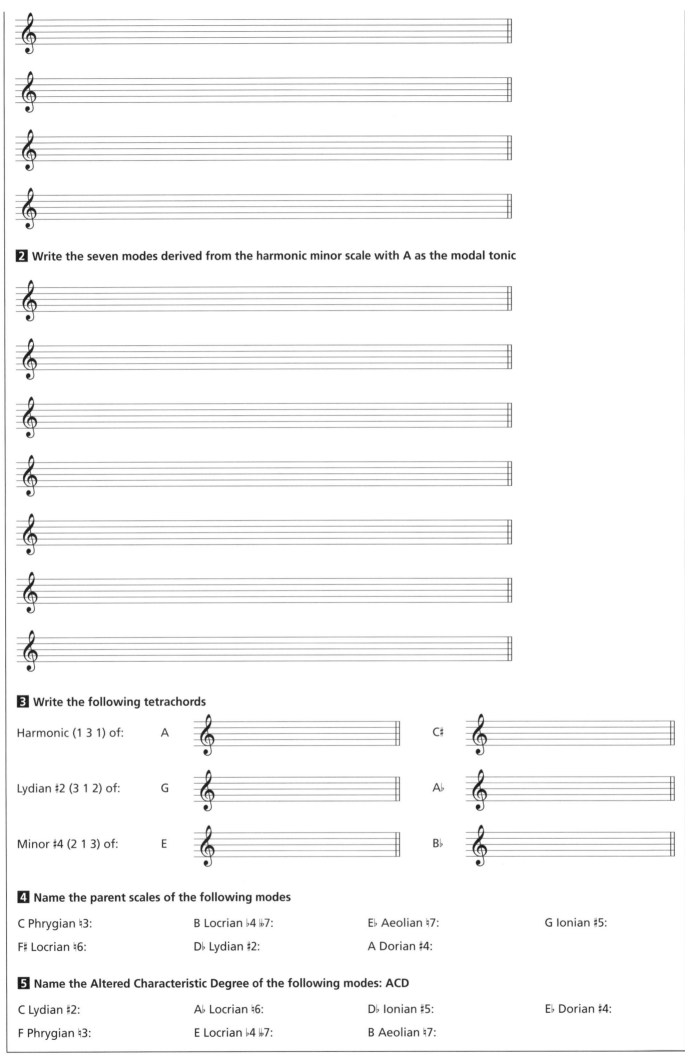

2 Write the seven modes derived from the harmonic minor scale with A as the modal tonic

3 Write the following tetrachords

Harmonic (1 3 1) of: A   C♯

Lydian ♯2 (3 1 2) of: G   A♭

Minor ♯4 (2 1 3) of: E   B♭

4 Name the parent scales of the following modes

C Phrygian ♮3:   B Locrian ♭4 ♭♭7:   E♭ Aeolian ♮7:   G Ionian ♯5:

F♯ Locrian ♮6:   D♭ Lydian ♯2:   A Dorian ♯4:

5 Name the Altered Characteristic Degree of the following modes: ACD

C Lydian ♯2:   A♭ Locrian ♮6:   D♭ Ionian ♯5:   E♭ Dorian ♯4:

F Phrygian ♮3:   E Locrian ♭4 ♭♭7:   B Aeolian ♮7:

Answers, p. 224-225

❷ Using harmonic minor modes in themes

2.1 Aeolian ♮7

The Aeolian ♮7 mode is associated with tonic minor chords (with a tonic function). In addition to the major 2nd and the perfect 4th, the presence of the NCD (minor 6th) and the ACD (major 7th) create a diminished tetrachord. When played over a tonic, this tetrachord creates a dominant/tonic (V/I). In the example below, measure 3 expresses all the notes in C Aeolian ♮7.

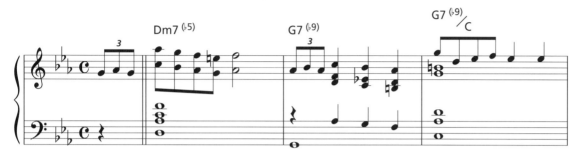

2.2 Locrian ♮6

Less frequently encountered than the Locrian ♮2, the Locrian ♮6 mode (with a major 13th ACD) is associated with Xm7(♭5) chords. Em13(♭5) in measure 1 below features C♯ (the ACD of E Locrian ♮6), the first note of a voice-leading passage ascending by half-step to reach F in measure 3.

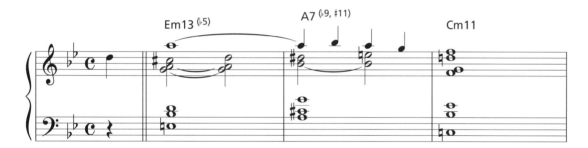

The F♯m13(♭5) chord below utilizes D♯, the ACD of F♯ Locrian ♮6.

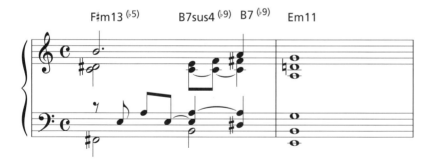

2.3 Ionian ♯5

The Ionian ♯5 mode is used with Xmaj7(♯5) chords. This mode sounds similar to the Lydian ♯5 (derived from the melodic minor), but differs in that it also features the augmented 5th and perfect 4th. The Ionian ♯5 is therefore recommended for harmonizing melodies where the 11th of the chord is voiced in the melody.

In major tonalities, this mode is often associated with a dominant/tonic (V/I) chord. In measure 2 below, the E♭maj7(♯5) chord voices the perfect 11th (A♭) in the melody and the augmented 5th (B♮) in the harmonization. This measure expresses all the notes of E♭ Ionian ♯5.

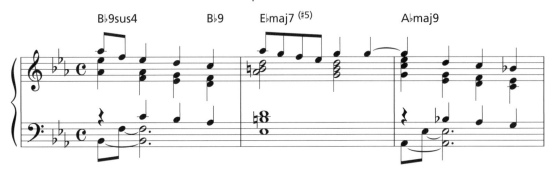

The melodic context in the following example is similar. All the notes of F Ionian ♯5 are voiced in measure 1. In the harmonization of the first beat of measure 1, we can hear a C♯dim7/F, which is the dominant/tonic chord, C7(♭9)/F. This mode is also used with appoggiatura[11] chords.

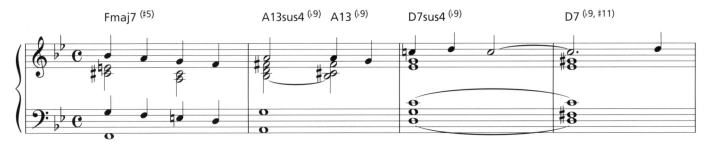

2.4 Dorian ♯4

The Dorian ♯4 mode is associated with tonic minor chords such as Xm6, Xm9, and Xm6/9. This mode features the augmented 11th of the chord, which, together with the major 6th (Dorian NCD) and the 9th, form a major triad, one whole-step above the root.

Because the 9th of the Cm9(♯11) chords in the examples above are voiced in the melody, it is possible to play a D major triad played over the C minor chords. This is an example of a polychord,[12] which may also be represented by the symbol:

$$\frac{D}{Cm}$$

---

11 An appoggiatura is a non-diatonic note that precedes the principal note in the melody, generally by half-step either from above or from below.
12 A polychord is a complex chord formed by stacking two (or more) different chords on top of each other.

The Cm9(♯11) chords in the previous example feature all the notes in C Dorian ♯4 (IVth degree of G harmonic minor). Voicing the root of the chord (in brackets) is optional, since it can be played by the bass player. The Dorian ♯4 mode can also be used when the theme expresses a modal plateau.

In the example below, the melody features all the notes of the Dorian mode, with the exception of the 4th. We could therefore opt to express Dorian ♯4 and its NCD by using a D major triad, which includes the 9, ♯11, and 13 of C Dorian ♯4.

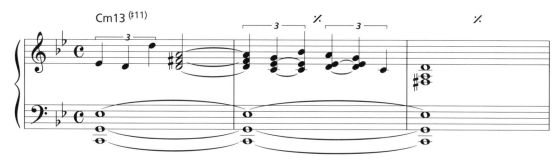

All the notes in D Dorian ♯4 are expressed in measure 2 below, notably with the ACD (G♯) voiced in the melody. Dorian ♯4 is also used with appoggiatura chords.

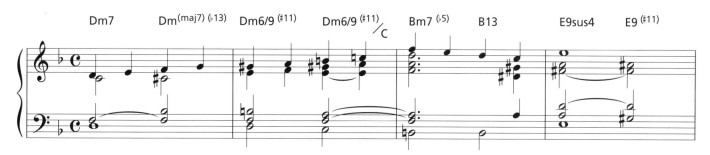

2.5 Phrygian ♮3

Harmonically, the Phrygian ♮3 is rarely used in a tonal context or in a cadence. From a melodic point of view, however, it can be used with X7(♭9, ♭13) chords when composing and in modal music (notably Spanish music).

In general, it is interesting to use modes (synthetic and natural) over a pedal.

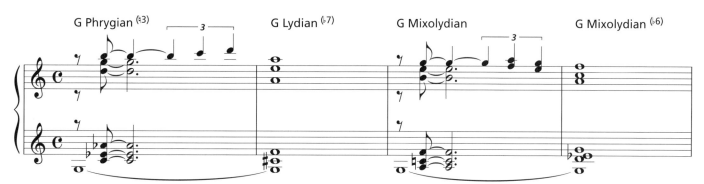

The first chord in the above example should be Gmaj7. However, we have chosen to include an E♭ and A♭ in the lower staff, which, with the addition of the C, form an A♭ major triad. These notes are derived from G Phrygian ♮3 and perceived as an unresolved descending appoggiatura.

Because of the G pedal throughout the passage, different modes can be used for each measure to express a change in mood, produce a strong contrast, and offer new colors for improvising.

2.6 Lydian ♯2

The Lydian ♯2 mode is often associated with tonic major chords such as Xmaj7, Xmaj7(♯11), and Xmaj7(♯9). This mode can be used when a diatonic note, the NCD, or the ACD is voiced in the melody.

In measure 1 below, the major 7th of E♭maj is voiced in the melody (D). While this suggests the Ionian mode, we have chosen to modify the mode. Our harmonization features all the notes of the E♭ Lydian ♯2 mode. Lydian ♯2 is also used with appoggiatura chords.

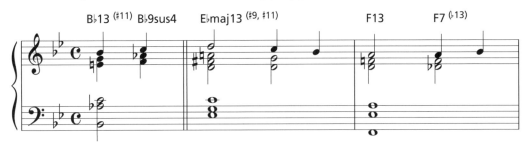

2.7 Locrian ♭4 ♭♭7

This mode is associated with Xdim7 chords. Although it can be used, performers generally prefer the H-W diminished scale.[13] Locrian ♭4 ♭♭7 nevertheless has a very rich sound that is interesting for composition purposes and in modal music.

❸ Answers

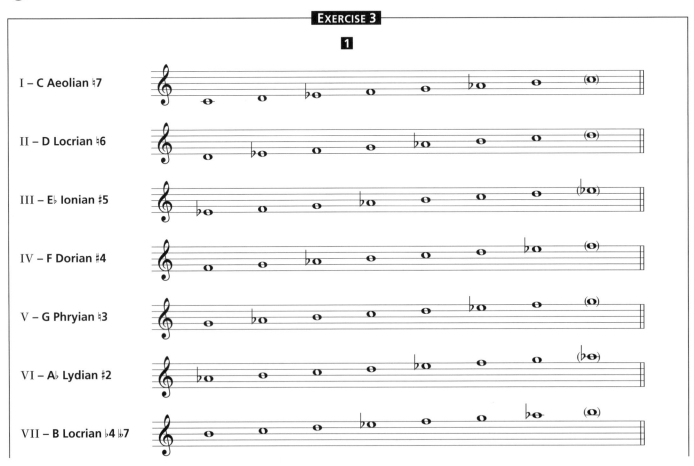

---

13 Also referred to as Messiaen Mode 2; a symmetrical scale comprising a progression of half-step/whole-step intervals with limited transposition possibilities.

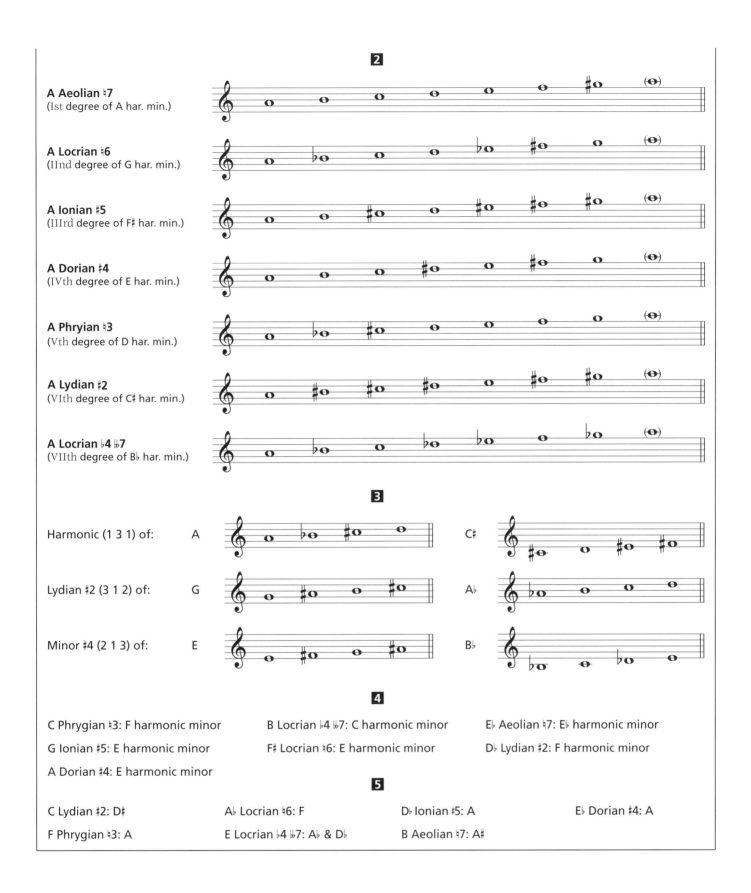

2

A Aeolian ♭7
(Ist degree of A har. min.)

A Locrian ♮6
(IInd degree of G har. min.)

A Ionian ♯5
(IIIrd degree of F♯ har. min.)

A Dorian ♯4
(IVth degree of E har. min.)

A Phryian ♮3
(Vth degree of D har. min.)

A Lydian ♯2
(VIth degree of C♯ har. min.)

A Locrian ♭4 ♭7
(VIIth degree of B♭ har. min.)

3

Harmonic (1 3 1) of: A   C♯

Lydian ♯2 (3 1 2) of: G   A♭

Minor ♯4 (2 1 3) of: E   B♭

4

C Phrygian ♮3: F harmonic minor   B Locrian ♭4 ♭7: C harmonic minor   E♭ Aeolian ♮7: E♭ harmonic minor

G Ionian ♯5: E harmonic minor   F♯ Locrian ♮6: E harmonic minor   D♭ Lydian ♯2: F harmonic minor

A Dorian ♯4: E harmonic minor

5

C Lydian ♯2: D♯   A♭ Locrian ♮6: F   D♭ Ionian ♯5: A   E♭ Dorian ♯4: A

F Phrygian ♮3: A   E Locrian ♭4 ♭7: A♭ & D♭   B Aeolian ♮7: A♯

Part 3: The harmonic major system

❶ Modes derived from the harmonic major scale

The harmonic major system differs from the diatonic major system in that the VIth degree is flatted. It is like a harmonic minor scale with a raised IIIrd degree.

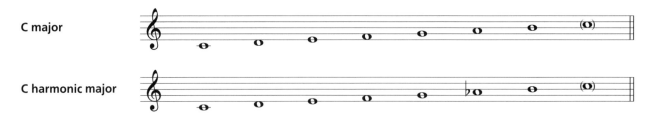

1.1 Sequence of descending 5ths

As in the harmonic minor, the harmonic major system cannot be organized as a series of perfect 5ths and, as such, produces a **synthetic diatonic sequence**.

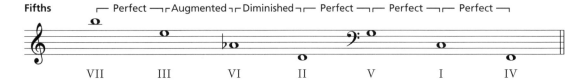

1.2 Symmetrical sequence

Although the seven degrees of the harmonic major system cannot be organized symmetrically, mirror writing can be used to identify the inverted and neighboring modes.

1.3 Origin of modes

The harmonic major scale is another parent scale that produces seven new synthetic modes built on the seven degrees of the scale. Taking the seven notes of the C harmonic major parent scale, we can determine the seven synthetic modes related to this system:

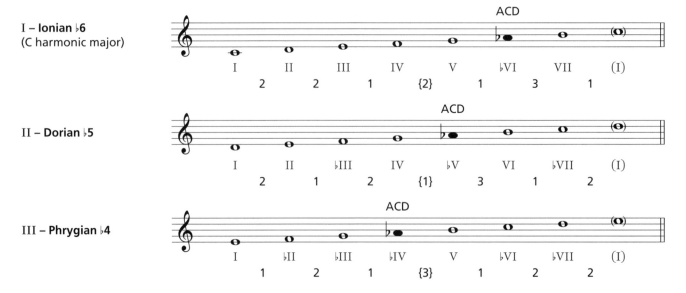

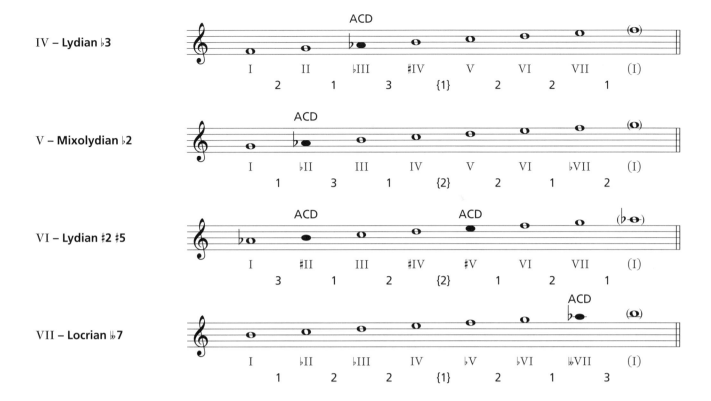

IV – Lydian ♭3

	I	II	♭III	♯IV	V	VI	VII	(I)
	2	1	3	{1}	2	2	1	

V – Mixolydian ♭2

	I	♭II	III	IV	V	VI	♭VII	(I)
	1	3	1	{2}	2	1	2	

VI – Lydian ♯2 ♯5

	I	♯II	III	♯IV	♯V	VI	VII	(I)
	3	1	2	{2}	1	2	1	

VII – Locrian ♭♭7

	I	♭II	♭III	IV	♭V	♭VI	♭♭VII	(I)
	1	2	2	{1}	2	1	3	

1.4 Analysis of modes

Transposing these seven synthetic modes onto the same modal tonic facilitates the analysis and makes it possible to draw comparisons between them. The major scale is still the reference scale used to indicate the altered degrees present in the synthetic modes derived from the harmonic major system.

The NCDs of these synthetic modes are the same as in the parallel natural modes; only the ACDs change, depending on the synthetic mode in question.

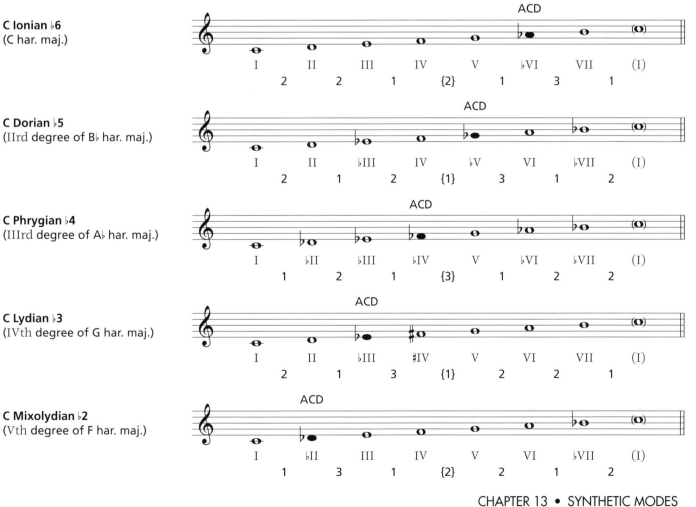

C Ionian ♭6
(C har. maj.)

	I	II	III	IV	V	♭VI	VII	(I)
	2	2	1	{2}	1	3	1	

C Dorian ♭5
(IIrd degree of B♭ har. maj.)

	I	II	♭III	IV	♭V	VI	♭VII	(I)
	2	1	2	{1}	3	1	2	

C Phrygian ♭4
(IIIrd degree of A♭ har. maj.)

	I	♭II	♭III	♭IV	V	♭VI	♭VII	(I)
	1	2	1	{3}	1	2	2	

C Lydian ♭3
(IVth degree of G har. maj.)

	I	II	♭III	♯IV	V	VI	VII	(I)
	2	1	3	{1}	2	2	1	

C Mixolydian ♭2
(Vth degree of F har. maj.)

	I	♭II	III	IV	V	VI	♭VII	(I)
	1	3	1	{2}	2	1	2	

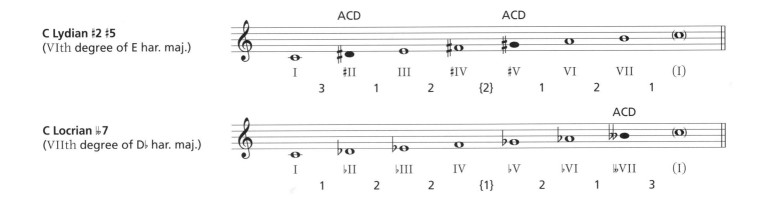

C Lydian ♯2 ♯5
(VIth degree of E har. maj.)

C Locrian ♭♭7
(VIIth degree of D♭ har. maj.)

1.5 Tetrachord analysis: harmonic-major modes

An analysis of the lower and upper tetrachords present in the seven synthetic modes derived from the harmonic major scale is presented in the table below.

Mode	Lower tetrachord	Connector interval {i}	Upper tetrachord
Ionian ♭6	2 2 1	2	1 3 1
Dorian ♭5	2 1 2	1	3 1 2
Phrygian ♭4	1 2 1	3	1 2 2
Lydian ♭3	2 1 3	1	2 2 1
Mixolydian ♭2	1 3 1	2	2 1 2
Lydian ♯2 ♯5	3 1 2	2	1 2 1
Locrian ♭♭7	1 2 2	1	2 1 3

This system offers no new tetrachords. As in the case of the modes derived from the other minor systems, none of the lower and upper tetrachords contained in these synthetic modes are the same. No palindromic modes are present.

1.6 Mirror harmony

In this system, mirror harmony is based on the harmonic minor and harmonic major scales. This nomenclature is interesting because of the logical correspondence between the names of the modes and their Altered Characteristic Degrees.

1.7 Tetrachord summary table

The chart below shows the harmonic minor modes and their harmonic major retrograde inversions:

Mode *harmonic minor*	Lower tetrachord	{i}	Upper tetrachord	Retrograde inversion *harmonic major*	Lower tetrachord	{i}	Upper tetrachord
Aeolian ♮7	2 1 2	2	1 3 1	Mixolydian ♭2	1 3 1	2	2 1 2
Locrian ♮6	1 2 2	1	3 1 2	Lydian ♭3	2 1 3	1	2 2 1
Ionian ♯5	2 2 1	3	1 2 1	Phrygian ♭4	1 2 1	3	1 2 2
Dorian ♯4	2 1 3	1	2 1 2	Dorian ♭5	2 1 2	1	3 1 2
Phrygian ♮3	1 3 1	2	1 2 2	Ionian ♭6	2 2 1	2	1 3 1
Lydian ♯2	3 1 2	1	2 2 1	Locrian ♭♭7	1 2 2	1	2 1 3
Locrian ♭4 ♭♭7	1 2 1	2	2 1 3	Lydian ♯2 ♯5	3 1 2	2	1 2 1

1 Write the seven modes derived from the F harmonic major scale

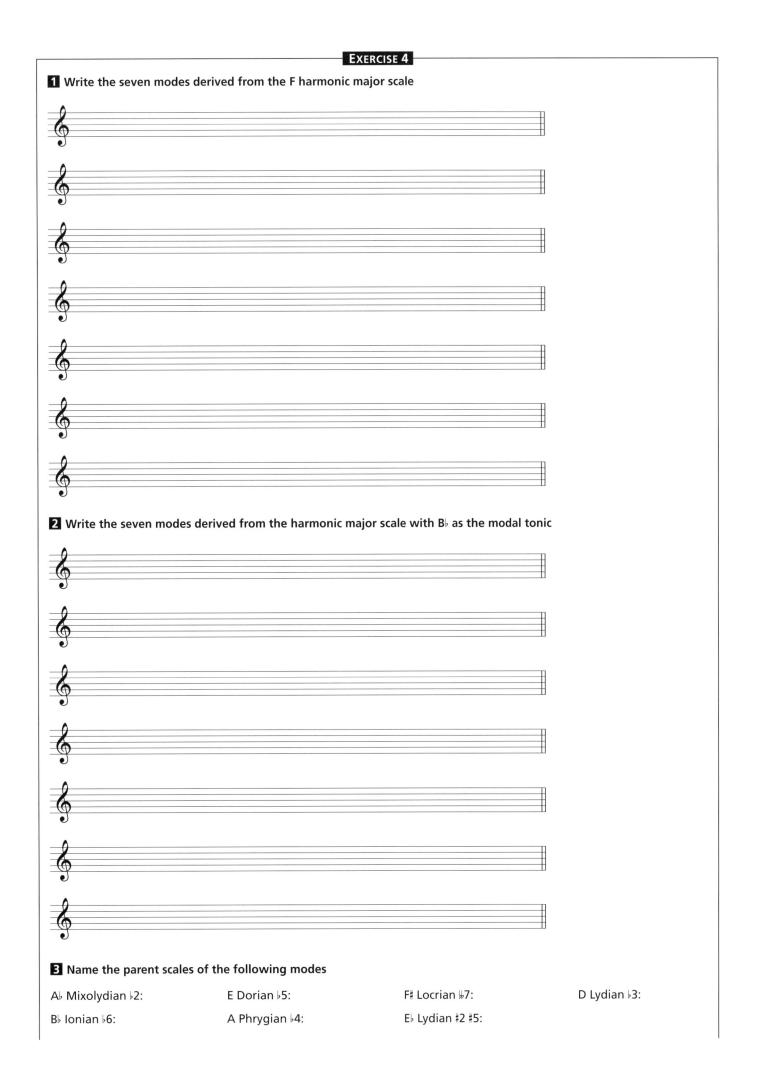

2 Write the seven modes derived from the harmonic major scale with B♭ as the modal tonic

3 Name the parent scales of the following modes

A♭ Mixolydian ♭2:   E Dorian ♭5:   F♯ Locrian ♮7:   D Lydian ♭3:

B♭ Ionian ♭6:   A Phrygian ♭4:   E♭ Lydian ♯2 ♯5:

Answers, p. 234-235

❷ Using harmonic major modes in themes

2.1 Ionian ♭6[14]

The Ionian ♭6 mode is associated with Xmaj9(♭13) chords that express the perfect 5th and the minor 13th. The presence of the perfect 4th in the chord makes it possible to play a descending appoggiatura movement in 6ths. This is the case in the following example, where A♭maj9(♭13) in measure 3 features a D♭ descending to C, and an F♭ descending to E♭. The 3rd of the chord is in the melody; this measure expresses all the notes of the A♭ Ionian ♭6.

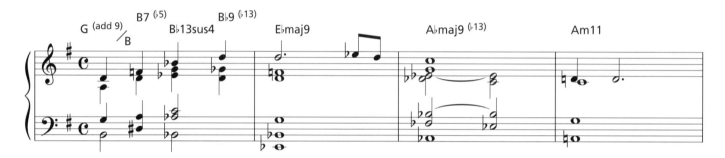

Measures 4 and 5 below feature all the notes of G Ionian ♭6. The modal identity of Gmaj9(♭13) is expressed on beat 1 in measure 4 with the 3rd (B) in the melody. In general, the minor 13th is voiced below the perfect 5th of the chord.

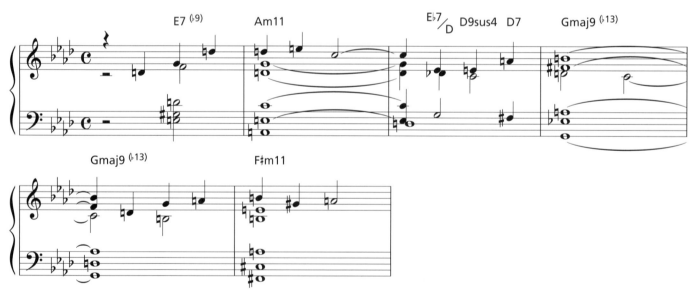

Note that these appoggiatura movements, although interesting, are not compulsory since the chord has its own modal identity and, therefore, does not have to be resolved.

---

14 Also known as the Rimsky-Korsakov Scale.

In the next example, we use the same mode to harmonize Fmaj9(♭13) in measure 2, which voices the major 7th (E) in the melody. The D♭, in the bass clef, continues its descent to C, then to B (the 5th of the tonic chord). This mode is also associated with appoggiatura chords.

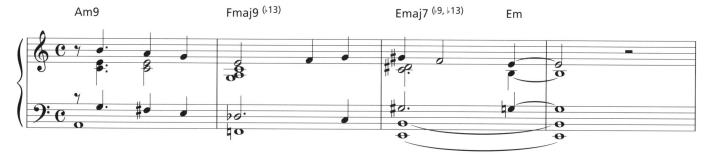

2.2 Dorian ♭5

We associate Dorian ♭5 with Xm7(♭5) chords, notably when the diminished 5th is in the melody. If we consider the diminished 5th as the enharmonic equivalent of the augmented 4th, this mode can be used to play a major triad whose tonic is one whole step above the root.

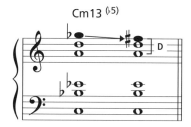

By treating the E♭ in measure 2 of the melody below as the enharmonic equivalent of D♯, we can play a B major triad above A minor. F♯ (the NCD of the Dorian mode) ascends chromatically to G, the minor 7th of the chord, while the B♮ rises to meet the C in the melody.

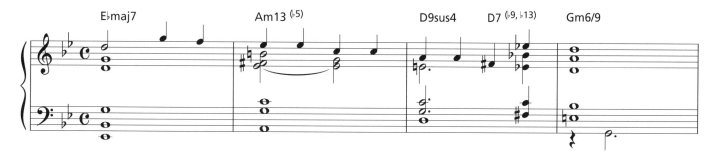

In the following example, the diminished 5th of the Bm13(♭5) chord in measure 1 is voiced in the melody. By adding the C♯ and the G♯ in the inner voices, we enharmonically obtain a C♯ major triad. The G♯ on the first eighth note of beat 2 in measure 1 rises to A on the second eighth note to form a major 3rd with the C♯ in the second voice. The two notes comprising this 3rd interval (A and C♯) ascend chromatically to reach the minor 7th and diminished 5th (B♭ and D) of the E7(♭9, ♭5) chord on the 3rd beat.

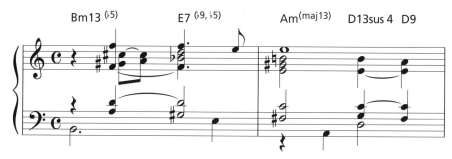

2.3 Phrygian ♭4

This mode is rarely used; because the diminished 4th is the enharmonic equivalent of the major 3rd, it suggests a dominant chord, in which case the most appropriate choices are the Mixolydian mode and the H-W scale, etc.

2.4 Lydian ♭3[15]

Lydian ♭3 is associated with minor Xm(maj9) chords, which also feature the augmented 11th and sometimes the major 13th. This is notably the case when one of the extension notes or the major 7th is voiced in the melody.

In the following example, the major 9th of the Gm(maj13#11) chord is featured in the melody in measure 2. This voicing makes it possible to express all of the notes in G Lydian ♭3. The Gm11 chord on beat 3 of the measure is voiced in its third inversion; D and B♭ remain in their original positions; F♯ drops to F♮, and E and C♯ converge toward D.

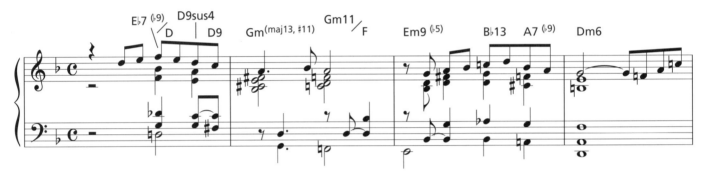

In the next excerpt, the major 7th of Dm(maj9) in measure 1 is voiced in the melody. The additions of the augmented 11th and major 13th produce a particularly rich harmonization of the chord, which is then expressed in a simpler way on beat 1 of measure 2.

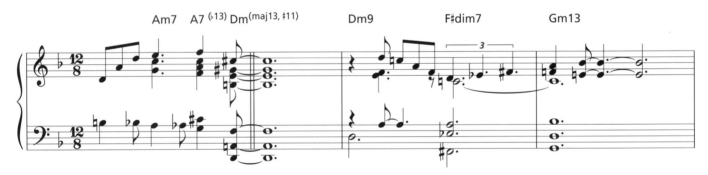

This mode is also associated with appoggiatura chords.

---

15 Lydian minor.

2.5 Mixolydian ♭2

Mixolydian ♭2 is associated with X13(♭9) chords. The following harmonization utilizes the natural Mixolydian mode (in measure 2) and the Mixolydian ♭2 (measure 4). By considering the minor 9th of the G13(♭9) chord (= A♭ as its enharmonic equivalent (= G♯), we obtain a major triad (E, G♯, B) whose tonic is the 13th of the chord, as in measure 4.

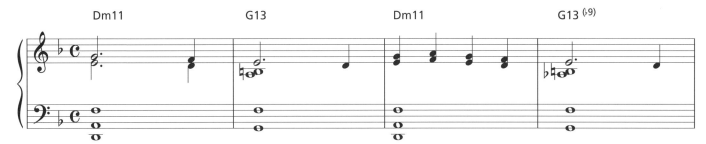

In the next example, the E13(♭9) in measure 2 features a C♯ major chord, where the F in the melody is heard as an E♯.

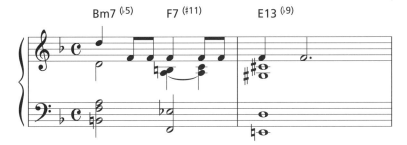

Although interesting, this mode is quite limited. The H/W diminished scale is a more appropriate scale choice for harmonizing dominant chords with major and minor triads.

2.6 Lydian ♯2 ♯5

Lydian ♯2 ♯5 is associated with major chords, such as the Xmaj7(♯5) with augmented 9ths and 11ths, and notably when the major 7th or one of the chord's extension notes is voiced in the melody. On beat 1 of measure 2 below, the 7th of E♭maj7 is voiced in the melody. We can amplify the impact of this chord by modifying its tetrachord structure (i.e., by augmenting the 5th) and adding two extension notes derived from G Lydian ♯2 ♯5, namely the augmented 9th (F♯) and the augmented 11th (A). Note that the introduction of these two notes (the ACDs of the mode) is prepared by a chromatic ascent in measure 1.

In the next example, measure 1 begins with a Cmaj7 chord harmonized with C Lydian ♯2 ♯5. The extension notes voiced in Cmaj7(♯5, ♯9, ♯11) then converge toward the major 9th and perfect 5th of the Cmaj9 chord (G and D).

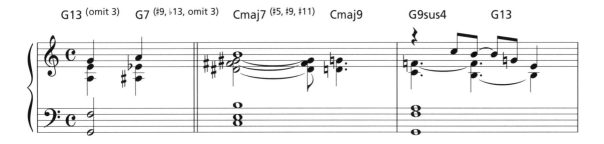

This mode is also associated with appoggiatura chords.

2.7 Locrian ♭♭7

While this mode is associated with Xdim7 tetrads, we recommend using the W/H diminished scale.

❸ Answers

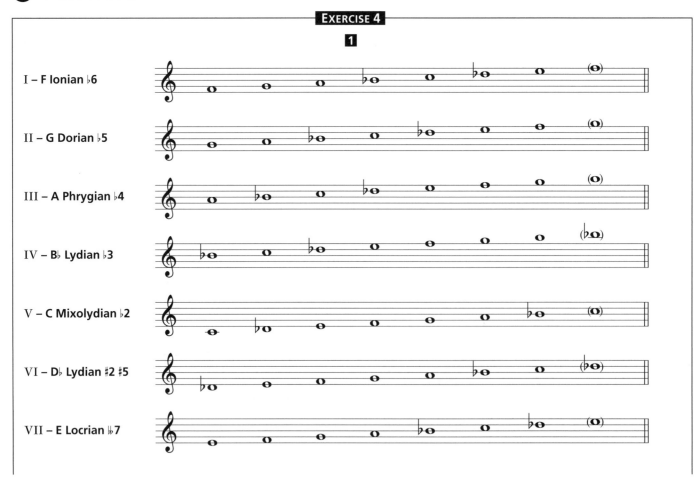

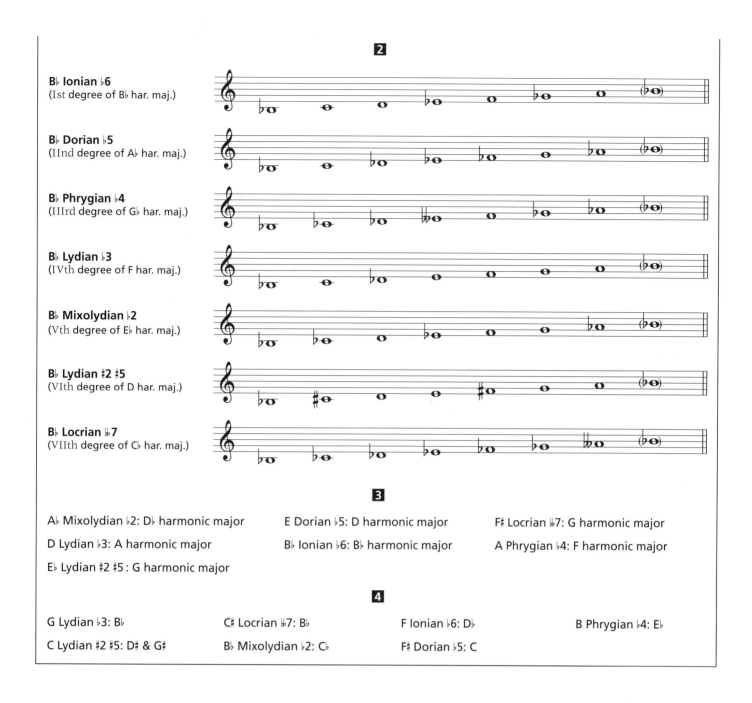

2

B♭ Ionian ♭6
(Ist degree of B♭ har. maj.)

B♭ Dorian ♭5
(IInd degree of A♭ har. maj.)

B♭ Phrygian ♭4
(IIIrd degree of G♭ har. maj.)

B♭ Lydian ♭3
(IVth degree of F har. maj.)

B♭ Mixolydian ♭2
(Vth degree of E♭ har. maj.)

B♭ Lydian ♯2 ♯5
(VIth degree of D har. maj.)

B♭ Locrian ♭♭7
(VIIth degree of C♭ har. maj.)

3

A♭ Mixolydian ♭2: D♭ harmonic major   E Dorian ♭5: D harmonic major   F♯ Locrian ♭♭7: G harmonic major

D Lydian ♭3: A harmonic major   B♭ Ionian ♭6: B♭ harmonic major   A Phrygian ♭4: F harmonic major

E♭ Lydian ♯2 ♯5 : G harmonic major

4

G Lydian ♭3: B♭   C♯ Locrian ♭♭7: B♭   F Ionian ♭6: D♭   B Phrygian ♭4: E♭

C Lydian ♯2 ♯5: D♯ & G♯   B♭ Mixolydian ♭2: C♭   F♯ Dorian ♭5: C

Part 4: The double harmonic major system

❶ Modes derived from the double harmonic major scale

The double harmonic major system differs from the diatonic major system in that both the IInd and VIth degrees are flatted.

C major

C double harmonic major

1.1 Sequence of descending 5ths

The seven degrees in the double harmonic major system cannot be organized as a series of perfect 5ths.

1.2 Symmetrical sequence

The double harmonic major system can be reorganized symmetrically.

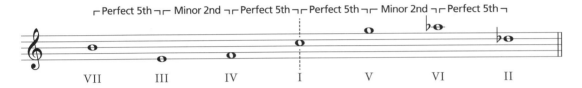

1.3 Origin of modes

The double harmonic major scale is another parent scale that produces seven new synthetic modes built on the seven degrees of the scale. Taking the seven notes of the C double harmonic major parent scale, we can determine the seven synthetic modes related to this system:

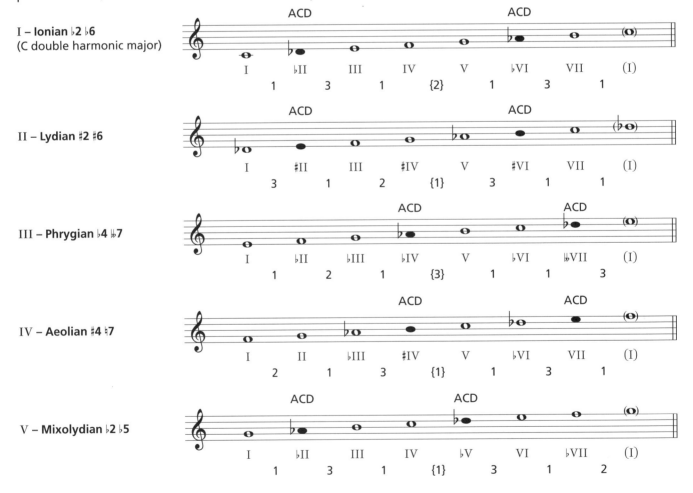

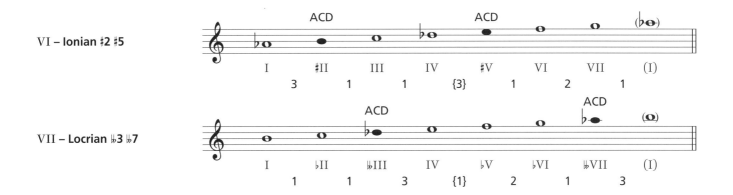

VI – Ionian ♯2 ♯5

VII – Locrian ♭♭3 ♭7

1.4 Analysis of modes

Transposing these seven synthetic modes onto the same modal tonic facilitates their analysis and makes it possible to draw comparisons between them.

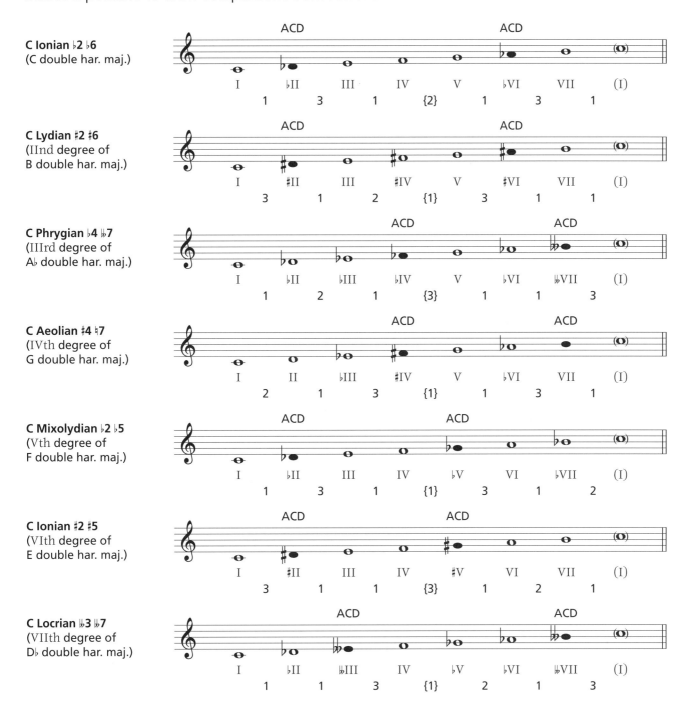

C Ionian ♭2 ♭6
(C double har. maj.)

C Lydian ♯2 ♯6
(IInd degree of
B double har. maj.)

C Phrygian ♭4 ♭♭7
(IIIrd degree of
A♭ double har. maj.)

C Aeolian ♯4 ♮7
(IVth degree of
G double har. maj.)

C Mixolydian ♭2 ♭5
(Vth degree of
F double har. maj.)

C Ionian ♯2 ♯5
(VIth degree of
E double har. maj.)

C Locrian ♭♭3 ♭7
(VIIth degree of
D♭ double har. maj.)

1.5 Tetrachord analysis

The chart below shows the lower and upper tetrachords present in the seven synthetic modes derived from the double harmonic major modes:

Mode	Lower tetrachord	Connector interval {i}	Upper tetrachord
Ionian ♭2 ♭6	1 3 1	2	1 3 1
Lydian #2 #6	3 1 2	1	3 1 1
Phrygian ♭4 ♭♭7	1 2 1	3	1 1 3
Aeolian #4 ♮7	2 1 3	1	1 3 1
Mixolydian ♭2 ♭5	1 3 1	1	3 1 2
Ionian #2 #5	3 1 1	3	1 2 1
Locrian ♭♭3 ♭♭7	1 1 3	1	2 1 3

The analysis above produces two new tetrachords:

- the **Phrygian ♭♭3 tetrachord** (1 1 3): *ambitus* of a perfect 4th;
- the **Major #2 tetrachord** (3 1 1): *ambitus* of a perfect 4th.

EXERCISE 5

1 Write the seven modes derived from the D double harmonic major scale

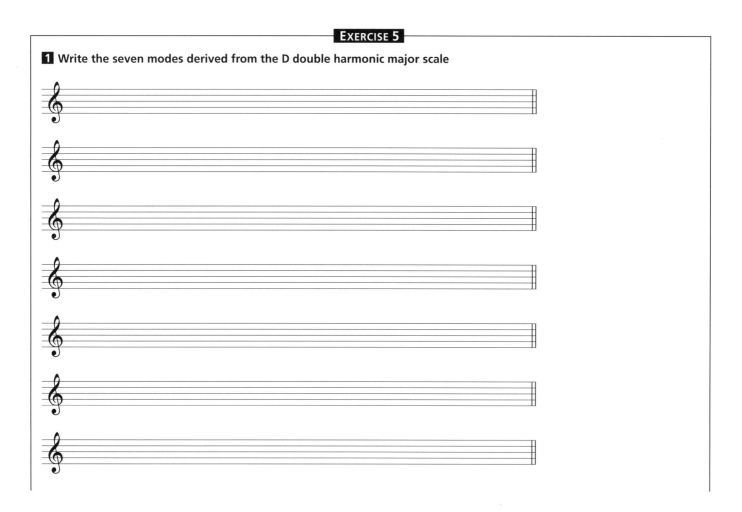

2 Write the seven modes derived from the double harmonic major scale with E♭ as the modal tonic

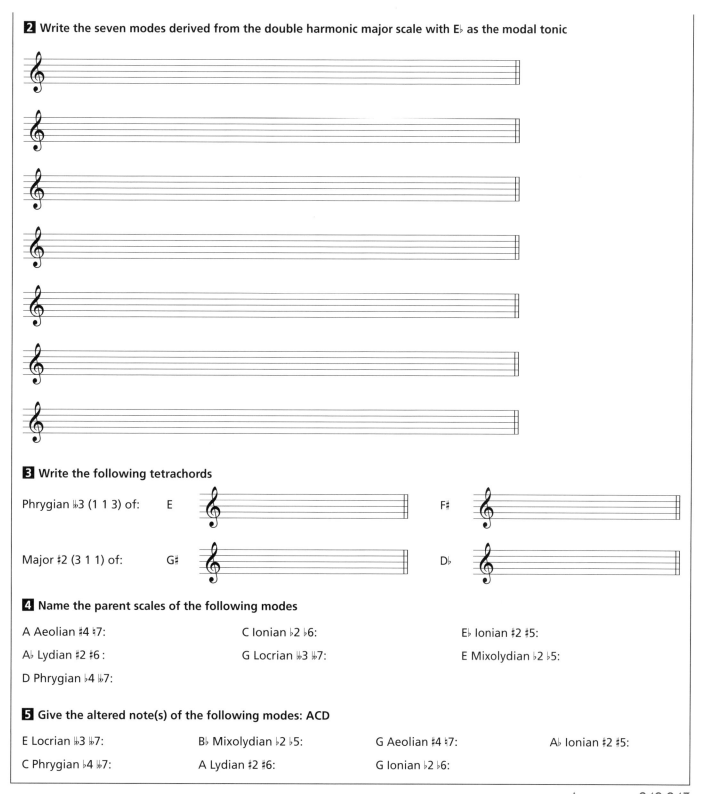

3 Write the following tetrachords

Phrygian ♭♭3 (1 1 3) of: E   F♯

Major ♯2 (3 1 1) of: G♯   D♭

4 Name the parent scales of the following modes

A Aeolian ♯4 ♮7:   C Ionian ♭2 ♭6:   E♭ Ionian ♯2 ♯5:

A♭ Lydian ♯2 ♯6 :   G Locrian ♮3 ♮7:   E Mixolydian ♭2 ♭5:

D Phrygian ♭4 ♭♭7:

5 Give the altered note(s) of the following modes: ACD

E Locrian ♮3 ♮7:   B♭ Mixolydian ♭2 ♭5:   G Aeolian ♯4 ♮7:   A♭ Ionian ♯2 ♯5:

C Phrygian ♭4 ♭♭7:   A Lydian ♯2 ♯6:   G Ionian ♭2 ♭6:

Answers, p. 242-243

1.6 Reorganization of the double harmonic major scale

By reorganizing the symmetrical scale, we can obtain the neighboring modes and thus classify the modes from "darkest" to "brightest."

Modes derived from C double harmonic major	Mode
	B Locrian ♭♭3 ♭7
	E Phrygian ♭4 ♭♭7
	F Aeolian ♯4 ♮7
	C Ionian ♭2 ♭6
	G Mixolydian ♭2 ♭5
	A♭ Ionian ♯2 ♯5
	D♭ Lydian ♯2 ♯6

1.7 Mirror harmony

Mirror writing is possible, based on the reorganization of the double harmonic major system. The inverted and neighboring modes are contained in the same system.

The relationships between the following modes remain the same:

- Lydian and Locrian;
- Phrygian and Ionian;
- Aeolian and Mixolydian.

Each mode has two ACDs that have to be inverted to obtain their inverted mode:

- Ionian ♭2 ♭6 remains unchanged because it is a palindrome;
- Lydian ♯2 ♯6 becomes Locrian ♭♭3 ♭7;
- Phrygian ♭4 ♭♭7 becomes Ionian ♯2 ♯5;
- Aeolian ♯4 ♮7 becomes Mixolydian ♭2 ♭5.

1.8 Tetrachord summary table

The chart below shows the double harmonic major modes and their retrograde inversions:

Mode	Lower tetrachord	{i}	Upper tetrachord	Retrograde inversion	Lower tetrachord	{i}	Upper tetrachord
Ionian ♭2 ♭6	1 3 1	2	1 3 1	Ionian ♭2 ♭6	1 3 1	2	1 3 1
Lydian ♯2 ♯6	3 1 2	1	3 1 1	Locrian ♭♭3 ♭♭7	1 1 3	1	2 1 3
Phrygian ♭4 ♭♭7	1 2 1	3	1 1 3	Ionian ♯2 ♯5	3 1 1	3	1 2 1
Aeolian ♯4 ♮7	2 1 3	1	1 3 1	Mixolydian ♭2 ♭5	1 3 1	1	3 1 2

❷ Using modes derived from the double harmonic major scale

Although we can attempt to attribute a color derived from the double major harmonic major scale to functional chords, in practice, some of these modes are rarely used because they are considered less interesting than the modes derived from the other parent scales we have studied.

Ionian ♭2 ♭6

♭II(♯6)/I.

Lydian ♯2 ♯6

Xmaj7(♯9, ♯11, ♯13).

Phrygian ♭4 ♭♭7[16]

Xdim7; we recommend using the W/H diminished scale.[17]

Aeolian ♯4 ♮7[18]

Xm(maj9, ♯11, ♭13); use the voicing 1 5 3 4 6 7 9 10.

Mixolydian ♭2 ♭5[19]

X7(♭5, ♭9, 13); use the H/W diminished scale.

Ionian ♯2 ♯5[20]

Xmaj7(♯5, ♯9); use Lydian ♯2 ♯5.

Locrian ♭♭3 ♭♭7

Not a functional chord. Its melodic use in jazz is rare.

---

16   Also known as the Ultraphrygian.
17   The W/H symmetric scale has limited transposition possibilities and comprises a progression of whole-step/half-step intervals.
18   Also known as the Hungarian minor.
19   Also known as the Oriental mode.
20   Also known as the Ionian augmented ♯2.

❸ Answers

Exercise 5

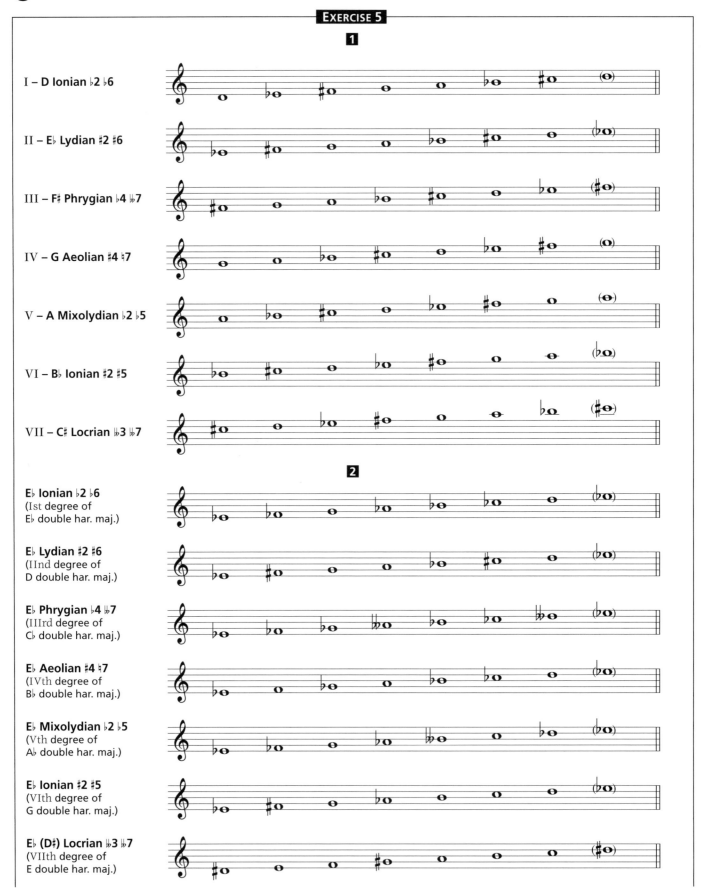

1

I – D Ionian ♭2 ♭6

II – E♭ Lydian ♯2 ♯6

III – F♯ Phrygian ♭4 ♭7

IV – G Aeolian ♯4 ♭7

V – A Mixolydian ♭2 ♭5

VI – B♭ Ionian ♯2 ♯5

VII – C♯ Locrian ♭♭3 ♭7

2

E♭ Ionian ♭2 ♭6
(Ist degree of
E♭ double har. maj.)

E♭ Lydian ♯2 ♯6
(IInd degree of
D double har. maj.)

E♭ Phrygian ♭4 ♭7
(IIIrd degree of
C♭ double har. maj.)

E♭ Aeolian ♯4 ♭7
(IVth degree of
B♭ double har. maj.)

E♭ Mixolydian ♭2 ♭5
(Vth degree of
A♭ double har. maj.)

E♭ Ionian ♯2 ♯5
(VIth degree of
G double har. maj.)

E♭ (D♯) Locrian ♭♭3 ♭7
(VIIth degree of
E double har. maj.)

Phrygian ♭♭3 (1 1 3) of: E

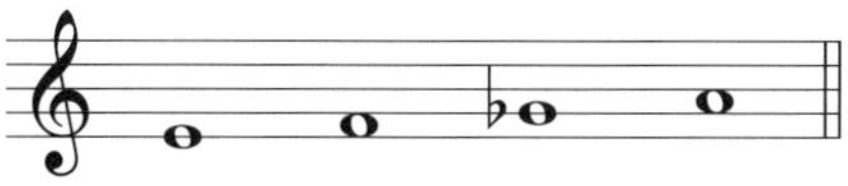

F♯

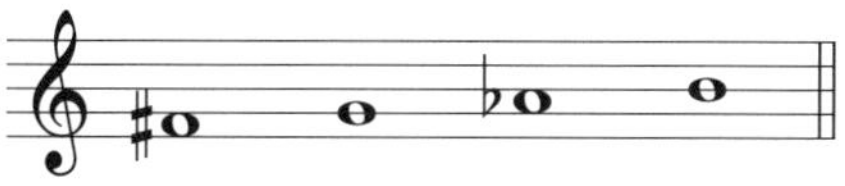

Major ♯2 (3 1 1) of: G♯

D♭

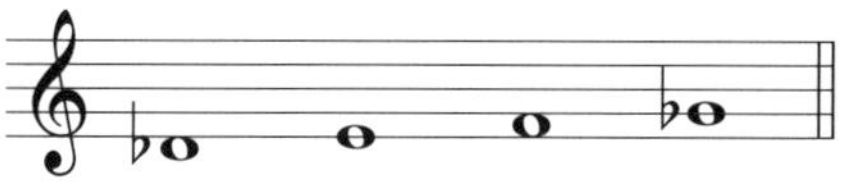

4

A Aeolian ♯4 ♮7 : E double har. maj.   C Ionian ♭2 ♭6: C double har. maj.   E♭ Ionian ♯2 ♯5: G double har. maj.

A♭ Lydian ♯2 ♯6: G double har. maj.   G Locrian ♭♭3 ♭♭7: A♭ double har. maj.   E Mixolydian ♭2 ♭5: A double har. maj.

D Phrygian ♭4 ♭♭7: B♭ double har. maj.

5

E Locrian ♭♭3 ♭♭7: G♭ & D♭   B♭ Mixolydian ♭2 ♭5: C♭ & F♭   G Aeolian ♯4 ♮7: C♯ & F♯   A♭ Ionian ♯2 ♯5: B & E

C Phrygian ♭4 ♭♭7: Fa♭ & B♭♭   A Lydian ♯2 ♯6: B♯ & F✕   G Ionian ♭2 ♭6: A♭ & E♭

Part 5: Summary of natural and synthetic modes

An analysis of the natural and synthetic modes derived from the five diatonic major and minor systems is given below.

❶ Tetrachords

From our study of the modes, we obtain six natural and four synthetic tetrachords:

Name	Interval	*Ambitus*	System
Major	2 2 1	Perfect 4th	Major
Minor	2 1 2	Perfect 4th	Major
Phrygian	1 2 2	Perfect 4th	Major
Lydian	2 2 2	Augmented 4th	Major
Diminished	1 2 1	Diminished 4th	Melodic minor
Harmonic	1 3 1	Perfect 4th	Harmonic minor
Lydian ♯2	**3 1 2**	**Augmented 4th**	**Harmonic Minor**
Minor ♯4	**2 1 3**	**Augmented 4th**	**Harmonic Minor**
Phrygian ♭♭3	**1 1 3**	**Perfect 4th**	**Double harmonic major**
Major ♯2	**3 1 1**	**Perfect 4th**	**Double harmonic major**

❷ Mirror harmony

The modes and their retrograde inversions are listed below:

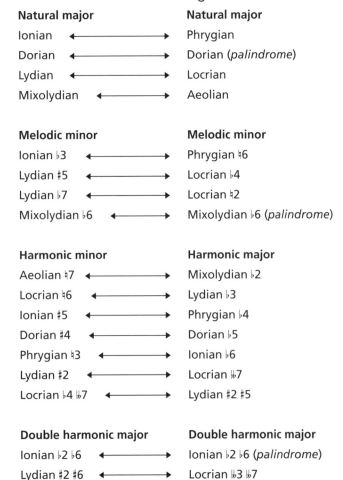

Natural major — **Natural major**

Ionian ⟷ Phrygian
Dorian ⟷ Dorian (*palindrome*)
Lydian ⟷ Locrian
Mixolydian ⟷ Aeolian

Melodic minor — **Melodic minor**

Ionian ♭3 ⟷ Phrygian ♮6
Lydian ♯5 ⟷ Locrian ♭4
Lydian ♭7 ⟷ Locrian ♮2
Mixolydian ♭6 ⟷ Mixolydian ♭6 (*palindrome*)

Harmonic minor — **Harmonic major**

Aeolian ♮7 ⟷ Mixolydian ♭2
Locrian ♮6 ⟷ Lydian ♭3
Ionian ♯5 ⟷ Phrygian ♭4
Dorian ♯4 ⟷ Dorian ♭5
Phrygian ♮3 ⟷ Ionian ♭6
Lydian ♯2 ⟷ Locrian ♭♭7
Locrian ♭4 ♭♭7 ⟷ Lydian ♯2 ♯5

Double harmonic major — **Double harmonic major**

Ionian ♭2 ♭6 ⟷ Ionian ♭2 ♭6 (*palindrome*)
Lydian ♯2 ♯6 ⟷ Locrian ♭♭3 ♭♭7
Phrygian ♭4 ♭♭7 ⟷ Ionian ♯2 ♯5
Aeolian ♯4 ♮7 ⟷ Mixolydian ♭2 ♭5

❸ The five systems

Degrees	Natural modes	Synthetic Modes			
	Major	Melodic minor	Harmonic minor	Harmonic major	Double harmonic major
I	**Ionian** Xmaj7 9, 11, 13 NCD: ♮4 & ♮7	**Ionian ♭3** Xm(maj7) 9, 11, 13 ACD: ♭3	**Aeolian ♮7** Xm(maj7) and V7 (♭9)/I 9, 11, ♭13 ACD: ♮7	**Ionian ♭6** Xmaj7 and V7 (♭9)/I 9, 11, ♭13 ACD: ♭6	**Ionian ♭2 ♭6** Xmaj7 and ♭II7/I* ♭9, 11, ♭13 ACD: ♭2 & ♭6
II	**Dorian** Xm7 9, 11, 13 NCD: ♮6	**Phrygian ♮6** X7sus4 ♭9, ♭10, 13 ACD: ♮6	**Locrian ♮6** Xm7 (♭5) ♭9, 11, 13 ACD: ♮6	**Dorian ♭5** Xm7 (♭5) 9, 11, 13 ACD: ♭5	**Lydian ♯2 ♮6** Xmaj7 ♯9, ♯11, ♯13 ACD: ♯2 & ♯6
III	**Phrygian** Xm7 ♭9, 11, ♭13 NCD: ♭2	**Lydian ♯5** Xmaj7 (♯5) 9, ♯11, 13 ACD: ♯5	**Ionian ♯5** Xmaj7 (♯5) 9, 11, 13 ACD: ♯5	**Phrygian ♭4** X7 ♭9, ♭10, ♭13 ACD: ♭4	**Phrygian ♭4 ♭♭7** *No tetrad* ♭9, ♭11, ♭13 ACD: ♭4 & ♭♭7
IV	**Lydian** Xmaj7 9, ♯11, 13 NCD: ♯4	**Lydian ♭7** X7 9, ♯11, 13 ACD: ♭7	**Dorian ♯4** Xm7 9, ♯11, 13 ACD: ♯4	**Lydian ♭3** Xm(maj7) 9, ♯11, 13 ACD: ♭3	**Aeolian ♯4 ♮7** Xm(maj7) 9, ♯11, ♭13 ACD: ♯4 & ♮7
V	**Mixolydian** X7 9, 11, 13 NCD: ♭7	**Mixolydian ♭6** X7 9, 11, ♭13 ACD: ♭6	**Phrygian ♮3** X7 ♭9, 11, ♭13 ACD: ♮3	**Mixolydian ♭2** X7 ♭9, 11, 13 ACD: ♭2	**Mixolydian ♭2 ♭5** X7 (♭5) ♭9, 11, 13 ACD: ♭2 & ♭5
VI	**Aeolian** Xm7 9, 11, ♭13 NCD: ♭6	**Locrian ♮2** Xm7 (♭5) 9, 11, ♭13 ACD: ♮2	**Lydian ♯2** Xmaj7 ♯9, ♯11, 13 ACD: ♯2	**Lydian ♯2 ♯5** Xmaj7 (♯5) ♯9, ♯11, 13 ACD: ♯2 & ♯5	**Ionian ♯2 ♯5** Xmaj7 (♯5) ♯9, 11, 13 ACD: ♯2 & ♯5
VII	**Locrian** Xm7 (♭5) ♭9, 11, ♭13 NCD: ♭5	**Locrian ♭4** X7 alt. ♭5, ♭9, ♭10, ♭13 ACD: ♭4	**Locrian ♭4 ♭♭7** Xdim7 ♭9, ♭11, ♭13 ACD: ♭4 & ♭♭7	**Locrian ♭♭7** Xdim7 ♭9, 11, ♭13 ACD: ♭♭7	**Locrian ♭♭3 ♭♭7** *No tetrad* ♭9, 11, ♭13 ACD: ♭♭3 & ♭♭7

* Here, the ♯6 is heard as a minor 7th (see the augmented 6th chord, p. 147).

♯ = augmented.

♮ = major.

♭ minor (diminished for the 4th and 5th).

♭♭ = diminished.

Part 6: Modal analysis

The following analyses illustrate how certain modes can be used in a tonal or modal context. These analytical choices are not exclusive. While each example proposes one harmonic treatment, many other choices exist, depending on the color you want to evoke.

"Some Day My Prince Will Come" (Frank Churchill)

Theme in B♭ major; 32 measures in AB form.

Meas. 1-8

|B♭maj7	|D7	|E♭maj7	|G7 (♭13)		
B♭ major	D Phrygian ♮3	B♭ major	G Phrygian ♮3	
|Cm7	|G7 (♭13)	|Cm7	|F7	‖
B♭ major	G Phrygian ♮3	B♭ major		

"The Days of Wine and Roses" (Henry Mancini)

Theme in F major; 32 measures in AB form.

Meas. 1-8

|Fmaj7	|E♭7	|D7			⁒		
F major	E♭ Lydian ♭7	D Locrian ♭4		
	Gm7		⁒		B♭m(maj7)		E♭7 (♯11)	‖
F major		B♭ Ionian ♭3	E♭ Lydian ♭7	

"Body and Soul" (Johnny Green)

Theme in D♭ major; 32 measures in AABA form.

This standard offers several modal analysis choices. In the key of D♭ major, it begins on the IInd degree of the scale (E♭), which we then refer to as E♭ Dorian rather than D♭ major. The notes are identical, but the sensation created by E♭ minor at the beginning is more marked than the tonality of D♭ major, which explains our choice to analyze this piece from a modal perspective. The first A section ends in D♭ major with a II–V–I cadence, then moves to the Vth degree of E♭m7, which takes us back for the second A section.

Meas. 1-8

|E♭m7	B♭7	|E♭m7	D7	|D♭maj7	G♭7	|Fm7	Edim7		
E♭ Dorian	B♭ Phrygian ♮3	E♭ Dorian	D Lydian ♭7	D♭ Ionian	G♭ Lydian ♭7	F Aeolian	E W/H	
|E♭m7		|Cm7 (♭5)	F7	|B♭m7 E♭7	E♭m7 A♭7	|D♭6		B♭7	:‖
E♭ Dorian		C Locrian ♮2	F Locrian ♭4	A♭ major	D♭ major		B♭ Phrygian ♮3	

"Fall" (Wayne Shorter)

No tonal center; 16 measures; one-part form.

Meas. 1-8

|C♯m13	|B7 (♭9)	|E7sus4	|Cm6		
C♯ Dorian	B Mixolydian ♭2	E Mixolydian	C Ionian ♭3	
|C♯m13	|B7 (♭9)	|E7sus4	|E♭maj7 (♯11)	‖
C♯ Dorian	B Mixolydian ♭2	E Mixolydian	E♭ Lydian	

"Very Early" (Bill Evans)

C major tonal center; 48 measures in AAB form.

Meas. 1-8

|Cmaj7	|B♭9	|E♭maj7	|A♭7 (♭9)	
C Ionian	B♭ Lydian ♭7	E♭ Ionian	A♭ H/W

|D♭maj7	|G9	|Cmaj7	|B♭7 (♯11)	‖
D♭ Ionian	G Mixolydian ♭6	C Ionian	B♭ Lydian ♭7

"Peace" (Horace Silver)

B♭ major tonal center; 10-measure tune; one-part form.

|Am7 (♭5)　　D7 (♭9)　　|Gm7　　　　C7　　　　|C♭maj7　　　Cm7 (♭5)　F7 (♯9)　|B♭maj7　　　　　　　　　|
A Locrian ♮2　D Locrian ♭4　G Dorian　　C Mixolydian　Lydian　　C Locrian ♮2　　B♭ Lydian
　　　　　　　　　　　　　　　　　　　　　　　　　　　　　　　　　　F Locrian ♭4

|Bm7　　　　E7　　　　|Amaj7　　　F♯m7　　|E♭m7 (♭5)　　D7　　　|D♭maj7　　　　　　　　　|
II　　　　　V　　　　　I　　　　　VI　　　　　E♭ Locrian ♮2　D H/W　　D♭ Lydian
└──────────── Cadence in A major ────────────┘

|C7　　　　　B7　　　　|B♭maj7　　　　　　‖
C Locrian ♭4　B H/W　　B♭ Ionian

"Re: Person I Knew" (Bill Evans)

16-measure theme; pedal on C throughout the theme.

We have proposed only one modal analysis example for this theme, as several modes can be used for improvising.

|C6/9	|Caug (add9)	|Gm9(maj7)	|Gm9	
C Ionian	C Lydian ♯5	C Lydian ♭7	C Mixolydian

|Fm13		⁄.	|Cm9		⁄.	
C Aeolian		C Dorian	

|Fm11	|Cm(maj7)	|Fm7	|Gm9(maj7)	
C Aeolian	C Ionian ♭3	C Aeolian	C Lydian ♭7

|Fm(maj7)	|Gm9	|Fm11	|D♭maj9	‖
C Mixolydian ♭6	C Mixolydian	C Aeolian	C Phrygian

APPENDIX

❶ 24 four-note chord voicings

There are six basic ways to voice tetrachords.

The tetrachord possibilities in Cmaj7 are:

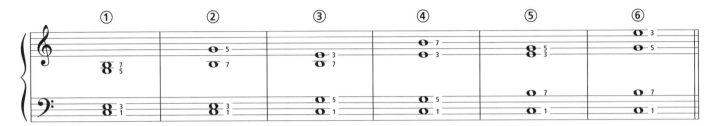

Each voicing may be expressed in one of four positions. A summary of all these chord voicings is given below:

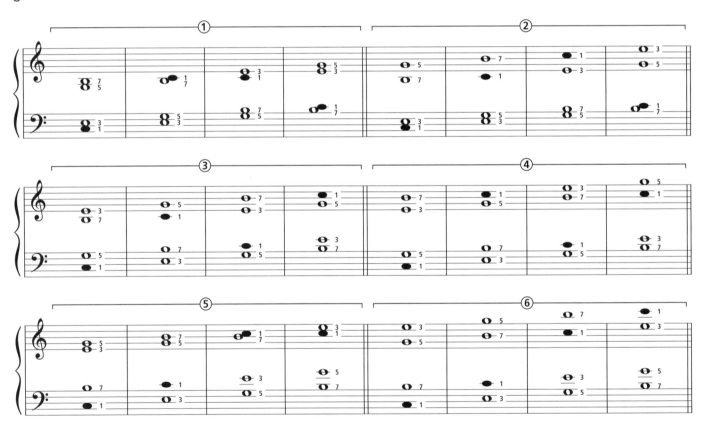

❷ Summary table of modes by parent scale

	Xmaj7	X7	Xm7	Xm7 (♭5)	Xmaj7 (♯5)	Xm(maj7)	X7 (♭5)	X7sus4	Xdim7
Natural major modes									
Ionian	9, 11, 13								
Dorian			9, 11, 13						
Phrygian			♭9, 11, ♭13						
Lydian	9, ♯11, 13								
Mixolydian		9, 11, 13						9, 10, 13	
Aeolian			9, 11, ♭13						
Locrian				♭9, 11, ♭13					
Melodic minor modes									
Ionian ♭3						9, 11, 13			
Phrygian ♮6								♭9, ♭10, 13	
Lydian ♯5					9, ♯11, 13				
Lydian ♭7		9, ♯11, 13							
Mixolydian ♭6		9, 11, ♭13							
Locrian ♮2				9, 11, ♭13					
Locrian ♭4	♭9, ♭10, 13								
Harmonic minor modes									
Aeolian ♮7						9, 11, ♭13			
Locrian ♮6				♭9, 11, 13					
Ionian ♯5					9, 11, 13				
Dorian ♯4			9, ♯11, 13						
Phrygian ♮3		♭9, 11, ♭13							
Lydian ♯2	♯9, ♯11, 13								
Locrian ♭4 ♭♭7									♭9, ♭11, ♭13
Harmonic major modes									
Ionian ♭6									
Dorian ♭5				9, 11, 13					
Phrygian ♭4		♭9, ♭10, ♭13							
Lydian ♭3						9, ♯11, 13			
Mixolydian ♭2		♭9, 11, 13							
Lydian ♯2 ♯5					♯9, ♯11, 13				
Locrian ♭♭7									♭9, 11, ♭13
Double harmonic major modes									
Ionian ♭2 ♭6	♭II7 / I*								
Lydian ♯2 ♯6	♯9, ♯11, ♯13								
Phrygian ♭4 ♭♭7	No related chord								
Aeolian ♯4 ♮7						9, ♯11, ♭13			
Mixolydian ♭2 ♭5							♭9, 11, 13		
Ionian ♯2 ♯5					♯9, 11, 13				
Locrian ♭♭3 ♭♭7	No related chord								
	Xmaj7	X7	Xm7	Xm7 (♭5)	Xmaj7 (♯5)	Xm(maj7)	X7 (♭5)	X7sus4	Xdim7

* Here, the ♯6 is heard as a minor 7th (see the augmented 6th chord, p. 153).

❸ Summary table of modes by name

Mode	Chord	Parent-scale degree
Ionian	Xmaj7	I in major
Ionian ♭3	Xm(maj7)	I in melodic minor
Ionian #5	Xmaj7 (#5)	III in harmonic minor
Ionian ♭6	Xmaj7	I in harmonic major
Ionian ♭2 ♭6	♭II7 / I*	I in double harmonic major
Ionian #2 #5	Xmaj7 (#5)	VI in double harmonic major

Mode	Chord	Parent-scale degree
Dorian	Xm7	II in major
Dorian #4	Xm7	IV in harmonic minor
Dorian ♭5	Xm7 (♭5)	II in harmonic major

Mode	Chord	Parent-scale degree
Phrygian	Xm7	III in major
Phrygian ♮6	X7sus4	II in melodic minor
Phrygian ♮3	X7	V in harmonic minor
Phrygian ♭4	X7	III in harmonic major
Phrygian ♭4 ♭♭7	No function	III in double harmonic major

Mode	Chord	Parent-scale degree
Lydian	Xmaj7	IV in major
Lydian #5	Xmaj7 (#5)	III in melodic minor
Lydian ♭7	X7	IV in melodic minor
Lydian #2	Xmaj7	VI in harmonic minor
Lydian ♭3	Xm(maj7)	IV in harmonic major
Lydian #2 #5	Xmaj7 (#5)	VI in harmonic major
Lydian #2 #6	Xmaj7	II in double harmonic major

Mode	Chord	Parent-scale degree
Mixolydian	X7	V in major
Mixolydian ♭6	X7	V in melodic minor
Mixolydian ♭2	X7	V in harmonic major
Mixolydian ♭2 ♭5	X7 (♭5)	V in double harmonic major

Mode	Chord	Parent-scale degree
Aeolian	Xm7	VI in major
Aeolian ♮7	Xm(maj7)	I in harmonic minor
Aeolian #4 ♮7	Xm(maj7)	IV in double harmonic major

Mode	Chord	Parent-scale degree
Locrian	Xm7 (♭5)	VII in major
Locrian ♮2	Xm7 (♭5)	VI in melodic minor
Locrian ♭4	X7	VII in melodic minor
Locrian ♮6	Xm7 (♭5)	II in harmonic minor
Locrian ♭4 ♭♭7	Xdim7	VII in harmonic minor
Locrian ♭♭7	Xdim7	VII in harmonic major
Locrian ♭3 ♭♭7	No function	VII in double harmonic major

* Here, the #6 is heard as a minor 7th (see the augmented 6th chord, p. 153).

ABOUT THE AUTHORS

Lilian Dericq studied piano under Samy Abenaïm and music harmony with Bernard Maury. He completed his musicology studies at the University of Paris VIII. He has been teaching piano and harmony at the Bill Evans Piano Academy in Paris since 1996 and teaching harmony at the University of Paris since 1999.

Étienne Guéreau is a French pianist born in Bretagne in 1977 and raised in Paris. He studied classical music at the Issy-Les-Moulineaux Conservatory, then jazz harmony under Bernard Maury. In 2005, he released his first piano solo record, drawing the attention of Clare Fischer, who encouraged him to pursue his artistic exploration. Today, Étienne performs regularly in public and is accomplished in a variety of musical styles, ranging from jazz to pop. He has published several educational books on piano and harmony and is one of the senior teachers in the Bill Evans Piano Academy. As a writer of fiction, he has published several novels in Europe with the Denoël publishing house.

INDEX

superstructure notes. See extension notes

supertonic chord, subdominant function of, 95–96

supertonic scale degree, 76
— as weak degree, 94

sus4 chords (X7sus4), 52–53
— chord symbols, 53
— chord symbols for extensions, 71
— as color chord, 131
— extension notes with, 71, 129n5, 205, 212
— function of, 53
— Mixolydian mode with, 186–87
— perfect 4th in, 52
— Phrygian ♮6 with, 212
— in subdominant function to prepare X7 chords, 129–30
— as target-chord preparation, 128, 129–31, 154
— tritone lacking in, 130
— using, 130

sus4 chords (X7sus4(♭9)), 205, 212

symmetrical scale, 224n13

symmetrical succession of pitches, 33

synthetic diatonic sequence, 204, 217, 226

synthetic modes, 203–4
— accidentals in, 164
— Altered Characteristic Degree in, 188, 203, 207
— analyzing, 203
— defined, 203
— derived from melodic minor scale, 203–14
— differentiating, 207
— harmonic minor as, 164
— names for, 169
— parent scales for, 203
— secondary dominants and, 134
— summary of, 245

systems
— chromatic, 165–66
— double harmonic major, 235–41
— harmonic major, 226–35
— harmonic minor, 217–24
— melodic minor, 203–14
— natural diatonic, 163–64

T

target chord, 92

temporary tonic function
— diminished seventh chords and, 145
— secondary dominants and, 128, 131
— secondary subdominants and, 151

tension chords, 92

tenths, 3, 4

tessitura, 180

tetrachords
— analysis of double harmonic major modes, 238
— analysis of harmonic minor modes, 219
— analysis of melodic minor modes, 206–7
— analysis of natural diatonic modes, 173
— in harmonic minor scale, 83
— Major ♯2, 238, 244
— in major scale, 75–76
— in melodic minor scale, 88
— Minor ♯4, 219, 244
— Phrygian ♭♭3, 238
— summary of, 244

tetrads, 41–61
— augmented major seventh chords (Xmaj7(♯5)), 53–54
— defined, 41
— diminished chords (Xdim7), 44, 47, 48
— forming, 2
— harmonizing harmonic minor scale with, 85
— harmonizing major scale with, 79
— harmonizing melodic minor scale with, 89
— identifying chords, 46–48
— inversions, 45–48
— major seventh chords (Xmaj7), 41–42, 47, 48
— minor-major seventh chords (Xm(maj7)), 51–52
— minor seventh chords (Xm7), 42–43, 47, 48
— minor-seventh flat-five chords (Xm7(♭5)), 43, 47, 48
— qualities of, 41–44
— root position voicings, 45
— seventh chord (X7), 42, 47, 48
— sus4 chords (X7sus4), 52–53
— triads with added 6ths, 50–51
— voicings, 248

third inversion, 45, 232

thirds, 10–11
— augmented, 4
— circle of, 164
— diminished, 4
— major, 11
— minor, 10

thirteenth chords
— X13, 64, 66–67
— X13(♯11), 213
— X13(♭9), 66, 233

— X13sus4, 129n5
— X13sus4(♭9), 205, 212
— Xm13, 67
— Xm13(♭5), 231
— Xm13(maj7), 70
— Xmaj13, 64, 65
— Xmaj13(♯11), 65
— Xm(maj13♯11), 232

thirteenths, 3, 4, 64–65
— major, 64, 65, 66, 67, 70, 71
— minor, 64, 66, 68

tonal cadences, 97–109
— I–I7/3–♯IVdim7–I/5, 117
— I–I7/7–IV/3–IVm/3–I/5, 117
— I–VI–II–V chord progressions, 111–12
— II–V chord progressions, 109–11
— II–V–I major, 101–2
— II–V–I minor, 102–6
— II–V–I minor/major, 102–3
— II–♭VII7–I, 114
— III–VI–II–V–I, 113
— IV–V–I major, 106
— IV–V–I minor, 107
— IV–V–I minor/major mixed, 107
— IV–♭VII–I, 114–15
— VI–V–I, 108
— ♭VII–I, 113–14
— deceptive, 98
— half, 98
— imperfect authentic, 98
— perfect authentic, 97–98
— plagal, 99–100, 114, 117–18, 192
— three-chord, 101–9
— turnaround, 113–14, 120–21
— two-chord, 97–101

tonal degrees, 7

tonal plateau, 157

tonal zone, 179

tonality
— determining key, 93–94, 156
— scale and mode distinguished from, 180–81
— scales and, 92–94

tonic chords
— determining mode from, 93
— function of, 95, 184
— major, 115–18
— minor, 118–19, 221, 222–23

tonic scale degree, 76
— chords built on, 115–21
— gravitational pull of, 92
— as strong degree, 94

tonicization (defined), 128n2

transposition, 181
— onto same modal tonic, 172, 205, 218, 222, 237

triads, 33–40

— with added 6ths, 50–51

— altered fifth, 37–38

— augmented, 38

— basic chord positions, 34–35

— defined, 33

— forming, 2

— harmonizing major scale with, 79

— identifying chord names, 36

— inversions, 35–36

— major, 34–37

— minor, 34–37

— naming, 34

— notation principles, 34

— voicings, 35, 36

trills, 165

triplum, 183

tritone, 14. *See also* augmented fourths; diminished fifths

— resolution of, 129–30

— in X7 chord, 95

tritone substitution, 135–39

— table for, 138

— using, 139–40

turnaround (turnback) cadences, 120–21

— "backdoor," 113–14

— one-measure, 121

— two-measure, 121

U

Ultraphrygian. See Phrygian ♭4 ♭♭7 mode

unisons, 7

V

Van Heusen, Jimmy, "I Thought About You," 140

voice leading, 139, 181, 186, 221

voicing (of chord)

— tetrads, 45, 51, 52, 53, 54, 248

— triads, 35, 36

W

W-H diminished scale, 234, 241

Wagner, Richard, extension notes used by, 62

Warren, Harry, "There Will Never Be Another You," 159

Washington, Ned (with Kaper), "On Green Dolphin Street," 181, 192

Webern, Anton, 165

Williams, Tony, "Pee Wee," 157

Y

Young, Victor, "Beautiful Love," 121

Great Harmony & Theory Helpers

HAL LEONARD HARMONY & THEORY – PART 1: DIATONIC
by George Heussenstamm

This book is designed for anyone wishing to expand their knowledge of music theory, whether beginner or more advanced. The first two chapters deal with music fundamentals, and may be skipped by those with music reading experience. Topics include: basic music-reading instruction; triads in root position; triads in inversion; cadences; non-harmonic tones; the dominant seventh chord; other seventh chords; and more.
00312062...$27.50

HAL LEONARD HARMONY & THEORY – PART 2: CHROMATIC
by George Heussenstamm

Part 2 – Chromatic introduces readers to modulation and more advanced harmonies, covering: secondary dominants; borrowed chords; the Neapolitan 6th chord; augmented 6th chords; 9th, 11th, and 13th chords; and more. In addition to text, the book features many musical examples that illustrate the concepts, and exercises that allow readers to test and apply their knowledge.
00312064...$27.50

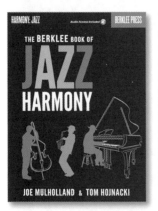

THE BERKLEE BOOK OF JAZZ HARMONY
by Joe Mulholland & Tom Hojnacki
Berklee Press

Learn jazz harmony, as taught at Berklee College of Music. This text provides a strong foundation in harmonic principles, supporting further study in jazz composition, arranging, and improvisation. It covers basic chord types and their tensions, with practical demonstrations of how they are used in characteristic jazz contexts; an accompanying recording lets you hear how they can be applied.
00113755 Book/Online Audio $27.50

A PLAYER'S GUIDE TO CHORDS AND HARMONY
Music Theory for Real-World Musicians
by Jim Aikin
Backbeat Books

If you'd like to know about music theory but don't want to get bogged down in a stuffy college-level textbook, this guide was written just for you! Covers: intervals, scales, modes, triads and advanced voicings; interpreting chord symbols and reading sheet music; voice leading, chord progressions, and basic song forms; classical, jazz & pop; and more, with helpful quizzes and answers.
00331173...$19.95

ENCYCLOPEDIA OF READING RHYTHMS
Text and Workbook for All Instruments
by Gary Hess
Musicians Institute Press

A comprehensive guide to notes, rests, counting, subdividing, time signatures, triplets, ties, dotted notes and rests, cut time, compound time, swing, shuffle, rhythm studies, counting systems, road maps and more!
00695145 ....$19.95

THE CHORD WHEEL
The Ultimate Tool for All Musicians
by Jim Fleser

Master chord theory ... in minutes! *The Chord Wheel* is a revolutionary device that puts the most essential and practical applications of chord theory into your hands. This tool will help you: Improvise and Solo – Talk about chops! Comprehend key structure like never before; Transpose Keys – Instantly transpose any progression into each and every key; Compose Your Own Music – Watch your songwriting blossom! No music reading is necessary.
00695579 ....$14.99

MUSIC THEORY WORKBOOK
For All Musicians
by Chris Bowman

A self-study course with illustrations and examples for you to write and check your answers. Topics include: major and minor scales; modes and other scales; harmony; intervals; chord structure; chord progressions and substitutions; and more.
00101379 ....$12.99

THE ULTIMATE KEYBOARD CHORD CHART

This convenient reference features 120 of the most commonly used chords, easy diagrams, and information on chord theory.
00220016 ....$3.50

Train Your Ears

HAL LEONARD PERFECT PITCH METHOD
A Musician's Guide to Recognizing Pitches by Ear
by Adam Perlmutter

Perfect pitch is largely a misunderstood phenomenon. The *Hal Leonard Perfect Pitch Method* is designed to help you develop a sense of perfect pitch. In the process, your overall musicianship will benefit and you'll start listening to music on a deeper level and getting more satisfaction from it. At the heart of this book is a series of 49 ear-training sessions, one per day for seven weeks, using the included CDs or the online audio.
00311221 Book with 3 CDs and
Online Audio Access . $29.99

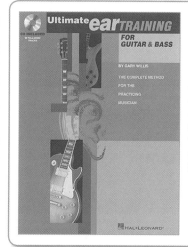

ULTIMATE EAR TRAINING FOR GUITAR AND BASS
by Gary Willis

Everything you need to improve your ear training, including a CD with 99 full-demo tracks, vital information on intervals, rhythms, melodic shapes, inversions, scales, chords, extensions, alterations, fretboard visualization, and fingering diagrams.
00695182 Book/CD Pack $17.99

BEGINNING EAR TRAINING
by Gilson Schachnik
Berklee Press

Introduces the core skills of ear training. Teaches how to: learn melodies by ear; sight-sing; internalize rhythms and melodies; improve pitch and timing; transpose; use solfege; transcribe and notate; and much more!
50449548 Book/Online Audio $16.99

ESSENTIAL EAR TRAINING FOR THE CONTEMPORARY MUSICIAN
by Steve Prosser
Berklee Press

The Ear Training curriculum of Berklee College of Music is known and respected throughout the world. Now, for the first time, this unique method has been captured in one comprehensive book by the chair of the Ear Training Department. This method teaches musicians to hear the music they are seeing, notate the music they have composed or arranged, develop their music vocabulary, and understand the music they are hearing. The book features a complete course with text and musical examples, and studies in rhythm, sight recognition, sol-fa, and melody.
50449421 .... $16.95

BERKLEE MUSIC THEORY – 2ND EDITION
by Paul Schmeling
Berklee Press

This essential method features rigorous, hands-on, "ears-on" practice exercises that help you explore the inner working of music, presenting notes, scales, and rhythms as they are heard in pop, jazz, and blues. You will learn and build upon the basic concepts of music theory with written exercises, listening examples, and ear training exercises. The online audio will help reinforce lessons as you begin to build a solid musical foundation. Now available with an answer key!
50449615 Book 1 .... $24.99
Also Available:
50449616 Book 2 .... $22.99

MUSIC THEORY
A Practical Guide for All Musicians
by Barrett Tagliarino

Get the rock-solid fundamentals of rhythm, pitch and harmony with this easy-to-use book/CD pack. Learn the universal language used by all musicians, regardless of instrument. Includes concise, detailed explanations, illustrations and written exercises with online audio examples and practice drills. This book will teach you how to: construct scales, chords and intervals; identify major and minor key centers and common chord progressions; accurately play various rhythm feels and figures; learn the basic principles of form and compositional analysis.
00311270 Book/Online Audio $15.99

Jazz Instruction & Improvisation

BOOKS FOR ALL INSTRUMENTS FROM HAL LEONARD

AN APPROACH TO JAZZ IMPROVISATION
by Dave Pozzi
Musicians Institute Press
Explore the styles of Charlie Parker, Sonny Rollins, Bud Powell and others with this comprehensive guide to jazz improvisation. Covers: scale choices • chord analysis • phrasing • melodies • harmonic progressions • more.
00695135 Book/CD Pack......................$17.95

THE ART OF MODULATING
FOR PIANISTS AND JAZZ MUSICIANS
by Carlos Salzedo &
Lucile Lawrence
Schirmer
The Art of Modulating is a treatise originally intended for the harp, but this edition has been edited for use by intermediate keyboardists and other musicians who have an understanding of basic music theory. In its pages you will find: table of intervals; modulation rules; modulation formulas; examples of modulation; extensions and cadences; ten fragments of dances; five characteristic pieces; and more.
50490581 ....$19.99

BUILDING A JAZZ VOCABULARY
By Mike Steinel
A valuable resource for learning the basics of jazz from Mike Steinel of the University of North Texas. It covers: the basics of jazz • how to build effective solos • a comprehensive practice routine • and a jazz vocabulary of the masters.
00849911 ....$19.99

THE CYCLE OF FIFTHS
by Emile and Laura De Cosmo
This essential instruction book provides more than 450 exercises, including hundreds of melodic and rhythmic ideas. The book is designed to help improvisors master the cycle of fifths, one of the primary progressions in music. Guaranteed to refine technique, enhance improvisational fluency, and improve sight-reading!
00311114 ....$16.99

THE DIATONIC CYCLE
by Emile and Laura De Cosmo
Renowned jazz educators Emile and Laura De Cosmo provide more than 300 exercises to help improvisors tackle one of music's most common progressions: the diatonic cycle. This book is guaranteed to refine technique, enhance improvisational fluency, and improve sight-reading!
00311115 ....$16.95

EAR TRAINING
by Keith Wyatt,
Carl Schroeder and Joe Elliott
Musicians Institute Press
Covers: basic pitch matching • singing major and minor scales • identifying intervals • transcribing melodies and rhythm • identifying chords and progressions • seventh chords and the blues • modal interchange, chromaticism, modulation • and more.
00695198 Book/Online Audio $24.99

EXERCISES AND ETUDES FOR THE JAZZ INSTRUMENTALIST
by J.J. Johnson
Designed as study material and playable by any instrument, these pieces run the gamut of the jazz experience, featuring common and uncommon time signatures and keys, and styles from ballads to funk. They are progressively graded so that both beginners and professionals will be challenged by the demands of this wonderful music.
00842018 Bass Clef Edition $17.99
00842042 Treble Clef Edition $16.95

JAZZOLOGY
THE ENCYCLOPEDIA OF JAZZ THEORY FOR ALL MUSICIANS
by Robert Rawlins and
Nor Eddine Bahha
This comprehensive resource covers a variety of jazz topics, for beginners and pros of any instrument. The book serves as an encyclopedia for reference, a thorough methodology for the student, and a workbook for the classroom.
00311167 ....$19.99

JAZZ THEORY RESOURCES
by Bert Ligon
Houston Publishing, Inc.
This is a jazz theory text in two volumes. **Volume 1 includes**: review of basic theory • rhythm in jazz performance • triadic generalization • diatonic harmonic progressions and analysis • substitutions and turnarounds • and more. **Volume 2 includes**: modes and modal frameworks • quartal harmony • extended tertian structures and triadic superimposition • pentatonic applications • coloring "outside" the lines and beyond • and more.
00030458 Volume 1 ....$39.95
00030459 Volume 2 ....$29.95

HAL•LEONARD®
7777 W. BLUEMOUND RD. P.O. BOX 13819 MILWAUKEE, WI 53213

Visit Hal Leonard online at
www.halleonard.com

JOY OF IMPROV
by Dave Frank
and John Amaral
This book/audio course on improvisation for all instruments and all styles will help players develop monster musical skills! Book One imparts a solid basis in technique, rhythm, chord theory, ear training and improv concepts. **Book Two** explores more advanced chord voicings, chord arranging techniques and more challenging blues and melodic lines. The audio can be used as a listening and play-along tool.
00220005 Book 1 – Book/Online Audio...............$27.99
00220006 Book 2 – Book/Online Audio...............$26.99

THE PATH TO JAZZ IMPROVISATION
by Emile and Laura De Cosmo
This fascinating jazz instruction book offers an innovative, scholarly approach to the art of improvisation. It includes in-depth analysis and lessons about: cycle of fifths • diatonic cycle • overtone series • pentatonic scale • harmonic and melodic minor scale • polytonal order of keys • blues and bebop scales • modes • and more.
00310904 ....$14.99

THE SOURCE
THE DICTIONARY OF CONTEMPORARY AND TRADITIONAL SCALES
by Steve Barta
This book serves as an informative guide for people who are looking for good, solid information regarding scales, chords, and how they work together. It provides right and left hand fingerings for scales, chords, and complete inversions. Includes over 20 different scales, each written in all 12 keys.
00240885 ....$19.99

21 BEBOP EXERCISES
by Steve Rawlins
This book/CD pack is both a warm-up collection and a manual for bebop phrasing. Its tasty and sophisticated exercises will help you develop your proficiency with jazz interpretation. It concentrates on practice in all twelve keys – moving higher by half-step – to help develop dexterity and range. The companion CD includes all of the exercises in 12 keys.
00315341 Book/CD Pack......................$17.95

Prices, contents & availability
subject to change without notice.